Corporate Bankruptcy

Chapter 11 Analysis & Financial Restructuring

The Case of Pierre Foods & Oaktree Capital
Featuring an Alternative Plan

Joe Gensor

The right of this work has been asserted in accordance with the Copyright, Designs and Patents Act of 1988.

No part of this publication may be reproduced, stored in a retrieval system, or transmitted in any form or by any means, electronic, mechanical, photocopying, recording, scanning, or otherwise, except as permitted under Section 107 or 108 of the 1976 United States Copyright Act, without prior written permission of the author.

Limit of Liability: While best efforts have been used in preparing this book, the author makes no representation or warranty with respect to the accuracy or completeness of the contents and disclaims any implied warranties of merchantability. The advice and strategies in the book may not be suitable for a particular situation and you should consult with a professional where appropriate.

Copyright 2009 by Joe Gensor
First Edition August 2009
Library of Congress Catalog in Publication Data
Gensor, Joe A, 1956 –
Corporate Bankruptcy: Chapter 11 Analysis & Financial Restructuring
The Case of Pierre Foods & Oaktree Capital
Featuring an Alternative Plan
Includes bibliographical references
IBSN-978-0-578-03613-7

To my wife Eda
To my mother Mary Roberts
To Christian, Elizabeth, and Rachel
To Barron and Cleo

Preface

In May 2009, Mergers and Acquisitions gave the 2008 acquisition deal of year award to Oaktree Capital Management's acquisition of Pierre Foods.

My first knowledge of Pierre Foods was from reading a December 2008 article in the Wall Street Journal (Lattman and McCracken) about Pierre Foods emerging from Chapter 11 bankruptcy. This started my informal case study of Pierre Foods, its bankruptcy, and the company's plan of reorganization. The informal case study gradually evolved into a book that has been published for educational purposes. The book includes the presentation of a feasible alternative plan of reorganization for the benefit of the bankrupt estate.

In Chapter 11 bankruptcy, a debtor's reorganization plan can be difficult to analyze and understand. It consists of a mixture of legal and financial information. In Chapter 11, the debtor has the exclusive right for the first 120 days to present a plan of reorganiztion. The debtor prepares the plan with the assistance of its hired legal experts and financial savants, who are likely to be compensated in a way and an amount that at least raises a question as to their true independence. Due dilgence requires objective analysis of the reorganization plan by the interested parties. It can be challenging to determine if a debtor's reorganizaton plan is the best feasible plan for the prepetition creditors and equity holders.

A primary focus of this book is to set forth basic methods and principles for the analysis of a debtor and its plan of reorganization in Chapter 11 bankruptcy. A real life bankruptcy case is presented for analysis and formulation of an alternative plan of reorganization.

Part I of the book begins with the the basics of bankruptcy on Chapter 11 of Title 11 of the United States Bankruptcy Code.

Part II covers valuing a company. One of the central questions in a bankruptcy is whether the debtor has greater value as a going-concern or in a liquidation of its assets. The estimate of Enterprise Value is one of the most difficult and critical estimates in a case.

Part III is a strategic guide to Chapter 11 case analysis with a 30 point checklist and reminders for analyzing a Chapter 11 case and for proposing an alternative plan of reorganization.

Part IV follows with a comphrehensive analysis of Pierre's: history, ownership, management, operations, acquistions, industry, competitors, legal structure, operating peformance, capital structure, liquidity, credit ratings, trading value of debt, prepetition claims, secured debt, unsecured debt, holders of debt, loan agreement terms, debtor-in-possession financing, first-day bankruptcy court orders, performance in bankruptcy, and the Pierre's Plan of Reorganization.

Part V is the estimate of Pierre's Alternative Enterprise Value. A comphrehenisve analysis is performed using various methods to estimate Pierre's Enterprise Value.

Part VI is the presentation of the alternative Plan of Reorganization for the benefit of the estate that provides a higher recovery for prepetition creditors and stockholders.

The Pierre Foods and Oaktree Capital case has important lessons for credit underwriting, distress work-out, and risk management.

How to Read This Book

For specific areas of interest:

Chapter	Title	Page(s)
Chapter 27:	Condensed Version: Case Study & Alternative Plan & Concluding Comments	243–263
Chapter 1 & 2:	Basic Knowledge of the Bankruptcy Code	1–46
Chapter 3:	How to Value a Company	48–61
Chapter 4:	30 Point Checklist & Reminders for Case Analysis	63–70
Chapter 5–23:	Full Case Analysis and Pierre's Plan	71–195
Chapter 16:	Rush to Exit Chapter 11 Summary of Pierre's Plan of Reorganization	159–169
Chapter 24:	Estimate of Alternative Enterprise Value for Pierre	197–221
Chapter 25:	Presentation of Alternative Plan of Reorganization	223–238

Contents

Part I	**Bankruptcy Basics**
Chapter 1	**Basics of the Bankruptcy Code**
Page 1	• Overview of Title 11 of the U.S. Code
	• Bankruptcy Courts and Judges • Place of Filing
	• Chapter 11 Filing • Why File Chapter 11 Bankruptcy?
	• Immediate Benefits and Objectives of a Chapter 11 Filing
	• Costs of Bankruptcy • U.S. Trustee vs. Case Trustee
	• Unsecured Creditors Committee • Examination of the Debtor
	• Powers & Duties of Appointed Committees
	• Equity Committee
	• Debtor's Reporting Requirements in Bankruptcy
	• Debtor's Use, Sale, and Lease of Property
	• Concept of Value in Bankruptcy • Adequate Protection
	• Bankruptcy Code Procedures for Obtaining Credit
	• DIP Financing • Moody's Default Study on DIP Loans
	• Bifurcation of a Claim into Secured Claim and Unsecured Claim
	• Principal & Interest on Unsecured & Secured Claims
	• Priority of Prepetition Claims
	• Prepetition Unsecured Vendor Claims • Executory Contracts
	• Employment Contracts • Labor Contracts
	• Real Estate Leases • Personal Property Leases
	• Structural Advantages of Leasing
	• Risk of Re-Characterizing a Lease as a Loan
	• Other Leasing Considerations • Assignment of Leases
	• Retaining an Asset Management Specialist
	• Structuring the Lease on One Lease Schedule
	• Debt Agreements and Structural Issues
	• Substantive Consolidation • Subordination
	• Preferences • Fraudulent Transfers • Securitizations
	• Pension Plan Termination Claims
	• Swap Agreements • Off-Balance Sheet Liabilities
	• Net Operating Loss Carry-Forward Issues
	• Taxes Due on Cancellation of Debt or Exchange
	• Warrants & Rights Offering

Chapter 2 **The Plan of Reorganization & Other Special Issues**
Page 30
- Debtor Exclusive Period to File a Plan • Impairment
- Minimum Requirements for a Plan
- Disclosure Statement • Voting on the Plan
- Confirmation of Plan—Minimum Requirements
- Section 1129 Cramdown • Fair & Equitable Treatment
- Challenges of Obtaining a Cramdown
- Limit on a Creditor Receiving a Recovery Greater Than Its Claim
- Undersecured Creditor Strategy and Section 1111(b) Election
- Absolute Priority—363 Sale Issue/Chrysler Bankruptcy
- Trend of Faster Reorganizations
- Issues Presented by Second-Lien Loans
- Distressed Investors & Hedge Funds
- Investing in Distressed Debt or Claims
- Recent Investing Case—Return on Spansion's Debt

Part II Estimating Enterprise Value

Chapter 3 **Enterprise Value**
Page 48
- Bias in the Estimate of Enterprise Value in Bankruptcy
- Enterprise Value at the Date of the Plan
- Determination of Enterprise Value
- Discounting Cash Flows
- Estimating the Cost of Equity
- Capital Asset Pricing Model
- Average Leverage Ratios & Other Key Financial Metrics for U.S. Exchange Traded Companies
- Equity Risk Premium Debate Among Experts
- Equity Premium for Firm Size • Industry Premium
- Bankruptcy Emergence Premium • Estimating the Cost of Debt
- Comparable Company Method of Valuing a Company
- Comparable Transactions Method of Valuing a Company

Part III Strategic Guide to Chapter 11 Case Analysis

Chapter 4 **Checklist for Case Analysis**
Page 63
- 30 Point Checklist for Strategic Case Analysis & Plan Structuring

Part IV — Case Analysis of Pierre Foods

Chapter 5
Page 72

Pierre's Bankruptcy Filing—Case Information and Parties
- Debtor • Date of Filing • Case Number
- Date of Reorganization Plan
- Date of Plan Approval
- Date of Emergence from Bankruptcy
- Bankruptcy Judge • U.S. Trustee • Organization Chart
- Debtor Subsidiaries • Corporate Structure
- Debtor's Professionals & Fees
- Unsecured Creditors Committee
- Trade Vendor Unsecured Claims vs. Unsecured Debt
- Creditor Committee Professionals
- Plan Sponsor: Oaktree Capital
- Legal Counsel for Oaktree Capital

Chapter 6
Page 77

Pierre's Business & History
- Pierre's Business
- Leading Market Share
- Products/End Markets
- Vending Sales • Convenience Store Sales
- Warehouse Clubs/Grocery Store Sales
- School Sales • Foodservice Sales
- Sales & Marketing • R&D
- Customer Concentration
- USDA Requirements
- Manufacturing Plants
- Raw Materials Required for Products
- Industry • Sandwich Market
- Sandwich Sales to Convenience Store Market
- Competition • Meat Processing Competition
- Sandwich Competition
- Biscuit/Yeast Roll Competition
- Seasonality • Employees
- History of Pierre's Ownership
- Background on James Richardson Jr. & David R. Clark—former Directors and 88% shareholders prior to Madison Dearborn buyout
- Management and Board at Date of Bankruptcy
- Compensation of Top Officers

Chapter 7 Page 87	**Acquisitions/Fairness of Price/Debt Leverage** • Background on Private Equity Firm Madison Dearborn • Madison Dearborn's Acquisition of Pierre Foods in June 2004 • Sources & Uses of Funds in Acquisition • Pre and Post Acquisition Balance Sheet • New Secured Loan From Wachovia Bank • Analysis of Madison Dearborn's Acquisition Price • Acquisition EBITDA Multiple Compared to Industry • Cash Flow and Debt Leverage Risk for Lenders • Debt to EBITDA—Post Acquisition • Post Acquisition Leverage: Secured vs. Unsecured Lender Risk • Financial Covenants in Wachovia Secured Credit Facility • Acquisition of Clovervale (August 2006) & Zartic (December 2006) • Impact of the Clovervale and Zartic Acquisitions • Secured Credit Facility: Lender Risk and Collateral Deficiency • Required Wachovia Loan Amortization • Unsecured $125 million Senior Notes: The Hope and Prayer Lenders

Chapter 8
Page 100
	Analysis of Pierre's Operating Results and Balance Sheet
	• Key Operating & Cash Flow Metrics: FYE March 2004 to 2008
	
	  • **Analysis of FYE March 2006:** Sales; Gross Profit; SG&A, Interest; Pre-Tax Income; Cash Flow Coverage; and Free Cash Flow
	
	  • **Analysis of FYE March 2007:** Sales; Gross Profit; SG&A, Interest; Pre-Tax Income; Cash Flow Coverage; and Free Cash Flow
	
	  • **Analysis of FYE March 2008:** Sales; Gross Profit; SG&A, Plant Fire in 2007; Closure of Cedartown Plant; Goodwill & Intangible Impairment Charges; Operating Lease Payments; Interest, Change in Interest Rate; Free Cash Flow; Change in CFO
	
	• Pierre's EBITDA Margins Compared to the Industry
	• Pierre's EBITDA Margins Compared to all U.S. Exchanged Traded Non-Financial Firms
	• Asset Turnover • Pierre's Sales & EBITDA During Bankruptcy
	• Balance Sheets Prior to Chapter 11 • Analysis of Liquidity
	• Substantial Decrease in Receivables Prior to Bankruptcy
	• Substantial Increase in Vendor Prepayments Prior to Bankruptcy
	• Substantial Decrease in Vendor Payables Prior to Bankruptcy
	• Analysis of Accrued Payroll • Debt Balances Prior to Bankruptcy
	• Analysis of Change in Net Worth
	• Analysis of Tax Loss Carry-forwards • Debt and Net Worth
	• Tax Loss Carry-forwards • Employee Benefits

Chapter 9 Page 116	**Pierre's Credit Ratings and Trading Value of Pierre's Debt** ● Credit Rating Agencies ● Issuer Rating ● Issue Rating ● Long-Term Issuer Ratings ● Issuer or General Corporate Credit Rating ● Issue Credit Rating ● Recovery Ratings for Issue Rating ● Analytical Framework for Determining Credit Ratings ● Financial Ratios as Determinants of Credit Ratings ● S&P Default Recovery Methodology ● Summary & Conclusions of Credit Agency Ratings ● S&P Median Credit Ratios vs. U.S. Exchange Traded Firms ● Market Trading Value of Pierre's Debt ● Trading Value of $125 million Senior Unsecured Notes ● Trading Value of $250 million Wachovia Loan
Chapter 10 Page 123	**Events Leading to Chapter 11 / First-Day Orders / DIP Loan** ● Black-Swan Events ● Oaktree Capital Begins Buying Debt & Proposes a Plan ● First-Day Order for Wages, Salaries, Other Compensation ● First-Day Order for Payments of Vendors ● First-Day Order for DIP Revolver ● DIP Financial Covenants ● Adequate Protection Granted to the Wachovia Credit Facility ● Preliminary DIP Loan Court Hearing and Order ● Final DIP Loan Court Hearing and Order
Chapter 11 Page 133	**Prepetition Claims** ● Summary of Prepetition Claims ● $252 million Prepetition Wachovia Secured Credit Facility ● $125 million Prepetition Senior Unsecured Notes ● Institutional Holders of Senior Notes ● Largest Unsecured Creditors ● Leases Rejected ● Rejection of Other Contracts by Debtor ● Analysis of $252 million Wachovia Secured Credit Facility ● Institutional Holders the Wachovia Secured Credit Facility

Chapter 12 Page 141	**Validity of Guarantees Securing Wachovia Credit Facility**
Chapter 13 Page 144	**Disgorgement of Preference Payments** • Preference Payments to the Wachovia Credit Facility • Preference Payments to the Trade Vendors
Chapter 14 Page 148	**Wachovia Loan: Under or Over Secured and Initial Estimate of Recoveries Based on Assets & Enterprise Value** • Matrix for Values and Recoveries for Classes of Claims • Under or Over Secured—Wachovia Credit Facility • Detail of Independent Analysis: Asset Values, Liquidation, and Recovery • Independent Analysis: Liquidation Assumptions
Chapter 15 Page 156	**Wachovia Claim: Unimpaired or Impaired Treatment**
Chapter 16 Page 159	**A Rush to Exit Chapter 11 & the Debtor's Plan** • A Rush to Exit Bankruptcy • Creditors Committee Reaches Plan Agreement in One Month • Compensation Structure for Financial Consultants Gives Incentive for Quick Plan • Make-up of Creditors Committee Favors Vendors over Sr. Notes • Concern Over an Enterprise Value Fight • Risk of Loss of Customer and Vendor Support • Did a DIP Trigger Cause a Rush to Submit a Plan? • Did Oaktree Capital's Proposed Cash Investment Rush a Plan? • Incentives for Pierre's Management & the Debtor Plan • Are the Financial Advisors Responsible for the Debtor's Plan? • Oaktree Capital: Hope for a Bigger & Brighter Future for Pierre • The Debtor's Plan • Dilution of Preferred Stock • Constraints on Selling Preferred Stock • Requirement to Sell Preferred Stock • Table Summarizing Debtor's Plan
Chapter 17 Page 170	**Exit Financing for Debtor's Plan** • $95 million First-Lien Exit Credit Facility • $85 million PIK Note (Second-Lien and Subordinate)

Chapter 18 Page 173	**Sources & Uses of Cash in the Debtor's Plan** • Debtor's Plan Missing a Sources & Uses of Funds Statement • Estimate of Sources & Uses of Funds—Debtor's Plan • Liquidity: Assuming Disgorgement of Preference Payments, Increase in Payables, Equipment Sale, and Zero Claim Payout
Chapter 19 Page 177	**Feasibility of Debtor's Plan—Debtor's Projected Balance Sheet** • Post Chapter 11 Balance Sheet Key Metrics (Debtor's Plan) • Ability to Retain Sufficient Liquidity & Capital (Debtor's Plan) • Balance Sheet Capital Structure (Debtor's Plan) • Feasibility of Debtor's Plan—Debt Structure and Debt Service
Chapter 20 Page 181	**Feasibility of Debtor's Plan—Debtor's Projected Income Statement &Cash Flow** • Reasonableness of Sales Forecast in Debtor's Plan • Reasonableness of the EBITDA Forecast in Debtor's Plan • Debtor's Plan Projected EBITDA to Debt Service Coverage • Debtor's Plan Projected Working Capital and CAPX • Debtor's Plan Projected CMLTD and Net Cash Flow • Reasonableness of the Projected EBITDA in the Debtor's Plan • Comparison of Normalized EBITDA to Debtor's Plan EBITDA • Debtor's Historical EBITDA Margins Compared to Industry • Debtor's Historical EBITDA Margins Compared to U.S. Firms • Feasibility of Debtor's Plan—Cash Flow
Chapter 21 Page 186	**Objections to the Debtor's Plan** • U.S. Trustee Objections • Rabobank Objections
Chapter 22 Page 190	**Voting Results for Debtor's Plan** • Class 1 and 2 Treated as Unimpaired and Do Not Vote • Voting Result for Class 3 Claims (Wachovia Credit Facility) • Voting Result for Class 4 Claims (Unsecured Claims) • Exit from Chapter 11 December 12, 2008 • New Chief Executive Officer and New Directors for Pierre
Chapter 23 Page 194	**Perella Weinberg's Estimate of Pierre's Enterprise Value** • Perella Weinberg Methods of Valuation • Perella Weinberg's Enterprise Value as a Multiple of FYE March 2009–2010 EBITDA Projected in Debtor's Plan • Missing Assumptions & Details

Part V	**Presentation of Alternative Enterprise Value for Pierre**
Chapter 24 Page 197	**Alternative Analysis Supporting a Higher Enterprise Value** • Review of Grant Thornton Enterprise Valuation Performed in 2001 • Comparable Firms Used in Grant Thornton's 2001 Valuation • Comparable Transactions in Grant Thornton's 2001 Valuation • Discounted Cash Flow in Grant Thornton's 2001 Valuation • Grant Thornton's Final Enterprise Value for Pierre in 2001 • October 2008 Enterprise Value on Grant Thornton 2001 Multiples • October 2008 Enterprise Value on Bridgford Foods Multiples • October 2008 Enterprise Value on Hormel Foods Multiples • October 2008 Enterprise Value on Madison Dearborn's Acquisition Multiple for Pierre in June 2004 • October 2008 Enterprise Value on Industry Peer Multiples • October 2008 Enterprise Value on Recent Comparable Transactions • October 2008 Enterprise Value Based on Discounted Cash Flow • Assumptions for the Pierre's Cost of Equity under Build-Up Method • Risk-Free Rate • Equity Risk Premium • Size Premium • Industry Premium & Method to Determine Industry Premium • Bankruptcy Emergence Risk Premium • Estimating Pierre's Cost of Debt • Discounted Cash Flow Model Present Value Formula • Pierre's Assumed Growth Rate • Detailed Calculation of Pierre's Enterprise Value—Build-Up Method • Detailed Calculation of Pierre's Enterprise Value—CAPM • Summary of Enterprise Values for all Valuation Methods • Final Estimate of Pierre's Enterprise Value for the Alternative Plan
Part VI	**The Presentation of an Alternative Reorganization Plan**
Chapter 25 Page 223	**Alternative Reorganization Plan** • Presentation of the Alternative Plan of Reorganization • Alternative Plan Assumes $1 million in Capital Leases Accepted • $248.7 million Wachovia Loan Reinstated on 8.5 Year Amortization • Wachovia Loan 4 Tranches: Each Succeeding Tranche Subordinate • Escrow for Loan if Collateral Falls Below Minimum Amount • Covenants for the Wachovia Loan • Allocation of Reorganized Debtor Stock in the Alternative Plan • If EBITDA to Debt Service < 1.0: at December 31, 2009, then Tranches 2, 3, & 4 of Wachovia Debt Convert to Preferred Stock

- Senior Management Incentive Compensation Plan
- Tax Implications of Alternative Plan
- Amortization of the Wachovia Loan Tranches
- Collateral Coverage Ratios for each Wachovia Loan Tranche
- Determination of the Wachovia Interest Rate for each Loan Tranche
- Fixed Interest Rate by Tranche
- Projected Debtor Liquidity at Emergence (Alternative Plan)
- Working Capital Required for Future Periods (Alternative Plan)
- Post Closing Balance Sheet (Alternative Plan)
- Projected Income Statement, Cash Flow, Cash, and Wachovia Loan Balance (Alternative Plan)
- Adequate Liquidity (Alternative Plan)
- Adequate Free Cash Flow/Debt Service Coverage (Alternative Plan)
- Sensitivity Analysis (Alternative Plan)
- Safety Net Structure for Alternative Plan
- Feasibility of Alternative Plan
- Credit Ratings Based on S&P Metrics (Alternative Plan)
- Final Credit Ratings Assigned for Pierre Corporate Credit Rating and for Wachovia Loan Tranches
- Recommended Cramdown for Classes of Creditors Not Approving the Alternative Plan

Chapter 26 Page 239	**Bankruptcy Prediction Z-Scores** • Z-Score Prior to Bankruptcy • Z-Score on Alternative Plan • Z-Score on Alternative Plan Assuming Conversion of Tranche 2, 3, and 4 to Equity
Chapter 27 Page 243	**Condensed Version of Pierre's Bankruptcy, the Alternative Plan, & Concluding Comments** • Pierre's Business • Madison Dearborn's Acquistion of Pierre in June 2004 • Acquistion of Clovervale and Zartic • Pierre's High Debt Burden • Wachovia Secured Credit Facility Collateral • $125 Million Senior Notes (Unsecured) • Pierre's Credit Rating • Credit Agency Rating Implications • Events Leading to Bankruptcy • Oaktree Capital Begins Buying Debt & Works on a Bankruptcy Plan • Oaktree Capital's Investment Strategy • Creditors Committee, Oaktree, & Pierre Agree to Speedy Plan • Debtor's Plan of Reorganization • Form of Wachovia Claim Recovery

- Plan Vote and Approval • Why the Rush for a Debtor Plan?
- Structure of Financial Advisor Fees
- Creditors Committee & Vendor Claims
- No Fight Over Enterprise Value From Senior Note Holders
- Loss of Customer and Vendor Support
- Oaktree Capital's DIP Loan Trigger for a Debtor Plan Submittal
- Did Oaktree Capital's Proposed Cash Investment Rush a Plan?
- Hypothesis for Debtor's Speedy Plan
- Managements Role in Debtor's Plan
- Registration Rights Agreement
- Management & Director Incentive & Severance Plan
- An Alternative Plan of Reorganization
- Comparison of Pierre's EBITDA Margins to Industry & U.S. Firms
- Estimate of an Alternative Enterprise Value
- Alternative Plan Structure
- Recovery Debtor's Plan vs. Alternative Plan
- Alternative Plan—Wachovia Loan Carved into Four Tranches
- $6.4 million Exit Revolver Without Impariment to Wachovia Loan
- Feasibility Test: Liquidity in Alternative Plan
- Feasibility Test: Cash Flow Coverage in the Alternative Plan
- Disgorgement of Preference Payments
- Pierre's Corporate Credit Rating B- for Alternative Plan
- Structural Enhancement in Alternative Plan
- Bankruptcy Prediction Model for Alternative Plan
- Alternative Plan Structured for Distress Event and Recapitalization without the need to Re-Enter Bankruptcy
- Tax Impact of Altnerative Plan
- Concluding Comments on Altnerative Plan
- Analysis of Oaktree Capital's Investment in Pierre
- Lesson for Institutional Lenders
- Epilogue

References
Page 264

Biblography
Page 267

About the Author
Page 271

List of Tables

Table		Page
2.0	Bankruptcy Debt Investing Example: Return on Spansion's Debt	44
3.0	Matrix Calculating Levered Beta Assuming Various Unlevered Betas and Debt to Equity Ratios	53
3.1	Matrix Calculating a Firms Equity Risk Premium Assuming Various Betas and the Market Equity Risk Premiums	53
3.2	Key Financial Metrics for U.S. Exchange Traded Firms in U.S.	54
3.3	Summary of U.S. Equity Risk Premium Estimates	56
4.0	Guide for Bankruptcies—Table to Estimate Asset Values	65
4.1	Guide for Bankruptcies—Table to Estimate Recoveries	66
5.0	Debtor's Professionals and Fees	71
5.1	Unsecured Creditors Committee Members	72
5.2	Creditors Committee Professionals	73
6.0	Pierre's Top Executive Officer Compensation	84
7.0	Sources & Uses of Funds—Madison Dearborn Acquisition of Pierre	87
7.1	Pierre's Balance Sheet Pre & Post Madison Dearborn Acquisition	89
7.2	Pro-Forma SG&A Expenses Eliminated Post Madison Dearborn Acquisition	89
7.3	2004 Enterprise Value to EBITDA and Debt—Pierre & Industry	90
7.4	S&P's Key U.S. Industrial Average Financial Ratios Compared to S&P's Credit Ratings	91
7.5	Pierre's EBITDA to Interest Expense Ratio FYE March 2004–2007	92
7.6	Ratio of Unsecured and Secured Debt to Adjusted EBITDA	93
7.7	Wachovia Credit Facility Maximum Debt to EBITDA Ratio	94
7.8	Post Acquisition Debt Compared to Pierre's Tangible Assets	95
8.0	Key Operating Metrics & Cash Flow Coverage Prior to Bankruptcy	99
8.1	EBITDA Margins for Firms in the Packaged Foods/Meats Industry	107
8.2	Key Financial Metrics for All U.S. Exchange Traded & U.S. Based Firms: EBITDA to Sales Ratio and Sales to Total Assets Ratio	108

Table		Page
8.3	Sales, COGS, and EBITDA during Bankruptcy	109
8.4	Balance Sheet Prior to Bankruptcy	109
8.5	Analysis of Current Liabilities	111
8.6	Change in Wachovia Loan Balance 136 Days Prior to Bankruptcy	111
9.0	Standard & Poor's Median Ratio of EBITDA to Interest Ratio for all U.S. Industrial Firms Rated by Standard & Poor's	116
9.1	Pierre's EBITDA to Interest Ratio FYE March 2004–2008	116
9.2	Standard & Poor's: Pierre's Credit Rating & Issue Recovery Rating	118
9.3	History of Market Trading Values for Pierre's Debt	120
10.0	Wachovia Credit Facility Financial Covenants	122
10.1	DIP Financial Covenants	128
11.0	Top Unsecured Creditors	133
11.1	Leases to be Rejected by Debtor	134
11.2	Initial Holders of the Wachovia Secured Credit Facility	137
12.0	Breakout of Balance Sheet for Pierre Foods, Inc. and Subsidiary Guarantors	141
13.0	Change in Wachovia Loan Balance 136 days prior to Bankruptcy	143
13.1	Analysis of Wachovia Credit Facility for Disgorgement	143
14.0	Recovery by Class of Claims in the Independent Analysis and Debtor's Plan	147
14.1	Independent Analysis of Asset Value Recovery, Liquidation Costs, and Recoveries for Claims	149
16.0	Table Summarizing the Debtor's Reorganization Plan	167
18.0	Estimated Sources/Uses of Cash at Plan Exit based on Debtor Plan	172
18.1	Balance on Debtor's Plan Exit Facility after Disgorgement & Increase in Vendor Float	173
18.2	Balance on Debtor's Plan Exit Facility Without 12% Cash Payouts After Disgorgement & Increase in Vendor Float	174
19.0	Debtor's Plan Projected Balance Sheets	176
19.1	Estimated Value of Preferred Stock in Debtor's Plan.	177

Table		Page
20.0	Debtor's Plan Projected Income Statement & Cash Flows	180
22.0	Class 3 Vote Outcome	189
22.1	Class 4 Vote Outcome	189
24.0	Comparable Firm EBITDA & Sales Multiples for the Year 2001	195
24.1	Implied EBITDA Multiples in 2001 Grant Thornton Discounted Cash Flow Method of Valuation of Pierre	197
24.2	Bridgford Food's Enterprise Value to EBITDA & Sales Multiples	199
24.3	Hormel Food's Enterprise Value to EBITDA & Sales Multiples	200
24.4	October 2008 Enterprise Value to EBTIDA for Industry Peers	201
24.5	Summary of Recent Comparable Sale Transaction Multiples	204
24.6	Calculation of Free Cash Flow for use in the Discount Cash Flow Method of Valuation (Alternative Plan)	206
24.7	Build-Up Method for Cost of Equity (Alternative Plan)	207
24.8	Industry Premiums for Cost of Equity and Industry Betas	211
24.9	Calculation of Alternative Enterprise Value—Build-Up Method	215
24.91	Calculation of Alternative Enterprise Value—CAPM based on Industry Beta and Comparable Firm Betas	217
24.92	Summary of Pierre's Enterprise Value under the Different Models.	219
25.0	Allocation of Stock to Classes of Claims (Alternative Plan)	222
25.1	Allocation of Stock to Claims in Event of Distress (Alternative Plan)	223
25.2	Amortization of Four Wachovia Loan Tranches (Alternative Plan)	225
25.3	Pricing of the Wachovia Loan Tranches (Alternative Plan)	225
25.4	Ratio of Prudent Lender Loan Values to the Wachovia Loan by Tranche	226
25.5	Fixed Interest Rate by Loan Tranche (Alternative Plan)	228
25.6	Projected Cash Liquidity at Exit from Chapter 11 (Alternative Plan)	228
25.7	Analysis of Working Capital Accounts (Alternative Plan)	229
25.8	Balance Sheet after Exit from Bankruptcy (Alternative Plan)	230

Table		Page
25.9	Alternative Plan Projected Income Statements, Cash Flows, Cash, Wachovia Loan Balance for Nine Years in the Future	231
25.91	Cash Flow Stress Analysis for Alternative Plan	233
25.92	Cash Flow Stress Analysis for Alternative Plan if Tranches 2–4 are Converted to Equity	234
25.93	Standard & Poor's U.S. Industrial Financial Ratios vs. Pierre's Ratios under the Alternative Plan	235
26.0	Pierre's Z-Score Results and Zones of Discrimination	238
26.1	Pierre's Z-Score FYE March 2008 & Quarter December 2007	238
26.2	Pierre's Z-Score Based on Alternative Plan Normalized & Distress EBITDA	239
26.3	Pierre's Z-Score based on Distress EBITA and Assuming Wachovia Tranches 2–4 Convert to Equity	240
27.0	Allocation of Stock to the Classes of Claims (Alternative Plan)	255

Chapter 1

Basics of the Bankruptcy Code

"If a man empties his purse into his head, no man can take it away from him. An investment in knowledge always pays the best interest." Benjamin Franklin

Overview of Title 11 of the U.S. Code

Knowledge of the U.S. Bankruptcy Code, as well as credit and financial analysis skills are required to analyze a debtor in bankruptcy and to structure a plan of reorganization. The purpose of Chapter 1 and 2 is to learn some of the key rules and procedures in the Bankruptcy Code to facilitate case analysis and structuring of a reorganization plan. Chapter 1 will discuss basics of the Bankruptcy Code. Chapter 2 will cover the plan of reorganization.

The Chapter 11 bankruptcy process is a mixture of law, finance, and the bargaining process that takes place between the parties of interest.

Title 11 of the United States Code is the Bankruptcy Code and it includes the following chapters:

Chapter	
1	General Provisions
3	Case Administration
5	Creditors, the Debtor, and the Estate
7	Liquidation
9	Adjustment of Debts of a Municipality
11	Reorganization
12	Adjustments of Debts of a Family Farmer or Family Fisherman with Regular Annual Income
13	Adjustments of Debts of an Individual with Regular Income
15	Ancillary and Other Cross-Border Cases
Appendix	Federal Rules of Bankruptcy Procedure and Official Bankruptcy Forms

Part I: Bankruptcy Basics

The Bankruptcy Code is available at the following website:
http://uscode.house.gov/download/title_11.shtml

Bankruptcy Courts and Judges

The bankruptcy courts are units of the district courts and a bankruptcy court exists in each district court. The court of appeals appoints bankruptcy judges.

In bankruptcy cases, the treatment of claims can conflict with the Bankruptcy Code or prior case law. The particular court and judge can often make a difference for each case.

The U.S. Trustee, the creditors committee, other creditors, equity holders, and other parties of interest are required to take initiative, perform due diligence, and evaluate the cost/benefit of enforcing their rights under the Bankruptcy Code. Bankruptcy courts have latitude to make judgments that can result in different outcomes based on the particular circumstances of the debtor, its creditors, and the perceived prospects of achieving an orderly reorganization.

There can be unexpected outcomes in a bankruptcy case even with full knowledge of the rules—an example is the Chrysler bankruptcy discussed in Chapter 2. Parties with significant financial interests in a case should retain bankruptcy counsel to discuss goals, strategies, and an action plan. This evaluation should include an estimate of the probability of success, the required time, and the cost.

Place of Filing

A company can file bankruptcy in either: (1) its domicile, (2) its place of residence, (3) location of its principal place of business, or (4) the location of its principal assets.

The Chapter 11 Filing

The date a company files Chapter 11 is the petition date. The entity in bankruptcy is the debtor-in-possession (DIP). The filing of Chapter 11 creates an estate that consists of all of the debtor's property.

In a Chapter 11 bankruptcy, unless a case trustee is appointed, the debtor retains control over its assets, business operations, and reorganization efforts.

Chapter 1: Basics of the Bankruptcy Code

Why File Chapter 11

- The debtor's management can continue to operate the company during the bankruptcy. The debtor can enter into transactions in the ordinary course of business, including the sale or lease of property;
- Often a company will attempt to restructure its debts without filing bankruptcy. Some creditors may not be willing to compromise. Chapter 11 brings the parties to the table. Each creditor claim is placed in a similar class and the Bankruptcy Code has rules for the treatment of the claims;
- A distressed debtor, who is attempting to sell assets, may find buyers unwilling to purchase because of the risk that other creditor claims will follow the purchased assets. The Bankruptcy Code provides procedures for the sale of assets and passing clear title to a buyer;
- Chapter 11 stays collection efforts unless the court determines otherwise;
- Chapter 11 can reduce debt service and preserve cash liquidity. The bankruptcy filing stops the payment of interest and principal payments on unsecured debt. Lenders are not permitted to receive principal payments on their debt, unless the court orders otherwise in an adequate protection order;
- The Bankruptcy Code has procedures to allow a debtor to request the use of cash balances and to borrow money. Chapter 11 can improve the debtor's chances of borrowing money;
- The Bankruptcy Code allows the debtor to reject burdensome cash outflow obligations for executory contracts, including union contracts, supply contracts, take-or-pay contracts, equipment leases, and real estate leases;
- The debtor has the exclusive opportunity for 120 days (up to 18 months with extensions) to propose a plan of reorganization. The debtor has up to 180 days from the petition date to obtain approval for the plan (up to 20 months with extensions);
- The debtor can use Section 363 of the Bankruptcy Code to sell assets;
- The final reorganization plan can be as a going-concern or an orderly liquidation of the business;
- The Bankruptcy Code allows a debtor to compromise debt under certain conditions. The debtor can reduce creditor claims and fresh start the business with a lower level of debt and obligations.

Part I: Bankruptcy Basics

Immediate Benefits and Objectives of Chapter 11

The immediate benefit of a company filing for Chapter 11 is the automatic stay, and, unless otherwise approved by the bankruptcy court, the bankruptcy filing stays all acts of a creditor to collect from the debtor. A party can file a court motion for relief from the stay, most typically filed by a secured creditor who is seeking adequate protection in the form of payments from the debtor or court approval to foreclose on its collateral.

The debtor's primary objectives in Chapter 11 are to increase cash liquidity, obtain new borrowing lines of credit, and to reduce cash outflows related to debt payments and other executory contracts. The bankruptcy code allows a company to improve liquidity, reduce obligations, and have a fresh start. A Chapter 11 reorganization is effective for a company who has too much debt and/or other significant obligations, subject to the company having reasonable prospects of making money in the future under a reorganized capital structure.

Cost of Bankruptcy

Professional fees can consume substantial assets of the debtor during bankruptcy. In the case of Pierre Foods, professional fees accounted for 8.3% of the Pierre's tangible assets during the five-month bankruptcy. Pierre's bankruptcy was relatively quick compared to the norm. The typical debtor spends an average of 6 to 18 months in bankruptcy. There are economies of scale in the cost of bankruptcy. Professional fees, as a percentage of total assets, will usually decrease as the size of the debtor's total assets increase.

A hidden cost of bankruptcy is the negative goodwill created by the stigma attached with the bankruptcy filing. The debtor's competitors will advertise to potential customers the financial distress of the debtor.

Different companies and industry face a greater risk loss of business because of the negative goodwill from a bankruptcy filing. The time it requires a debtor to deliver a product from the date of a customer order and the importance of product warranty may impact the future prospects for a business. Potential customers may be concerned that a distressed company may not be around in the future to deliver the product and honor long-term product warranties.

U.S. Trustee vs. Case Trustee

After a debtor files bankruptcy, the bankruptcy judge assigns a U.S. Trustee to the case. The debtor's management typically remains in possession of the business operations and has all of the powers granted to a trustee.

The U.S. Trustee appoints an unsecured creditors committee and also convenes and oversees the first creditors committee meeting. Along with the

Chapter 1: Basics of the Bankruptcy Code

creditors committee, the U.S. Trustee acts as a watchdog in the case to ensure compliance with the Bankruptcy Code. Any party with an economic interest in a case may request court approval for additional creditor or equity committees, and, if approved, the U.S. Trustee is responsible for appointing the members of those committees.

Parties of interest in a case may seek the appointment of a Chapter 11 case trustee or examiner, for cause and if in the best interest of the estate. The appointment of a case trustee is rare in a Chapter 11 bankruptcy. The Court typically orders the appointment of a case trustee for cause, such as fraud, dishonesty, incompetence, or gross mismanagement.

Unsecured Creditors Committee

Within the first month of the bankruptcy filing, the U.S. Bankruptcy Trustee will appoint an unsecured creditors committee based on a questionnaire sent out to the largest unsecured creditors. The creditors committee has three to eleven members and typically consists of between five and seven of the largest unsecured creditors who are willing to serve (a list of the 20 largest unsecured creditors must be filed by the debtor on the bankruptcy petition date).

The U.S. Bankruptcy Trustee will attempt to select members that have different types of unsecured claims. The unsecured creditors committee is typically a mixture of unsecured trade creditors and unsecured debt holders that have different economic interests. Vendors stand to benefit from the successful reorganization of a debtor through continued sales to the debtor. Unsecured trade creditors have high gross profit margins compared to a lender. The trade vendor also turns sales to the debtor many times in a year. The higher vendor profit margins and sales turnover can quickly offset the loss from the account receivable balance due from the debtor. In contrast, an unsecured lender has a small gross margin compared to a trade vendor, the lender does not receive interest during bankruptcy, and the lender does not earn profits from on-going sales of product to the debtor.

In the case of Pierre Foods, trade vendors had claims of $15.2 million at the date of bankruptcy and unsecured Senior Notes had claims of $131 million. Pierre's unsecured trade debt was 11% of total unsecured debt, suggesting the creditors committee should have had one member from the unsecured vendor class and six members from the Senior Note holders. The Bankruptcy Trustee chose to appoint three trade vendors and four Senior Note holders to the creditors committee.

The U.S. Bankruptcy Trustee may also appoint several creditors committees for the various classes of creditors or a committee for the equity holders.

Part I: Bankruptcy Basics

Because of the costs involved, smaller bankruptcy cases will typically limit the number of committees.

The bankruptcy judge and debtor value the creditors committee's opinions and recommendations, as opposed to the self-interested view of one creditor.

A member of the committee does not receive compensation but is entitled to reimbursement of reasonable expenses. The committee member has a fiduciary responsibility to all unsecured creditors; but within this obligation, a member of the committee can influence the treatment of their claim as well as those for other classes of claims.

Examination of Debtor

The U.S. Bankruptcy Trustee is required to call a meeting of creditors within 20 to 40 days from the date of the bankruptcy filing. The U.S. Bankruptcy Trustee is responsible for notifying the debtor and all creditors of the meeting within 20 days of the meeting, either through the mail or by posting public notice if it is impractical to notify by mail. The U.S. Bankruptcy Trustee or one of his/her assistants typically presides over the meeting. Prior to the end of the meeting, the debtor must appear and submit to examination under oath. The U.S. Bankruptcy Trustee or <u>any creditor</u> may examine the debtor. The debtor examination can include inquiry into the financial condition of the debtor, the operation of the business, the desirability of continuing the business, other matters relevant to the case, and questions as to the formulation of the plan of reorganization. The U.S. Bankruptcy Trustee must sound record the meeting and is required to provide a copy of the recording or transcript to any requesting party.

Powers and Duties of Appointed Committees

The Bankruptcy Code gives the unsecured creditors committee authorization to:
- Meet with the U.S. Trustee as soon as possible after the Chapter 11 filing to transact such business as may be necessary and proper;
- Select and authorize the employment of one or more attorneys, accountants, or other agents, to represent or perform services for the committee. Subject to court approval of the professionals, the reasonable expenses of the professionals will be paid from the assets of the debtor's estate;
- Concerning the administration of the case, consult with the U.S. Bankruptcy Trustee, the case trustee, or the debtor. Because the creditors committee plays an important role, the debtor will keep the

Chapter 1: Basics of the Bankruptcy Code

creditors committee and its professionals informed. The debtor will typically seek the consent of the creditors committee on major decisions, including sale of assets and the plan of reorganization;

- Investigate the debtor's acts, conduct, assets, liabilities, and financial condition, the operation of the business, the desirability of the continuance of the business, and any other matter relevant to the case or to the formulation of a plan;
- Participate in the formulation of a plan, advise those represented by the creditors committee of the creditors committee's recommendations as to any plan formulated, and collect and file with the court acceptances or rejections of a plan;
- If the creditors committee determines it necessary, request court approval for the appointment of a case trustee or examiner;
- Perform such other services as are in the interest of those it represents.

A committee member has a fiduciary duty to act in the best interest of all unsecured creditors. The committee members cannot use confidential information gained in their service on the committee to their own advantage or for trading on claims or securities.

The creditors committee is required to:

- Provide access to information for creditors: (a) who hold claims of the kind represented by the creditors committee and (b) who have not been appointed to the creditors committee;
- Solicit and receive comments from unsecured creditors.

The creditors committee can provide access to privileged information as long as it is not confidential information.

Any information received by the creditors committee in the initial required examination of the debtor in the meeting held by the U.S. Trustee is not subject to privileged and confidential information. If the creditors committee declines to provide any requested information, a creditor has the right to a court hearing to compel disclosure.

A bankruptcy judge will often authorize the use of a web site by the creditors committee to disclose information and to solicit comments from unsecured creditors.

Part I: Bankruptcy Basics

Equity Committee

A fiduciary responsibility of a company's board of directors is protecting the economic interest of the shareholders of a company. After a company files bankruptcy, the company's board of directors owes a heightened fiduciary responsibility to creditors; shareholders lose status in a favored position in the corporate structure.

A creditors committee has a fiduciary responsibility to act in the best interests of the unsecured creditors. Under the Bankruptcy Code, the creditors committee does not have a fiduciary responsibility to represent the interests of shareholders. Shareholders are not at the table with the creditors committee. When a party is not at the table, the party does not eat; little food delivered to the absent party. Although any party of interest in a case has the right to enforce its rights under the Bankruptcy Code in court, it is at their own expense. Moreover, the party does not have access to confidential debtor financial and business information that is critical in valuing a company. Shareholders do not have the right actively participate in the formulation of a plan of reorganization without a court approved equity committee.

If the court approves an equity committee, the equity committee has the same rights as the creditors committee, including the right to require the debtor to pay reasonable professional expenses, investigate the financial affairs of the business, and participate in the formulation of a plan of reorganization. The equity committee gains greater access to the debtor's confidential financial and business information.

The first step to forming an equity committee is the request of an official equity committee to the U.S. Trustee, petitioning the Trustee to solicit interest among shareholders to serve on an equity committee. It is typical that the debtor will not welcome the formation of an equity committee and often opposes the formation of an equity committee. The U.S. Trustee may be more receptive of the formation of an equity committee if the U.S. Securities & Exchange Commission supports the formation of an equity committee.

If the U.S. Trustee does not support the formation of an equity committee, the only alternative is to file a motion in bankruptcy court for the formation of any equity committee. Under the Bankruptcy Code, the court may order the appointment of an equity committee to assure adequate representation of equity holders. The bankruptcy courts typically look at the following factors: (1) the number of shareholders, (2) the complexity of the case, (3) the solvency of the debtor, (4) whether the cost to the estate is greater than the benefit of shareholder representation, and (5) the timing of the formation of the equity committee.

Chapter 1: Basics of the Bankruptcy Code

A party seeking the formation of an equity committee has a better chance of succeeding, with all else being equal, if the request for formation comes early in the case.

Case complexity is not typically an issue that prevents the court from approving an equity committee; the debtor's own bankruptcy first day court filings generally argue the complexity of the case.

Assuming sufficient number of shareholders in the case, the solvency of the debtor issue is often the key issue in the court decision for the formation of an equity committee. The argument for the formation of an equity committee is often that economic indicators demonstrate that there is value for the shareholders. This could be in the form of the market capitalization based on the stock trading price.

The creditors committee, and most likely the debtor, will oppose the formation of the equity committee because an equity committee will slow down the reorganization process and result in greater expense for the estate. The formation of an equity committee increases the risk that the creditors will be forced to share a portion of the estate with equity holders. If management and the board of directors of the debtor do not hold significant prepetition stock in the debtor, it is more likely that they will not look after the interest of the shareholders. Management understands that the company has a better chance of long term survival if the debtor emerges from bankruptcy with as little debt as possible. If debt can be compromised, then there is no value left over for shareholders. Moreover, management may be rewarded in the future from continuing to have employment with a reorganized company with a sound capital structure that rewards management with stock options in the reorganized debtor.

Those in opposition to the formation of court approval of an equity committee will argue for a more stringent solvency test, one that requires a substantial likelihood that the equity holders will receive a meaningful distribution under the strict application of the absolute priority rule. The party pursuing approval of an equity committee does not have full access to the debtor's financial and business information in order to value the business, and the valuation would be at its own expense. If it can be established that equity is in the money, many courts will take the view that equity holders need an equity committee. The trading value of the stock and expert financial testimony can persuade the court that equity is in the money.

Part I: Bankruptcy Basics

Debtor's Reporting Requirements in Bankruptcy

The debtor's duties include filing the following information with the bankruptcy court:

- File a list of names, addresses, and claims for the 20 largest unsecured claims;

- File a "Summary of Schedules" which includes a report on the amount of the debtor's assets and liabilities as of the petition date. The report includes the amount of real property, personal property, exempt property, secured claims, unsecured priority claims, unsecured non-priority claims, executory contracts, unexpired leases, and co-debtors. Supporting detailed schedules are required for each of the foregoing categories. The debtor is also required to provide a list of names and addresses for each creditor claim and for unexpired executory contracts. The court will typically give the debtor an extension of several months to file the schedules;

- File a "Statement of Financial Affairs" which includes the following: the debtor's income for two years prior to the petition date; payments to creditors 90 days prior to the petition; payments to insiders one year prior to the petition; property seized; property repossessed; property assigned to creditors; gifts within one year of the petition; payments for bankruptcy related legal and professional fees one year prior to the petition, distributions to insiders, information on lawsuits, environmental proceedings, and a list of officers/directors/partners. The court will typically give the debtor an extension of several months to file the Statement of Financial Affairs;

- File a notice for the initial meeting of creditors, examination of the debtor, and deadlines. The schedule identifies the time and location of the initial meeting of creditors for the examination of the debtor and the deadline for creditors to file claims,

- Within 30 days after each month, file the following schedules: cash receipts and disbursements, bank reconciliation, professional fees paid, copies of bank statements, cash disbursements journal, an income statement, balance sheet, status of postpetition taxes, summary of unpaid postpetition debts, accounts payable aging, and accounts receivable aging.

Chapter 1: Basics of the Bankruptcy Code

Debtor's Use, Sale, and Lease of Property

The debtor can enter into transactions, including the use, sale and lease of property in the ordinary course of business, without notice or court hearing. The debtor may use cash after court hearing and approval. The use of cash by the debtor is of concern because: (1) a secured creditor may have a lien on cash and (2) the cash is property of the estate. If the debtor spends the cash, it can decrease the value of the estate and harm creditors.

Two of the biggest events in a bankruptcy are sale of assets and the reorganization plan. After court hearing and approval, the debtor may use, sell, and lease property <u>other</u> than in the ordinary course of business. A party of interest in property retains the right of adequate protection with respect to the debtor's use, sale, and lease of property, whether in the ordinary course of business or other than in the ordinary course of business.

For the sale of property outside of the ordinary course of business, Section 363 of the Bankruptcy Code permits the debtor to sell property free and clear of the interest of an entity other than the estate, if one of the following conditions exists:

- The entity with the interest in the property consents;
- Non-bankruptcy law permits the sale of the property free and clear of such interest;
- The interest in the property is a lien and the property is sold for a price that equals or exceeds the value of the liens on the property;
- The interest in the property is in bona fide dispute;
- The entity with the interest in the property could be compelled in a legal or equitable proceeding to accept money in satisfaction of its interest.

For a Section 363 sale of property, a holder of a claim may bid at the sale of the property and can offset its claim against the purchase price.

In recent years, rather than going through a reorganization plan, debtors' have increasingly used Section 363 sales to sell major segments of the business. The process typically begins with a stalking horse, a party that has agreed to buy the assets. If the stalking horse losses in the bidding process for the debtor's assets, it is typically paid a breakup fee and its other expenses in connection with the bid. A 363 sale can be very appealing to many debtors and creditors because a sale can be an efficient and quick method of restructuring.

A major benefit of a 363 sale is that the purchaser takes the assets free and clear of liens. If a company has a buyer for the business prior to bankruptcy, many corporate charters require the approval of a majority its shareholders to sell substantially all of the assets of the company. By filing bankruptcy, the company can escape the shareholder approval requirement.

There are many caveats for Section 363 sales. Section 363 of the Bankruptcy Code provides that the debtor "may sell property… free and clear of any interest in such property of an entity other than the estate…"

The Bankruptcy Codes does not define "interest in such property" and courts have different opinions on whether this is sufficient to protect a successor from the obligations of the debtor under state and federal laws. The issue of whether environmental liabilities and product liabilities follow assets in a sale is complex. A debtor can sell assets free and clear of labor related liabilities without binding a successor employer to the debtor's prior labor agreement. Claims for unfair labor practices have been found to survive a sale.

Concept of Value in Bankruptcy

One of the most important issues in bankruptcy is the estimation of the value of the debtor's assets and the value of the business as a going-concern. This issue becomes critical in disputes involving adequate protection, automatic stay, and creditor treatment in the reorganization plan.

The bankruptcy court does not attempt to determine value on it own. It is up to the debtor and other parties in the case to agree on value or to file a motion for court hearing on the determination of value.

The bankruptcy courts have generally held that "value" is to be determined in light of the purpose of the valuation and of the proposed use of the property. If the debtor plans to continue to hold and use the collateral, the courts generally determine value to be "the price a willing buyer in the debtor's trade, business, or situation would pay to a willing seller to obtain property of like age and condition" (*Associates Commercial Corp. v. Rash*, 2007). In Granite Broadcasting (*Granite Broadcasting Corp. et al.*, 2007), the Southern District of New York Bankruptcy Court issued the following opinion on value:

> "…the market value of a piece of property is the price which it might be expected to bring if offered for sale in a fair market; not the price which might be obtained on a sale at public auction or a sale forced by the necessities of the owner, but such a price as would be fixed by negotiation and mutual agreement, after ample time to find a purchaser, as between a vendor who is willing, but not compelled, to sell and a purchaser who desires to buy, but is not compelled, to take the particular piece of property."

Chapter 1: Basics of the Bankruptcy Code

If a debtor plans to hold and use property, the *Rash* and *Granite Broadcasting Corp.* court decisions on value are similar to the American Society of Appraisers definition of fair market value:

> "The price, expressed in terms of cash equivalents, at which property would change hands between a hypothetical willing and able buyer and a hypothetical willing and able seller, acting at arm's length in an open and unrestricted market, when neither is under compulsion to buy or sell and when both have reasonable knowledge of the relevant facts."

There can be a significant difference between the fair market value of the assets of the debtor and the value of the debtor's business as a going-concern. The going-concern fair market value includes the intangibles of a highly skilled workforce, an operational plant, customer relationships, employment agreements, trademarks, trade secrets, patents, required licenses, systems, and procedures specific to a company.

Often the debtor's primary lender will take a blanket-lien on all of the debtor's assets, including intangibles, trademarks, and the common stock of the debtor. It is important to determine the extent of the lender's lien. If the creditor does not have a lien on the stock of the debtor, the value of the assets on which the creditor has a lien could be less than the going-concern value of the business.

The Bankruptcy Code makes it clear that value is determined for the purposes of the specific hearing, for example, value could be determined at the date of a court motion for adequate protection (early in the case) and another value could apply at the date of the plan of reorganization.

In summary, the key takeaway is that the courts generally hold that the value of the debtor's property is the fair market value if the debtor plans to use the property in the business.

Adequate Protection

The Bankruptcy Code allows a secured creditor to be protected against a decrease in the value of its collateral during the bankruptcy. If the debtor proposes to use the collateral during bankruptcy, a secured creditor has the right to adequate protection. This does not imply that an oversecured lender (collateral value greater than claim) will receive adequate protection for a decrease in the value of the collateral—the court may determine that the creditor continues to have an adequate collateral cushion.

Part I: Bankruptcy Basics

Adequate protection can be in many forms, including but not limited to, interest payments, principal payments, additional liens, or a continuing security interest in inventory and receivables.

The bankruptcy court may grant a lender superpriority status as adequate protection. A superpriority claim is a powerful right as the party with a superpriority claim has a right to receive payment prior to an administrative claim. In addition, the debtor is required to pay off the superpriority claim prior to emerging from bankruptcy.

The bankruptcy court may give a prepetition lender superpriority status as adequate protection for a priming lien given to a DIP lender, but the court will often limit the superpriority status to the loss in the value of creditor's collateral that results from the priming lien.

If a creditor files a motion to foreclosure on its property, after court hearing, the court can lift the stay and allow an undersecured creditor to foreclose on its collateral, subject to the creditor proving the collateral is not critical to the debtor's restructuring or the liquidation plan. Generally, an oversecured creditor is not allowed to foreclose on the property if the debtor requires the use of the collateral.

Bankruptcy Code Procedures for Obtaining Credit

Subject to court approval, the debtor may obtain new unsecured credit in the ordinary course of business during bankruptcy as an administrative expense, which then takes priority over other unsecured prepetition claims. If the debtor is unable to obtain unsecured credit as an administrative expense, the court, after notice and hearing, may give a lender extending new credit:

- Superpriority status for the extension of credit;
- A lien on property of the estate that is not subject to a lien; or
- A junior lien on property of the estate.

The court, after notice and hearing, may authorize new credit secured by a senior or equal lien on property of the estate only if:

- The debtor is unable to obtain credit otherwise; and
- Adequate protection is provided to the holder whose lien is being primed. The debtor has the burden of proof on the issue of adequate protection.

DIP Financing

One of the first motions after bankruptcy will be for a court hearing on the approval of DIP financing or the use of cash. In return for a DIP priming lien,

Chapter 1: Basics of the Bankruptcy Code

or use of cash, the Bankruptcy Code gives the prepetition lender the right to adequate protection for impairment caused by the priming lien.

If the debtor has not arranged DIP financing, the debtor will seek court approval to use a limited amount of cash. The bankruptcy court may approve the use of cash, subject to constraints and limits; but prior to approval, the court must hold a hearing to determine that the benefit to the estate from the use of cash outweighs the diminution in collateral value for the estate or for the secured party with a lien on the cash. The argument for the use of cash is that it allows the debtor to continue to operate which ultimately provides a higher recovery for the estate as compared to an immediate liquidation of the business. The approval for the use of cash will typically carry restrictions, often including an expiration period and a requirement that the debtor's expenditures comply with a weekly or monthly budget.

The debtor may attempt to arrange a continuation of its prepetition revolving line of credit secured by receivables/inventory. If the debtor and creditor cannot reach agreement on a continuation of the revolver, they will try to negotiate a limited amount of cash collateral usage or a DIP priming lien to keep the business going. The situation may be that the prepetition secured lender does not want to invest any more cash, but lender believes a shut down of the business will have unfavorable consequences, or the prepetition lender may believe the court will approve a DIP priming lien or the use of cash collateral. In some cases, the prepetition secured lender may be willing to loan additional money to preserve value for its own interest and/or to improve its position. The prepetition lender could try to improve its position by requesting cash payments, cross-collateralization of loans, and superpriority status to cover the unsecured portion of its loan. Other interested parties will most likely object to the prepetition lender who attempts to improve its position in return for DIP financing.

When the primary collateral is inventory/receivables, a prepetition lender will often receive a replacement lien on postpetition inventory/receivables as adequate protection. This form of adequate protection is significant for the lender because the bankruptcy filing cuts-off any lien on postpetition created property. The debtor can then spend the proceeds of the receivables that are subject to the prepetition lender's lien in exchange for a lien on new replacement inventory/receivables. If the debtor generates new receivables at the same rate as it spends the proceeds of prepetition receivables, then the lender has adequate protection.

If the debtor is unable to obtain DIP financing, the Bankruptcy Code allows the court to grant the DIP lender a priority lien over the lien on the collateral of prepetition creditors, subject to adequate protection of the party being primed. As a condition to the extension of credit in bankruptcy, DIP lenders generally demand superpriority status and they typically require some form of priming lien over the collateral held by other creditors.

A court approved superpriority claim granted to a DIP lender will often have a carve-out for a certain dollar amount of professional fee expense. Few bankruptcy professionals are willing to work without compensation. In turn, the DIP lender will often reduce the borrowing availability under the approved DIP loan by the amount of the carve-out.

Moody's Default Study on DIP Loans

A lender's risk of loss for extending credit to a debtor in bankruptcy decreases when the bankruptcy court grants a DIP lender superpriority status and a priming lien. Moreover, the DIP loan to the debtor in bankruptcy is often small compared to the value of the collateral securing the DIP loan. In the case of Pierre Foods, the $35 million DIP loan was 18% of Pierre's tangible assets. In the event the business is liquidated in bankruptcy, the superpriority status requires the loan to be paid off before administrative claims. On the other hand, if the debtor successfully reorganizes, the DIP lender with superpriority status has the right to be paid off before the debtor can emerge from bankruptcy.

Moody's has studied (Mulvaney, Fahy, Gates, 2009) the default experience for DIP loans created between 1988 and 2008 for a number of large public firms. The study found a default probability consistent with a low investment-grade credit rating. The loan pricing spreads charged by lenders to debtors in bankruptcy have historically been at interest rate spreads substantially above those for low investment-grade credits. DIP lenders also charge substantial upfront loan fees.

Bifurcation of Claim into Secured Claim and Unsecured Claim

If a creditor has a lien on property, it is a secured claim to the extent of the value of the property and an unsecured claim to the extent the value of property is less than the amount of the claim. In other words, if a creditor's total claim is less than the value of the collateral, the claim can be bifurcated into a secured claim for the value of the collateral and an unsecured claim for the balance of the claim. There is one exception to this rule: a secured creditor has the option to have its claim treated under Section 1111(b) of the Bankruptcy Code. Section 1111(b) allows a creditor, secured by collateral, to treat its entire claim as a secured claim, <u>but only for the treatment of its claim in the plan of reorganization</u>. Chapter 2 discusses the Section 1111(b) option at greater length.

Chapter 1: Basics of the Bankruptcy Code

Principal and Interest on Unsecured and Secured Claims

The Bankruptcy Code does not permit an unsecured creditor to receive interest or principal payments. If all other creditors receive a 100% recovery under a plan of reorganization, it is possible for an unsecured creditor to receive interest on its claim.

If the value of the lender's collateral exceeds its claim, the lender is entitled to interest during bankruptcy. If the loan is $1 million and the value of the collateral is $1.1 million, the lender is entitled to interest up to $100,000.

If the value of a lender's collateral is less than its claim, the Bankruptcy Code does not provide for interest on the lender's loan. If a lender is undersecured and the claim is bifurcated into a secured and unsecured claim, a question arises as to whether the lender is entitled to interest on the secured portion of its claim. Various court decisions have held that the payment of interest extends only to oversecured lenders.

An undersecured lender, in contrast to an unsecured lender, has the right under the Bankruptcy Code to adequate protection for a decrease in the value of the collateral. If the bankruptcy court approves adequate protection payments, some courts have required the application of the payments to the loan balance rather than interest because the lender is undersecured.

During bankruptcy, a lender does not generally receive principal payments on its prepetition loan, even if they were regularly scheduled payments under the prepetition loan. Depending on the adequate protection order, a lender may be entitled to receive payments that can be applied to principal.

In analyzing a Chapter 11 case, it is important to estimate the monthly cash flow relief from the nonpayment of interest, principal, and rejection of executory contracts. If the debtor has a significant amount of unsecured debt in its capital structure, or undesirable equipment and real estate leases, the cash flow relief can be significant and is a major benefit of filing bankruptcy. The payment relief will often allow the debtor to build cash balances during bankruptcy.

Priority of Prepetition Claims

Secured claims generally take priority over unsecured claims with exceptions for: (1) certain taxes, (2) other statutory liens, and (3) for the preservation or sale of a secured creditor's collateral.

Ordinarily, even the expenses of administrating the estate are junior to secured claims. The Bankruptcy Code makes an exception for administrative expenses for the preservation or sale of collateral because the expenses benefit the secured creditor. If the trustee operates the debtor's business to facilitate the sale of the collateral, the trustee can charge the secured creditor with the trustee's cost. These charges can represent a significant portion of the value of the debtor's assets. In the case of Pierre Foods, the Debtor's Plan projected that the cost of liquidating the business would equal 15% of Pierre's tangible assets in a 12-month liquidation period.

Examples of statuary liens with priority are claims arising under the Packers and Stockyards Act of 1921 and the Perishable Agricultural Commodities Act of 1930. These claims impose a statutory trust on the debtor's inventory of livestock and perishable agricultural commodities and all products, receivables, and proceeds. These liens will prime the lien of a properly perfected first-lien lender.

After the priority claims of secured creditors, the priority of unsecured claims is in the following order:

- Superpriority claim granted by the Bankruptcy Court in connection with the debtor obtaining credit during bankruptcy;
- Administrative Expenses approved by the court related to professional fees and other costs associated with bankruptcy. These expenses include fees for the trustee, examiner, debtor's attorney, official Chapter 11 committees, and other fees for professionals approved by the court. Administrative expense also includes monetary obligations for leases assumed in bankruptcy and subsequently rejected as well as for the value of any goods received by the debtor within 20 days before the date of bankruptcy. Administrative expense includes other claims that arise postpetition so long as such claims are beneficial to the estate. These expenses would include most all of the debtor's on-going expenses in connection with the necessary operation of the business, including those for wages and payments to vendors who delivered goods and services postpetition;
- Prepetition wage claims, subject to certain limitations;
- Prepetition federal and state tax claims;
- Prepetition general unsecured claims;
- Prepetition non-compensatory fines, penalties, and punitive damages;
- Postpetition interest on unsecured claims, only if there is enough to first pay all other unsecured creditors in full;
- Prepetition preferred stock;
- Prepetition common stock.

Chapter 1: Basics of the Bankruptcy Code

Super-priority and administrative claims have priority of payment rights over prepetition unsecured claims, but if the debtor is liquidated, a risk exists that net liquidation proceeds will be insufficient to pay some or all of the claims after the payment of priority secured claims. If a reorganization plan is approved, before the debtor can emerge from bankruptcy, the super-priority claims and administrative claims have the right to be paid off in cash. A super-priority or administrative claim holder can consensually agree to a payment other than in cash, a party may agree to this treatment when the debtor cannot raise the liquidity to pay the claims.

Suppose two claims arising after bankruptcy, one from an attorney for professional fees and the other from a trade vendor. At the exit from bankruptcy, the debtor pays both claims in cash. The payment to the attorney represents a permanent cash flow outflow for the debtor. Although the payment to the trade vendor is a cash outflow, if the vendor continues to sell to the debtor on regular trade terms after the exit from bankruptcy, then the debtor has a cash inflow from the extension of credit on a post reorganization basis. As discussed in the next section, a vendor has strong incentive to continue to extend credit to a debtor during and after bankruptcy.

Prepetition Unsecured Trade Creditor Claims

Trade creditor claims are unsecured claims. The Bankruptcy Code grants a creditor an administrative claim for the value of any goods delivered to the debtor within 20 days prior to the petition date, for goods sold to the debtor in the ordinary course of business. Suppliers also have certain rights to reclaim goods that were shipped to the debtor 45 days prior to the petition date, subject to the supplier making a written reclamation demand by the later of the following dates: (1) 45 days from the receipt of the goods by the debtor and (2) 20 days after the petition date. If the supplier fails to give the written notice, the supplier has the right to an administrative claim for goods delivered 20 days prior to the petition date.

In addition, the Bankruptcy Code has a provision for the payment of critical prepetition vendor claims. The fear is that vendors may refuse to ship to the debtor because of unpaid prepetition claims, causing a collapse of the business.

Some bankruptcy courts and judges have the reputation of being more agreeable to paying vendor prepetition claims on the basis that the vendors are critical to the business. Vendors have high gross profit margins and can turnover sales to a customer six times a year. In 2008, the average gross profit margin was 31.5% for all non-financial companies traded on U.S. based stock exchanges. A vendor's gross profit from a year of sales to a debtor can often offset the receivable balance it carries with the debtor under 30-60 day credit terms. In return for the bankruptcy court approval of the payment of critical vendor prepetition claims, the bankruptcy court will often require the debtor to execute vendor agreements that require the vendor to extend credit on similar terms to those prior to bankruptcy.

Executory Contracts

An executory contract is a contract where a party has not performed its duties as stipulated in the contract. A debtor has numerous ongoing and future obligations under executory contracts. The executory contracts can be a burden on the debtor's cash flow. The Bankruptcy Code gives the debtor wide latitude in rejecting executory contracts for the benefit of the estate. The debtor can reject union contracts, take-or-pay contracts, equipment leases, real estate leases, and other executory contracts.

The debtor may assume or reject an executory contract or an unexpired lease of commercial personal property at any time before the confirmation of the plan of reorganization. The bankruptcy court must give its final approval for the acceptance and rejection of executory contracts. Absent a finding of bad faith or carelessness, courts generally will not disturb a debtor's business decision to reject an executory contract or unexpired lease. The test for business judgment is if the rejection is in the best interest of the estate.

If the debtor agrees to assume an executory contract, it must cure: (1) all prior monetary defaults, (2) all curable non-monetary defaults, and (3) pay damages due under the contract.

If a debtor accepts an executory contract and fails to perform under the contract, the non-debtor party is entitled to an administrative priority claim for the obligations due under the contract.

Prior to plan confirmation, the debtor is required to file a list of accepted and rejected executory contracts. If the bankruptcy court confirms a plan that fails to deal with any of the debtor's executory contracts or leases, the bankruptcy court assumes the contracts and leases are accepted.

In the analysis of a bankruptcy case, it can be difficult to estimate the dollar amount of claims that will exist for rejected executory contracts. A review of the debtor's schedule of court filed rejected leases and the financial statements for lease/rent expense may provide insight into the significance of the potential claims. It may be difficult to determine the amount of pro-forma savings from the rejection of executory contracts. A party of interest has the right to ask the creditors committee to request the information from the debtor, but the debtor may request, and the court may approve, non-disclosure of renegotiated

Chapter 1: Basics of the Bankruptcy Code

contract pricing for competitive reasons. The debtor's final decision on the acceptance or rejection for some of its executory contracts may be immediately prior to plan confirmation.

Executory Contracts—Employment Contracts

The debtor can reduce cash payment obligations by rejecting employment contracts. The Bankruptcy Code limits employee claims for the breach of employment contracts to one year of compensation.

Executory Contracts—Breach of Labor Contracts

The rejection of labor contracts requires a stricter standard than the debtor's business judgment. After the debtor has set forth the proposed revised labor agreement, it must furnish the union with complete information on the debtor's financial condition and must bargain in good faith to try to reach a settlement. If the debtor and union cannot reach agreement, it is generally up to the court to decide if changes in the labor contract are required for a successful reorganization.

Executory Contracts—Real Estate Leases

A debtor is required to reject or accept a non-residential real estate lease in Chapter 11 within the earlier of:

- 120 days from the petition date (can be extended for 90 days with cause);
- Prior to court confirmation of the reorganization plan.

Until the debtor rejects a real estate lease, the debtor must continue to pay the real estate lease obligations as they become due from the date of the bankruptcy filing.

The Bankruptcy Code caps the recovery for damages for the rejection of a real estate lease to the greater of:

- one year of rent;
- 15% of the remaining cumulative payments under the lease, but limited to three years of rent payments.

The claim of a lessor for a rejected real estate lease becomes an unsecured claim, unless the debtor has accepted the lease and the debtor then subsequently rejects the lease—in which case the lessor may claim up to two years rent as an administrative claim.

Part I: Bankruptcy Basics

Executory Contracts—Personal Property Leases

For commercial personal property leases, the Bankruptcy Code requires the debtor to perform all of the lease obligations, first arising 60 days after the petition date, until the lease is assumed or rejected, unless the Bankruptcy Court orders otherwise based on the equities of the case.

Effectively, the bankruptcy code gives the debtor a 60 day skip period for personal property lease payments, thereafter the debtor is obligated to make all payments and perform all obligations under the lease until the lease is assumed or rejected. The clause: "unless the court, after notice and hearing, and based on the equities of the case, orders otherwise", leaves a door open for the debtor or other interested parties to seek some other type of undefined relief. On occasion, a debtor has attempted to use this provision to delay payment due to hardship or to reduce the lease payment pending a challenge of a re-characterization of the lease as debt.

If the debtor does not perform the lease obligations as they become due under the lease 60 days after the petition date, then the lessor has the right to seek relief from the stay by compelling the debtor to make payments or to reclaim the property from the debtor. If the debtor rejects the lease, the treatment for the claim is as if the rejection occurred immediately before the petition date, for all of the debtor's obligations under the lease and the claim becomes an unsecured claim.

The debtor may assume or reject a personal property lease at any time prior to the confirmation of the plan of reorganization. If a debtor accepts a lease, the debtor must cure all defaults under the lease, other than non-curable, non-monetary defaults. If the debtor accepts the lease and subsequently rejects the lease or is unable to pay, the lessor's claim becomes an administrative claim.

Section 363(e) of the Bankruptcy Code also provides the lessor with the right to adequate protection. If the value of the leased property is less than the lessor's investment balance, the lessor will most always be satisfied to receive lease payments rather than run the risk of a lease rejection and the return of the property.

Structural Advantage: Personal Property Leases in Bankruptcy

In underwriting the extension of credit, it may be desirable to structure the extension of credit as a lease transaction because of the treatment provided for leases in Bankruptcy Code.

Imagine the case of a loan or a lease on high-tech memory equipment. Assume the transaction opened two years ago and the lender/lessor financed 100% of the $4.6 million equipment cost. The loan or lease balance is currently

Chapter 1: Basics of the Bankruptcy Code

$2.8 million. Assume an economic recession and industry over supply, causing the fair market value of the equipment to decrease to $400,000. It is assumed the equipment remains critical to the debtor's business.

The debtor can continue to use the equipment as long as it performs the obligations under the lease, as they become due 60 days after the petition date. The debtor has until the confirmation of the plan of reorganization to accept or reject the lease as long as it continues to perform the obligations under the lease as they became due 60 days after the petition date.

If the debtor rejects the lease or does not pay the obligations under the lease as they become due after 60 days after the petition date, the lessor gets back the equipment and has an unsecured claim for obligations due under the lease.

If the lease is accepted, the debtor is required to cure all prepetition and postpetition obligations under the lease. If the debtor accepts the lease and then subsequently rejects the lease, or the debtor cannot pay on the accepted lease, the lessor is entitled to an administrative claim for the obligations under the lease.

The treatment for the same equipment on a loan is that the lender is entitled to accrue interest to the extent the value of the collateral exceeds the loan balance. This may or may not include the collection of cash interest during bankruptcy. The bankruptcy stops the regularly scheduled principal payments on the loan. Moreover, because the value of the collateral has decreased and the lender is undersecured, a party of interest could file a motion to bifurcate the loan into a secured claim and an unsecured claim, which also could prevent the lender from receiving interest. Because the lender is undersecured, the lender could file motion to foreclose, but only if the debtor does not require the property in its business. Moreover, the lender has the burden of proving the debtor does not need the property in the business. If the value of the collateral is continuing to decline, the lender could request a hearing and court approval for adequate protection payments on the secured portion of its claim, but the lender is not entitled to adequate protection on the unsecured portion of its claim.

In the example, it is most likely that the equipment lessor will continue to receive lease payments because the equipment is critical to the debtor's business. Each lease payment reduces the lessor's net investment balance. The lease payments are equivalent to interest and principal on a loan.

Even under a lease structure, the debtor may continue to have negotiating advantage—the debtor may threaten to reject the lease unless the lessor agrees to reduce the lease payment.

Part I: Bankruptcy Basics

Risk of Re-Characterizing a Lease

A risk to a lessor in leasing personal property is that the debtor, or other parties of interest in the estate, may seek to re-characterize the lease as a loan because the underlying structure of the transaction is in substance a loan disguised as a lease.

If the lease is small in dollar amount as compared to other matters in the bankruptcy, the larger issues will take priority and interested parties may not waste time and money on the re-characterization issue. A party challenging the re-characterization also has the risk/cost that the challenge will prove unsuccessful.

In the test to determine if a lease is in substance a loan, many bankruptcy courts will first look to true lease tests under the relevant state Uniform Commercial Code law, often referred to as the bright-line test. Under the bright-line test, a transaction creates a security interest (a loan) if:

- The lessee is required to pay a significant penalty to terminate the lease, and
- Any one of the following is present: (a) the lessee is required to purchase the property at the end of the lease, (b) if the lease term, including any required renewal term, is for the economic life of the property, (c) the lease has a purchase option price for the property that is nominal or the lease renewal payment is nominal.

If the transaction does not pass the bright-line test, the bankruptcy judge can re-characterize the lease as a loan.

If the transaction passes the bright-line test, the bankruptcy court will continue with additional tests to determine if the transaction is a loan. The court will look to the economic substance of the transaction. The case law varies on the tests the court will use. In underwriting a lease transaction, the lessor should test for the following conditions out of an abundance of caution:

- The end of lease purchase option price is for fair market value;
- The present value of the rental stream is less than 90% of the equipment cost;
- The early buy-out option does not create a bargain purchase price,
- The lessee is not required to pay excessive fees for the return of the equipment.

Chapter 1: Basics of the Bankruptcy Code

Other Leasing Considerations

Assignment of Leases

Although most leasing contracts prohibit the assignment of a lease without the consent of the lessor, this provision is not enforceable in bankruptcy. If a debtor holds long-term leases with favorable terms, the debtor may be able to sell the leases for value. This typically happen in cases involving long-term real estate leases where the leased locations are desirable or have value because the current pricing for the property is substantially in excess of the rate negotiated when the lease originally opened.

Retaining an Asset Management Specialist

A secured lender/lessor should retain an internal asset management specialist or department to inspect and value property. The importance of internal expertise for the valuation of assets is critical. The importance extends beyond assigning a final valuation. In structuring a lease, it is essential to determine if the asset is critical not only to the company but also to evaluate if the asset is highly desired in the industry. The best time to evaluate the risk is in the underwriting stage, prior to credit approval. This evaluation requires an experienced asset manager who has industry knowledge and the people skills to extract information from the borrower's plant managers during the inspection phase of the asset due diligence.

The checklist for asset due diligence is significant and beyond the scope of this book. The due diligence by an asset management department can prevent the approval and funding of a transaction that would eventually result in a loss. The knowledge gained from asset management due diligence can also result in better transaction structures.

Structuring the Lease on One Lease Schedule

One method to enhance a lease structure is to place all of the equipment on one lease schedule, for critical and less than critical assets. If all of the property is on one lease schedule, the Bankruptcy Code does not allow the debtor to accept or reject specific items on a schedule; the requirement is for the debtor to accept all of the property or reject all of the property on the lease schedule.

For separate lease schedules, the lessor may attempt to require the lessee to accept all of the property for all of the lease schedules or return all of the property for all of the lease schedules. This may be successful if the schedules are close together in time and the schedules are for one general transaction credit approval.

Debt Agreements and Structural Issues

In analyzing a Chapter 11 case, the analyst should carefully examine and analyze debt instruments, guarantees, relationships between the debtor's parent and subsidiaries, and the claims against each of the related entities that have filed bankruptcy. The analyst should review key terms and conditions, including subordination because the bankruptcy courts recognize the subordination rights in debt agreements.

A claim can be against a parent or subsidiary. It is important to determine what debtor entity is obligated for the claim. For example, assume: (1) a lender has an unsecured or undersecured loan to a subsidiary that has minimal assets and (2) the loan has the guarantee of the parent company. In this case, the lender may be looking for the parent to recover its loan, but, if the only asset of the parent guarantor is stock in other corporate entities in the bankruptcy, then the other entities must first satisfy their direct claims before they can distribute funds to the parent.

Substantive Consolidation

Most companies have complex organizational ownership structures. Every corporation has specific assets and claims. A risk in bankruptcy is that a party will seek to consolidate all of the various related corporations as if they were one entity.

Bankruptcy courts have looked to a number of tests for substantive consolidation. Bankruptcy courts may review the following factors in making a decision on substantive consolidation:

- Is each entity integral to the other entities;
- Did creditors rely on the separate entity for the extension of credit;
- Will the consolidation harm creditors;
- Did creditors treat the entities as one economic unit;
- Is it impossible or too difficult to separate all of the entities.

If an unsecured note holder has debt with a parent company without guarantees from subsidiaries, and further assuming all assets are at the subsidiary level, then the unsecured note holder would generally benefit by substantive consolidation.

Chapter 1: Basics of the Bankruptcy Code

Subordination

The recovery prospects for debt can also depend on the contractual terms of the debt instruments, such as, senior secured, senior unsecured, senior-subordinated, and junior subordinated.

The courts recognize subordination of claims in three general classes:

- The creditor has agreed to subordination by contract;
- Stockholder claims for damages from the sale of equity securities by the debtor. In this case, the stockholder claim is subordinated to the claims of other creditors;
- The bankruptcy court can subordinate creditor claims from insiders, which includes but is not limited to relatives, partners, officers, directors, and related entities.

Preferences

The debtor has avoiding powers to undo a transfer of money or property made 90 days prior to the petition date. For transfers to insiders (relatives, partners, officers, directors), the period extends to one year prior to the petition date. This preference period is a look-back period to see if creditors or insiders were able to improve their position compared to other creditors prior the bankruptcy.

Payments by the debtor can be clawed-back if the payment benefited a creditor, for or on account of a debt, while the debtor was insolvent and made within 90 days prior to the bankruptcy petition date (up to one year for an insider and two years for fraudulent transfers). In the case of a payment to a creditor, the payment must have also enabled the creditor to receive more than it would have received in a Chapter 7 liquidation of the debtor. Moreover, the foregoing does not apply if the payment was on a debt in the ordinary course of business or the debtor made the payment according to ordinary business terms. With respect to preferences payments, the Bankruptcy Code presumes the debtor is insolvent for any transfer made 90 days prior to the petition date.

The debtor is required to file with the bankruptcy court a report of all payments to creditors and insiders in the Statement of Financial Affairs. The creditors committee, or other parties of interest, should carefully review the debtor's schedules of payments to other creditors and insiders for preference payments.

Part I: Bankruptcy Basics

Fraudulent Transfers

Section 548 of the Bankruptcy Code provides that transfers of property within two years before bankruptcy may be voided under certain conditions. The issues are complex and beyond the scope of this book.

Securitizations

Accounts receivable securitizations are the sale of receivables to a special purpose entity. The programs provide financing for a company by purchasing its receivables. The receivables sold are not legally part of the debtor's estate. When a debtor files for bankruptcy, the special purpose entity owns the receivables and reduces its net investment through collection of the receivables.

Pension Plan Termination Claims

The ability to terminate a defined benefit pension plan is permitted in the U.S. Employee Retirement Income Security Act (ERISA). The debtor may voluntarily terminate pension plan or the Pension Benefit Guaranty Corporation (PBGC) may terminate the pension plan. To terminate a defined benefit pension plan, the debtor must show that it is necessary to eliminate the pension plan to achieve a successful reorganization.

The PBGC assumes the liabilities of the terminated pension plan up to the limits under ERISA. PBGC receives an unsecured claim for the unfunded benefits. The unsecured PBGC claim can be substantial for certain debtors. An analyst should review the footnotes to a company's financial statements to review the funding status of a company's pension plans.

Swap Agreements

The U.S. Bankruptcy Code accords special treatment for counterparties to financial contracts, such as swaps, repurchase agreements, securities contracts, and forward contracts. The Bankruptcy Code permits the contracts to settle under contractual terms as if the debtor did not file bankruptcy.

Off-Balance Sheet Liabilities

An analyst should review off-balance sheet items. Large potential claims may exist for equipment leases, real estate leases, purchase agreements, take-or-pay contracts, derivative contracts, guarantees, pension liabilities, health-care liabilities, and environmental claims.

Chapter 1: Basics of the Bankruptcy Code

Net Operating Loss Carry-Forwards

The Internal Revenue Tax Code allows a company to use prior year tax losses to offset income on its tax return for 20 years in the future. A company emerging from bankruptcy can carry-forward losses if 50% or more of the reorganized company's stock remains under the ownership of the prepetition shareholders and creditors. A creditor only counts toward the fifty percent threshold if it has held the debt for at least eighteen months prior to bankruptcy. The use of tax loss carry-forwards is restricted if there is a change of ownership control within two years after the debtor emerges from bankruptcy.

Preserving tax losses can be important to the Enterprise Value of the reorganized debtor. It is often difficult to comply with the change of control requirement because of significant changes in ownership in bankruptcy. On occasion, bankruptcy courts have approved orders that restrict the transfer of a debtor's stock and debt when tax losses are expected to have significant value to the reorganized debtor.

Taxes Due on Cancellation of Debt or Exchange

A company can have taxes due on the cancellation of debt and exchange of debt for securities. The tax is created when the value of the debt extinguished is greater than the cash or the fair market value of the securities given in exchange for the debt. Special Internal Revenue Code rules apply for companies in bankruptcy. The gain is first used to reduce any operating loss carry-forwards. The remaining gain can be used to reduce the tax basis of depreciable property, in effect deferring the tax on the gain to the date the property is sold.

Warrants and Rights Offering

A debtor may use a stock right offering to raise cash. The stock right allows the holder to acquire shares of stock, usually at a discount to the fair market value of the stock. Warrants and rights offerings have been used to give stockholders the opportunity to invest in the debtor at a discount to help recover their loss in the debtor's prepetition stock. The right offering typically has an expiration of several months vs. two to five years for warrants.

Chapter 2

Plan of Reorganization & Special Issues

"The reports of my death are greatly exaggerated." Mark Twain

Debtor Exclusive Period to File a Plan

The debtor has the exclusive opportunity for 120 days (up to 18 months with court extensions) to propose a plan of reorganization to emerge from bankruptcy under a revised capital structure. The debtor has up to 180 days from the petition date to obtain approval of the plan (up to 20 months with court extensions). After the expiration of the exclusivity period, any party of interest can file its own proposed plan of reorganization.

Impairment

An unimpaired class is not entitled to vote on a plan. This becomes important in the scheme of creditor recovery and court approval for a plan. For example, if the unsecured creditors can classify the secured creditors as unimpaired, this could improve the chances of the unsecured creditors receiving a higher recovery in the form of either debt and/or equity in the reorganized debtor, subject to the plan being feasible.

Chapter 2: Plan of Reorganization & Other Special Issues

Under the Bankruptcy Code, a claim is unimpaired if the reorganization plan does not alter the legal, equitable or contractual rights of the creditor.

If a loan agreement accelerates the maturity date of the loan because of an event of loan default, the plan can reinstate the maturity date that existed prior to default without impairing the claim as long as:

- The plan cures other defaults and compensates the creditor for damages for its reasonable reliance on the covenants that caused the default, and
- The plan compensates the creditor for actual money losses relating to non-monetary defaults under the prepetition agreement.

The Historical and Revision Notes to the Bankruptcy Code commented on impairment as follows:

> "a claim or interest is unimpaired by curing the effect of a default and reinstating the original terms of an obligation when maturity was brought on or accelerated by the default. The intervention of bankruptcy and the defaults represent a temporary crisis which the plan of reorganization is intended to clear away. The holder of a claim or interest who under the plan is restored to his original position, when others receive less or get nothing at all, is fortunate indeed and has no cause to complain. Curing of the default and the assumption of the debt in accordance with its terms is an important reorganization technique for dealing with a particular class of claims, especially secured claims."

The debtor may violate loan covenants that are difficult to restore. Creditor loan agreements customarily have financial covenants and other affirmative and negative covenants, including covenants for a change in control of the debtor's stock ownership. It is unusual for the prepetition stockholders to remain in control of the reorganized debtor.

The requirement for the reinstatement of the original maturity date could be problematic: the due date of a debt instrument may have been one of the primary reasons the debtor filed bankruptcy. If the plan restores the maturity date and the maturity date is in the near future, then the plan may not meet the Bankruptcy Code feasibility requirement.

If bank lenders control a creditor class, the bank lenders may be more likely to support a plan that restores the basic terms of their prepetition debt. They may even support less favorable terms than contained under the terms of the prepetition debt in return for full reinstatement of the debt in lieu of receiving stock. By charter, banks prefer debt to stock. This fact could improve the recovery chances for junior creditors. If the creditor class is controlled by an opportunistic hedge fund, who is seeking to control the debtor and realize future upside profit from operating or selling the company, then the hedge fund may prefer claim impairment in order to obtain stock in addition to debt. The hedge fund may also desire a low valuation for the debtor's business in order to capture a larger allocation of the debtor's stock over junior creditors. In contrast to the relationship bank, whose charter directs it to hold debt, the hedge fund may negotiate for a strict definition of impairment to capture greater value. If successful, this will reduce the recovery to junior creditors.

Minimum Requirements for a Plan of Reorganization
At minimum, a plan of reorganization should include the following:

- Designate the classes of claims. The Bankruptcy Code does not define the requirements for a class other than the claims in each class should be substantially similar;
- Specify any class of claims that is not impaired under the plan;
- Specify the treatment of any class of claims that is impaired under the plan;
- Provide the same treatment for each claim, unless the holder of a particular claim agrees to a less favorable treatment;
- Provide adequate means for the implementation of the plan, including: (1) retention of property by the debtor, (2) transfer of property to one or more entities, (3) merger or consolidation, (4) sale of property, (5) satisfaction or modification of any lien, (6) cancellation or modification of any debt instrument, (7) curing or waiving of any default, (8) extension of a maturity date or a change in an interest rate or other terms of the debt, (9) issuance of securities;
- Include a provision in the debtor's corporate charter that provides for an appropriate distribution of voting power among different classes of securities and a provision that prohibits the issuance of non-voting equity securities.

Chapter 2: Plan of Reorganization & Other Special Issues

A reorganization plan may do the following:
- Impair or leave unimpaired any class of claims;
- Provide for the assumption, rejection, or assignment of any executory contract;
- Provide for the settlement or adjustment of any claim of the debtor;
- Provide for the sale of all or substantially all of the property of the estate and the distribution of the proceeds of the sale among holders of claims;
- Modify the rights of holders of either unsecured or secured claims, or leave unaffected the rights of holders of any class of claims.

Disclosure Statement

The party filing a reorganization plan is required to file a disclosure statement with the bankruptcy court. The purpose of the disclosure statement is for the bankruptcy court to determine if the plan has provided adequate information to the holders of claims and parties of interest to make informed judgments about the plan. A party cannot solicit the acceptance or rejection of a plan until the bankruptcy court has approved the disclosure statement. The court will hold a hearing to determine if the plan contains adequate information.

Voting on the Plan of Reorganization

The Bankruptcy Code requires the placement of creditors with similar claims into classes for voting on the plan of reorganization. The plan will place secured and unsecured creditors into classes based on the terms and conditions of their claims. The plan proponent will attempt to create classes to ensure a favorable vote on the plan—at least one impaired class must vote to approve a plan before the bankruptcy court can force a plan on any other impaired non-consenting class of claims (called a cramdown).

An unimpaired class is presumed to have accepted a plan and does not vote on the plan.

If a class is not entitled to receive a distribution, the class is deemed to have rejected a plan and the class does not vote on the plan. This often turns out to be the treatment for prepetition stockholders because the Enterprise Value of many bankrupt companies is less than prepetition creditor claims.

Voting acceptance by a class requires over 50% of the number of claims and 75% of the dollar amount of the claims. Only those claims who actually vote on the plan count in terms of calculating the required majority approval. Therefore, the failure to vote is a no vote.

A party may attempt to acquire at least 25% of the claims in a class to block the voting consent of a class, but the Court can approve a plan without the required voting approval (75% dollar, 50% number) from a class in a cramdown of the class.

Confirmation of Plan—Minimum Requirements for Plan Approval
After the vote on the plan, the court must hold a confirmation hearing to approve and hear any objections to the plan.

The debtor, or plan proponent seeking confirmation of a plan, will ask for plan confirmation under two circumstances. The first is when all impaired classes of creditors and equity holders have accepted the plan. The second is when one or more of the classes of creditors or equity holders have rejected the plan but the plan proponent wants the court to confirm the plan over the dissenting class (a cramdown).

The key minimum requirements for the court to approve a plan include:
- The plan was proposed in good faith. Reason for denial would include that the primary purpose was tax avoidance or to work a fraud on creditors or equity holders;
- The claims have been classified properly in the plan;
- The plan is not likely to be followed by the liquidation or need for further financial reorganization (this is referred to as the feasibility test);
- If a class of claims is impaired and does not vote to approve a plan and the plan proponent is seeking plan approval, at least one impaired class must have voted to approve the plan;
- With respect to each impaired class of claims, **each holder** of a claim has accepted the plan or will receive or retain property of a value (as of the plan date) that is not less than the amount such holder would receive or retain if the debtor were liquidated under Chapter 7. This test is called the best interest of creditors test (every plan should have a liquidation analysis for this test);
- With respect to **each class** of claims, the class has accepted the plan or the class is not impaired under the plan; notwithstanding this requirement, Section 1129(b) of the Bankruptcy Code provides that a **plan proponent** can request that the court confirm a plan if the plan does not discriminate unfairly and is **fair and equitable** to each impaired class that has not accepted the plan (a cramdown).

Chapter 2: Plan of Reorganization & Other Special Issues

Section 1129(b) of Bankruptcy Code—Cramdown

The best interest of creditor test requires that **each claim holder** is entitled to receive a recovery at least equal to the amount it would receive in the liquidation of debtor. This test is for each holder of a claim.

With respect to **each class** of claims, if any class of claims does not consent to the plan of reorganization, and the plan meets other tests for court confirmation, then a **plan proponent** can ask the court to approve the plan over the dissent of an impaired class, if the plan does not discriminate unfairly and is fair and equitable with respect to each class of claims. Such a request and approval is commonly referred to as a cramdown.

Not discriminating means that the holders of claims with similar legal rights cannot be treated differently.

Secured claims and unsecured claims each have a different fair and equitable test under the Bankruptcy Code. A class of creditors can consent to any plan (over 50% in number and 75% in dollar amount), as long as the plan meets the best interest of creditors test.

Cramdown of Secured Creditors: Fair and Equitable Treatment

Section 1129(b)(2)(A) of the Bankruptcy Code covers the fair and equitable treatment of secured claims and requires one of the following treatments:

1. If the plan intends to sell the property, the secured creditor's lien against the property must follow the sale proceeds with treatment of the liens under item 2 or 3 below;

2. Each holder of a secured claim must retain the lien securing its claim and receive deferred cash payments at least equal to the amount of the claim and the payments must have a net present value at least equal to the value of property as of the plan date. Courts have generally interpreted the value of the property at the date of the plan as the fair market value of the property, if the debtor plans to retain the property in the business. Courts have generally held that the future payments must be discounted back to the fair market value of the property at a risk adjusted interest rate, or

3. The plan provides the realization for the secured claim of the indubitable equivalent of the claim. Indubitable means "too evident to be doubted" (Webster's Ninth New Collegiate Dictionary 1985). Indubitable equivalent gives the courts some flexibility to consider other types of treatment to satisfy the cramdown of a dissenting class of secured claims. The Historical and Revision Notes to Section 1129 of

the Bankruptcy Code elaborates on what constitutes the indubitable equivalent of a secured claim as follows:

> "Abandonment of the collateral to the creditor would clearly satisfy indubitable equivalence, as would a lien on similar collateral. However, present cash payments less than the secured claim would not satisfy the standard because the creditor is deprived of an opportunity to gain from the future increase in value of the collateral. Unsecured notes as to the secured claim or equity securities of the debtor would not be the indubitable equivalent."

Cramdown of Unsecured Claims—Fair and Equitable Treatment

To be fair and equitable to a class of dissenting unsecured creditors, the plan must provide that either:

- Unsecured creditors must receive a recovery equal to the allowed amount of their claims, or
- Claims junior to their claims cannot receive any recovery (the absolute priority rule).

Challenges of Obtaining Court Approval of a Cramdown

One of the challenges in attempting to obtain court approval for a cramdown is that at least one class of claims must be impaired and accept the plan. It requires only slightly more than 25% of the dollar amount of claims in a class to block acceptance of the class. A class that is being crammed down could purchase enough claims to gain control of more than 25% of the dollar claims of the impaired classes in order to block acceptance of the plan. In each bankruptcy case, it is necessary to analyze each class of claims, the size of the claims in each class, significant holders of claims, and determine the strategy and goals of the significant holders.

If the unsecured creditors committee or other interested party attempts to bifurcate a secured creditor's claim into a secured and unsecured claim, and if the challenge is successful, then the undersecured creditor's unsecured claim may end up in the voting class with the other general unsecured creditors, raising the possibility their votes could block plan approval of the unsecured class. This could be significant because at least one impaired class must approve the plan for a cramdown of the secured creditor class. Although the plan proponent may try to place the undersecured creditor's unsecured claim in a separate class, the undersecured creditor might successfully fight this classification scheme.

Chapter 2: Plan of Reorganization & Other Special Issues

Strategies can be complex in bankruptcy, depending on the motivations of the parties. A debtor and a secured creditor may prefer to have the lowest possible estimate of business valuation for the reorganized debtor in order to minimize the distribution to junior classes. Likewise, the prepetition equity and unsecured creditors will seek the highest possible estimate of business valuation to achieve a higher recovery for their claims.

Limitation on Creditor Receiving Recovery Greater Than Its Claim

If a plan is approved without the consent of a class, courts have interpreted the fair and equitable requirements in Section 1129(b)(2) of the Bankruptcy Code to require that no class will receive a recovery greater than the amount of their claim. Although the Bankruptcy Code does not specifically require a valuation of the debtor's business, most courts require an Enterprise Valuation of the business to ensure that a class of claims is not receiving a recovery greater than 100% of its claim, otherwise harm could be caused to junior classes.

The requirement that senior classes receive no more than 100 percent of their claims can involve other considerations. For example, if senior and junior claims are receiving the same amount of common stock, this does not compensate for the loss of priority of the senior claim. Therefore, the value of common stock given to the senior claim might exceed the amount of the senior claim without violating the fair and equitable requirement for the dissenting class.

Undersecured Creditor Strategy and Section 1111(b) Election

A secured creditor has the option to have its claim treated under Section 1111(b) of the Bankruptcy Code, which allows a creditor, secured by property, to treat its entire claim as a secured claim but only for purposes of the treatment of its claim in the plan of reorganization. The option must be exercised by the conclusion of the disclosure statement hearing. The Section 1111(b) election can only be of benefit to an undersecured creditor.

Section 506(a) of the Bankruptcy Code provides that an allowed claim, secured by a lien on the property, is a secured claim to the extent of the value of the property and an unsecured claim to the extent the value of the property is less than the allowed claim. This bifurcated claim has a vote in a class of secured claims and a vote in an unsecured class.

If the creditor elects the Section 1111(b) option, the definition of an undersecured creditor's claim is altered for the purpose of the plan of reorganization: the allowed creditor claim increases from the secured claim

Part I: Bankruptcy Basics

(value of property) to the full claim. This can be important if a creditor is undersecured and there is an attempt to cramdown the undersecured creditor.

There are two requirements that must be satisfied for a cramdown of a secured creditor:

- The creditor must retain its lien to the extent of the allowed amount of the claim, and
- The creditor must receives deferred pay cash payments at least equal to the allowed claim and those payments must also have a net present value, discounted at an appropriate risk adjusted rate, at least equal to the value of the property.

The following case example will illustrate Section 1111(b):

- Collateral: dry-bulk ship 15 years of age with a remaining useful life of 15 years;
- Loan opened in December 2007 for $16,500,000;
- Bankruptcy filed November 2008. The loan balance is $15,000,000 at the petition date;
- The fair market value of ship was $18,750,000 when the loan opened. Due to the 2008/2009 worldwide economic and financial crisis, the fair market value of the ship decreased to $7,500,000 at the date of the plan, a decrease of 60% in 18 months (this is based on actual decreases in ship values experienced in 2008/2009);
- It is assumed marine lenders customarily finance between 60% to 100% of the market value of a ship, with a loan amortization of 4 to 10 years for a 15 year old ship;
- Although market conditions are weak, the debtor requires the use of the ship in its operations;
- The interest rate is a fixed rate of 7% based on the long-term historical interest rate spread for secured loans;
- The debtor offers to pay the lender's claim in monthly payments. The loan amortization is eight years.

Assume the undersecured lender does not elect Section 1111(b) option, then the lender's $15,000,000 claim is then bifurcated into a $7,500,000 secured claim (fair market value of the ship) and a $7,500,000 unsecured claim for the balance. The plan proposes to pay the lender 96 monthly payments of $102,255. The deferred amount of the payments are $9,816,480 (96 x $102,255). The first

Chapter 2: Plan of Reorganization & Other Special Issues

Bankruptcy Code test passes; total deferred payments equal or exceed the amount of the $7,500,000 secured claim. The second Bankruptcy Code test also passes; the net present value of the payments discounted at the 7% rate equals $7,500,000 (the fair market value of the ship). The lender will also have an unsecured claim for $7,500,000. The undersecured portion of the claim receives the same recovery as other general unsecured creditors. Assume the recovery for unsecured claims is 10%, therefore the lender recovers $750,000 (10% x $7,500,000) on the unsecured portion of its claim. In summary, the lender who did not elect 1111(b) recovers $8,250,000, consisting of the $7,500,000 secured claim recovery and $750,000 unsecured claim recovery.

Let's compare this $7,500,000 recovery to the lender who elects the Section 1111(b) option. The undersecured creditor decides to elect the Section 1111(b) option because it has good reason to believe the value of the ship will recover in the future. The lender's market research forecasts a recovery in ship values within several years because:

- Recent significant order cancellations for new-build ships;
- The worldwide fleet is aged and a significant number of ships will be retired;
- China and India, with over 50% of the world population, will continue to industrialize and drive the demand for ocean going freight shipments.

If the lender elects the 1111(b) option, the entire $15,000,000 claim is treated as the full claim for purposes of the plan. The plan must pay the lender deferred cash payments of at least $15,000,000 and the payments must have a net present value of at least $7,500,000 (the current fair market value of the ship). The loan payments offered by the debtor are the same 96 monthly payments of $102,255 at the interest rate of 7% (for the secured portion of the claim), followed by one balloon payment of $5,183,520 due at the end of the eighth year. The gross monthly payments and the balloon are $15,000,000, meeting the Bankruptcy Code test that the total deferred payments must at least equal the $15,000,000 claim. The net present value of the monthly payments and balloon at the 7% discount is $10,465,695, exceeding the $7,500,000 fair market value of the ship. Therefore, the second Bankruptcy Code test passes which requires the net present value of the payments to equal or exceed the value of the ship. In conclusion, the lender who selected the 1111(b) option received a net present value recovery $2,215,695 greater than the lender who did not select the 1111(b) option.

Further, assume the market for ships recovers quickly and within 12 months the fair market value of the ship increases to $16,500,000. In the improved market, the lender sells the loan and monetizes its higher recovery.

What if the debtor offered the same 96 payments of $102,255 and the same $5,183,520 balloon amount but the debtor attempts to move the balloon date to month 180 (year 15), a balloon date that is at the end of the ships useful life. The secured lenders would object to these terms because it is non-market for ship financing. If the debtor pursued an attempt to cramdown the lender on this structure, the debtor might argue its case based on the scrap value of the ship at the end of its 15-year remaining useful life (a well established scrap market exists for ocean-going ships). The scrap value of the ship is $3,800,000 today, and in 15 years, the ship scrap value is projected at $5,183,520 based on 2% inflation. If the court approved the extended balloon date cramdown based on the protection afforded by the scrap value of the ship, the present value of the monthly payments and balloon at the 7% discount rate would equal $9,351,540, or $1,101,540 more than for the lender who did not elect the 1111(b) option.

For creditors electing the Section 1111(b) options, some courts have held that the plan proponent cannot pay the creditor cash (at plan exit) equal to the value of the collateral and then assert that the creditor is receiving the indubitable equivalent of its claim; the plan proponent is required to pay the full amount of the creditor's claim. In the case example, the payoff to satisfy the claim immediately at plan exit is $10,045,695 for the lender who elected the 1111(b) option. In contrast, the payoff to satisfy the creditor who did not elect the 1111(b) option is $7,500,000.

There are a number of significant factors for a creditor to evaluate prior to electing the 1111(b) option. If an undersecured creditor elects 1111(b) option, it gives up the right to treat a portion of the claim as unsecured claim. It therefore gives up the right to vote as an unsecured creditor and loses power to influence the recovery to unsecured creditors, in the amount of the recovery and in the form of the recovery. The lender is also making a decision today based on its belief that the ship will have a higher value in the unknown future.

If a creditor plans to elect the Section 1111(b) option, the creditor should evaluate whether this will have any impact on the feasibility of a plan. If the loan value of the ship in eight years is substantially below the loan balloon balance, a creditor could argue the plan is not feasible because it would be unlikely for another lender to refinance the balloon.

The creditor should also analyze the debtor's cash flow coverage with and without the Section 1111(b) election to determine if the change in debt service affects the plan feasibility.

Chapter 2: Plan of Reorganization & Other Special Issues

Absolute Priority—363 Sale Issue/Chrysler Bankruptcy

In late 2008, the U.S. Government established an auto task force to work with GM and Chrysler to restructure the auto companies. The U.S Treasury had already loaned Chrysler $4 billion to keep the Chrysler in business. Chrysler subsequently filed bankruptcy in April 2009. In bankruptcy, Chrysler and the U.S. Governement proposed a 363 sale of most all of Chrysler's goods assets to "Chrysler Newco" as a quick way to restructure Chrysler.

Chrysler and the auto task group offered Chrysler's secured lender group, a syndicate of 46 banks, a cash settlement of $2 billion for their $6.9 billion secured loan. Many of the big bank lenders in the group had pre-negoitated with Chrysler on the proposed terms. A small group of secured debt holders (the Non-TARP lenders) objected. Chrysler filed bankruptcy without an agreement from all of the lenders in the secured lender group.

The Obama administration and Chrysler believed that a quick 363 sale of Chrysler was necessary because of the substantial economic impact the Chrysler bankruptcy would have on the national economy. Chrysler had tried for many months to find a partner, investor, and buyer for the business. Chrysler's lender and investor of last resort was the U.S. Government and Fiat.

Chrysler Newco would be owned:
- 55% by the United Auto Workers Union (UAW);
- 25% by the U.S. and Canadian governments;
- 20% by Fiat.

In the 363 sale, Chrysler Newco would pay $2 billion for the purchase of Chrysler's assets and the proceeds would applied to the $6.9 billion secured debt. The secured lenders would receive no further recovery and would charge-off their remaining $4.9 billion loan balance.

The UAW had a $9.8 billion unsecured health care claim against old Chrysler. In the 363 sale, Chrysler Newco would assume the $9.8 billion health care claim and then pay the UAW $5.2 billion cash and issue the UAW a promissory note for $4.6 billion. The UAW also agreed to a wage cut. In return for the wage cut, the UAW would own 55% of the stock of Chrysler Newco.

The minority group of the secured Non-TARP Lenders objected to the 363 sale because:
- The sale price did not exceed the secured loan;
- The debtor would pay the $8 billion of unsecured claims and satisfy the secured loan for 30% of the loan;
- The sale would strip the collateral away from the secured lenders for the benefit of unsecured creditors;

Part I: Bankruptcy Basics

- A holder of a secured claim had a right to recover the liquidaiton value of the collateral. The lender group believed the liquidation value of the collateral was greater than the secured loan balance;
- The 363 sale was an illegal sub rosa plan of reorganization, improperly transfering value from senior creditors to junior creditors. Prior court decisions have prohibted the use of a 363 sale to abrogate the protections afforded creditors by Section 1129 of the Bankruptcy Code;
- Bids for the purchase of Chryslers assets were due May 15, 2009, only 15 days after the bankruptcy filing and the case was complex;
- The debtor mandated the key terms of competing bid, with restrictions designed to discourage bids. The purchase price and the terms of the bids were required to be substanially the same as those in the purchase agreement between Chrysler Newco and the debtor. The debtor required a bidder to assume billions in liabilities held by certain favored unsecured creditors, including the UAW bargaining agreements. No valid reason existed for the limitation;
- The DIP loan required "case milestones" to avoid an event of default, including the requirement that the court hold a hearing on the 363 sale by no later than June 1, 2009 and for all significant transactions to be completed by June 27, 2009. It was an event of default under the DIP loan if the secured lender submitted a credit bid for the amount of its claim.

The political pressure and news media took a heavy toll on the Non-TARP lender group. After the bankruptcy filing, President Obama attempted to exert pressure on the dissenting secured creditors by vilifing them in the national press. On May 9, 2009, the Non-TARP lender group announced they were withdrawing their objection to the Chrysler 363 sale.

On May 19, 2009, the Indiana State Teachers Retirement Fund, who held a portion of Chrysler's secured debt, filed an objection with the Bankruptcy Court. The objection argued that the 363 sale was illegal and trampled the secured creditor rights under a plan of reorganization. The objection asserted "Indeed, not a single court has ever approved a sale and distribution of proceeds as proposed here". The case was appealed to the Supreme Court who ruled that the Indiana Retirement Funds had not carried the burden of proving that their greivances merited the Supreme Court's attention.

The Chrysler bankruptcy illustrates how political and economic pressures can influence a case. Chrysler and the U.S. Government were able to exert

Chapter 2: Plan of Reorganization & Other Special Issues

considerable pressure on the bank TARP lenders. The absolute priority rule in the Bankruptcy Code was violated by paying unsecured claims prior to a full recovery for the secured claims.

Debtors have been increasingly using the Section 363 sale provision in the Bankruptcy Code as a method to speed up the reorganization process. The Chrysler case may change underwriting standards for the extension of credit. Secured and unsecured creditors may be more cautious in lending to companies with significant unfunded health-care and pension liabilities, especially when the companies have significant market share in an industry that is important to the U.S. economy.

Trend of Faster Chapter 11 Reorganizations

There is evidence that Chapter 11 reorganization plans have been filed and approved faster than in the 1980s and 1990s. Some researchers believe this is because DIP lenders have been structuring their loan agreements to control the debtor in bankruptcy. It is more common for DIP loan agreements to have provisions that establish outside hurdle dates for a debtor to submit and to obtain approval for a plan of reorganization. DIP lender loan agreements have also contained provisions requiring the sale of certain assets and operations of the debtor.

Skeel (2003) found evidence that DIP financing and management pay-to-stay contracts have been key factors in debtors selling assets or divisions faster and emerging earlier from Chapter 11. Skeel's research showed that key executives received performance based compensation packages in Chapter 11. The most common strategy was to promise the executives a large bonus if they completed the reorganization quickly.

In theory, a company's board of directors' remains in control during bankruptcy, but the ability of the board to run the company is constrained by the rules and procedures in the Bankruptcy Code. Creditors can influence the decisions of board members and management by making it clear that the creditors will control the reorganized debtor.

Ayotee and Morrison (2001) reported strong evidence that senior creditors had provisions in their loan agreements to control distressed firms. Seventy-five percent of the bankrupt debtors arranged for financing immediately prior to bankruptcy. The majority of the loans contained covenants imposing line-item budgets, profitability targets, or deadlines for submitting a plan of reorganization. If the debtor violated covenants, the lender was generally free to seize collateral unilaterally, without first seeking court approval.

Ayotee and Morrison (2008) also reported a statistically significant relationship between the debtor's asset to debt ratio and the time to resolve a case. When secured creditors were undersecured, or when the debt was all unsecured, the cases were relatively long and more likely to result in a traditional reorganization. A quicker case resolution occurred when creditors were oversecured.

Issues Presented by Second-Lien Loans

Su's (2007) research found that companies have obtained financing on an increasing basis through second-lien loans. His research showed that most second-lien loans are significantly impaired because the collateral value is less than the debt. This impairment had allowed second-lien lenders to place a stranglehold on the reorganization process. Su found that second-lien lenders were not hesitant to challenge cash collateral and DIP financing. Prior to the second-lien loans becoming a popular form of financing, reorganization was delineated by secured claims and unsecured claims. Secured debt was typically made whole in the plan of reorganization, leaving the majority of the debtor's stock to the unsecured lenders. After second-lien loans became widespread in use, Su found that impairment shifted from unsecured lenders to second-lien debt. Su's research reported many hedge funds were buying second-lien distressed debt for the bargaining position offered by the impaired status of the claims. The difficulty in cramming down the impaired second-lien debt provided additional leverage in reorganization negotiations. Second-lien debt holders recovered greater equity in the reorganized debtor.

Distressed Investors and Hedge Funds

If unsecured creditors receive any recovery in a Chapter 11, it is often in the form of the reorganized debtor's stock which can have a greater value than the prepetition stock because the reorganized company has less debt and has eliminated unfavorable contractual obligations. The investing strategy for distressed funds and hedge funds may often include a strategy of recovering value through ownership of stock in the reorganized company.

Private-equity funds are more likely to take an active approach to investing in bankrupt companies. As a result, some corporate borrowers have requested provisions in their loan agreement that prohibits or restricts certain hedge funds or distressed investment funds from participating in the loan. Borrowers have generally regarded banks as being more predictable and relationship oriented as compared to non-bank institutional lenders.

Chapter 2: Plan of Reorganization & Other Special Issues

Investing in Distressed Debt or Claims

If a company's stock is listed on a major stock exchange and it files for bankruptcy, the company's stock will soon be de-listed from trading on major stock exchanges. Subsequently, the stock will often trade on the over-the-counter electronic markets. The stock price could even increase substantially over a short period. The purchase of a debtor's stock in bankruptcy is generally extremely speculative. Even though a case analysis may show that the prepetition stock is expected to receive a zero recovery, the stock price will often continue to trade for some nominal value. Generally, the best way to view the stock price of a debtor in bankruptcy is similar to stock options that are way out of the money. There is nothing to preclude a 100% recovery for the prepetition stockholders in a reorganization plan, as long as there is sufficient Enterprise Value and the plan is feasible.

A purchase of a distressed debtor's debt is a safer investment than stock because of the absolute priority rule. There is an opportunity cost of investing in unsecured debt because the holder of unsecured debt does not receive interest income while the debtor lingers in bankruptcy.

The buyer of distressed debt, or of a claim in bankruptcy, will seek to pay a price for the claim that is below the projected recovery value for the claim in a liquidation of the company's assets.

Prior to investing in distressed debt, an investor should perform a complete case analysis.

Recent Bankruptcy Investing Case

Spansion, a NASDAQ exchange traded company, filed bankruptcy on February 28, 2009. Spansion was a leading worldwide manufacturer of memory products for cell-phones. Spansion had tangible assets of $3.3 billion and liabilities of $2.4 billion. Liabilities included $1.5 billion of debt.

Spansion's senior secured debt traded at 17 cents on the dollar prior to bankruptcy and 65 cents on the dollar by June 23, 2009.

The Table 2.0 shows the trading price of Spansion's unsecured and secured debt on January 15, 2009 as compared to the trading price on August 5, 2009.

An investor would have earned an annualized return of over 807% by purchasing a blend of Spansion's debt on January 23, 2009 and the selling the debt on August 5, 2009.

Part I: Bankruptcy Basics

Table 2.0—Bankruptcy Debt Investing Example: Return on Spansion's Debt
($ millions)

Debt Instrument	Par Debt	Trading Price of Debt				Return on Debt	
		January 15, 2009		August 5, 2009		1-15 to 8-05	Annualized
		$	% Par	$	% Par		
Senior secured	$ 625	$106	17%	$515	82.5%	386%	697%
Senior unsecured	$ 250	$ 18	7%	$168	67.5%	833%	1,500%
Senior subordinate	$ 207	$ 8	4%	$39	19.0%	388%	702%
Total trading debt	$1,082	$132		$722		447%	807%
Non-trading debt	$ 473						
Total debt	$1,555						

Source: Capital IQ

Part II: Estimating Enterprise Value

Chapter 3

Estimating Enterprise Value

"Faced with the choice between changing one's mind and proving there is no need to do so, almost everyone gets busy on the proof." John Kenneth Galbraith

Enterprise Value

Enterprise Value is the value of a business. The estimate of Enterprise Value is one of the most important factors determining the recovery for the classes of claims.

The estimate of the Enterprise Value can vary significantly among valuation experts because the value is sensitive to the variables that must be assumed in the valuation models. The valuation must provide full disclosure of the assumptions used in the estimate of a company's Enterprise Value.

After the Enterprise Value of a company has been estimated, the value is allocated to the company's debt and equity.

Financial and credit analysis modeling can be used to determine the appropriate amount of the debt for the firm, as well as the structure of the debt. The proposed debt and debt service must be structured to meet the Bankruptcy Code test for plan feasibility. The feasibility test requires that the court cannot confirm a plan unless the plan is not likely to be followed by the debtor's liquidation or need for further financial reorganization. The Bankruptcy Code does not attempt to define the specific financial metrics for the feasibility test.

Chapter 3: Enterprise Value

Under generally accepted principles of credit analysis, the Bankruptcy Code requirement for plan feasibility implies the debtor has: (1) adequate cash flow coverage for its financial obligations and capital expenditures and (2) adequate financial flexibility.

Financial flexibility can be a combination of any number of factors, including cash balances, bank line borrowing availability, the prospective sale of assets/divisions, and the capacity to borrow money and/or raise equity based on the debtor's capital structure and cash flow coverage. A company's primary liquidity is from cash and borrowing availability under bank lines of credit.

Evidence of Bias in the Estimate of Enterprise Value in Bankruptcy

The estimate of the Enterprise Value of a firm not only affects the recovery value for claimants receiving stock but it also affects the recovery for the other junior classes of claims. By estimating a lower Enterprise Value, senior claimants can benefit by gaining control of more stock.

Management of the debtor may have an incentive to estimate lower earnings and cash flows in its reorganization plan to increase the value of their stock options in the reorganized debtor. On the other hand, if management owns a large amount of the prepetition stock, management has an incentive to overestimate Enterprise Value to increase the recovery for their prepetition stock claims. Likewise, junior claimants have incentive to estimate a higher Enterprise Value to increase their recovery.

Gilson, Hotchkiss, Rubak (2000) performed research to determine if the estimate of Enterprise Value is biased by the interest of various parties in bankruptcy. The study statistically compared estimates of Enterprise Value in bankruptcy to the post bankruptcy values based on the trading price of the stock after the debtor emerged from Chapter 11. The analysis was based on a sample of 63 public firms who reorganized under Chapter 11 of the U.S. Bankruptcy Code during 1984–1993. The cross-sectional regression analysis showed estimated Enterprise Values tended to be lower (relative to post-bankruptcy market values) when a creditor gained control through a large block of senior debt, but larger when the creditor used junior debt to gain control. The regression analysis results supported the hypotheses that estimated Enterprise Value will be lower when senior claimants have an influential position in the restructuring plan and higher when junior claimants have an influential position in the restructuring plan. The regression results also supported their hypothesis that managers "low-balled" the financial projections when they received stock or stock options.

Part II: Estimating Enterprise Value

Enterprise Value at the Date of the Plan

Many courts have cited the U.S. Supreme Court's Consolidated Rock (1941) opinion in determining the value of the debtor's business as of the date of the plan of reorganization. In Consolidated Rock, the Supreme Court held that the key criteria in valuing a company should be the company's earning capacity rather than the market value of the business during the bankruptcy, because, among other things, being in bankruptcy harms market value. Furthermore, this estimate of earning capacity should be based on an informed judgment which embraces all facts relevant to future earning capacity, including, the nature and condition of the properties, the past earning records record, and all circumstances which indicate whether or not that record is a reliable criterion of future performance.

In Nellson Nutraceutical (2007), the Delaware Bankruptcy Court reconfirmed the prior opinion in Exide Technologies (2003), with the opinion that modern finance had caught up with the Supreme Court's decision in Consolidated Rock because modern finance provides valuation methodologies focusing on earning capacity, comparable company analysis, and discounted cash flow analysis.

Determination of Enterprise Value

There are four primary approaches used by practitioners to estimate the value a company:

1. An income approach that discounts future free cash flows to a present value;
2. A comparable companies approach where a comparable firm in the same industry is used to value the company based on ratios of Enterprise Value to earnings, Enterprise Value to EBITDA, Enterprise Value to sales, or based on other comparable financial metrics;
3. Comparable transactions method where recent comparable companies that have sold in the market are used to value a company based on financial metrics of the sale transaction;
4. The valuation of the assets of the company less its obligations.

Under the income approach, the future free cash flows are discounted to a present value using an appropriate discount rate. The income model approach is sensitive to the assumed cash flows and discount rate. The analysis should fully disclose all of the assumptions used in the model.

Chapter 3: Enterprise Value

The free cash flows to be discounted are the free cash flows available to debt and equity as follows:

(Earnings before interest & tax) x (1 – tax rate)
+ Depreciation
− Capital expenditures
− Change in working captial
= Free cash flow

The factor used to discount the cash flow in the model is the company's average cost of capital based on the weighting of the cost of debt and equity for the firm. A target capital structure can be used to weight the cost of equity and cost of debt. If known, the market value of the debt and equity should be used for the weighting. For a reorganized debtor, the debt to equity weighting can be based on the targeted pro-forma debt determined by the financial and credit analysis modeling.

The Enterprise Value is extremely sensitive to a small change in the discount rate. For example, decreasing the discount rate from 11% to 9% increases the Enterprise Value by 22.2%. A decrease in the discount rate from 14% to 9% increases the Enterprise Value by 55.5%.

Discounting Cash Flows

There are a number of models that can be used to discount the free cash flow to determine Enterprise Value, including (1) stable firm model that uses a stable rate of growth in earnings, (2) two stage model that assumes an intial high rate of growth in earnings followed by a stable growth, and (3) three stage growth model that assumes three different growth rates for various periods of time.

The well-known cash flow perpetuity formula for the stable firm model is:

$$\text{Enterprise Value} = \frac{\text{Free Cash Flows Available to all Capital}}{(\text{Required Rate of Return}) - (\text{Growth Rate})}$$

The above cash flow perpetuity formula assumes a constant free cash flow in each future period rather than forecasting a different cash flow for each future period. The growth rate of future free cash flow is accounted for in the denominator of the model by subtracting the assumed growth rate from the required rate of return.

Part II: Estimating Enterprise Value

Estimating the Equity Cost Component in the Cost of Capital

There are two commonly used methods for estimating the cost of equity: (1) the build-up method and (2) the Capital Asset Pricing Model (CAPM).

For the build-up method, one of the most widely accepted sources of information is the annual *Ibbotson SSBI (Stocks, Bonds, Bills, and Inflation) Yearbook* that has been published for 25 years by Ibbotson (owned by Morningstar).

The cost of equity under the build-up method, consists of the sum:

1. Risk-free rate. Ibbotson uses a risk-free rate equal to the income return for U.S. Treasury bonds with a 20-year maturity. Ibbotson considers the 30-year U.S. Treasury bond income return as the appropriate risk free rate, but the 30-year bond has limited history while a U.S. Treasury bond with a 20-year remaining maturity can be traced back to 1926. From 1926-2008, the income yield on the 20-year U.S. Treasury has averaged 3.00%, as reported in Table C-1 in the *Ibbotson SSBI 2009 Valuation Yearbook*;

2. Equity risk premium. The equity risk premium is the difference between the return on the S&P 500 stock index and the risk-free rate. Ibbotson's data for the equity risk premium is from 1926 to the end of the most recent year. This equity risk premium was 6.5% from 1926–2008, as reported in Table C-1 in the *Ibbotson SSBI 2009 Valuation Yearbook*;

3. A premium based on the market capitalization. Table C-1 of the *Ibbotson SSBI 2009 Valuation Yearbook* reports premiums for firm sizes that range between -0.36% for the largest firms to 9.53% for firms with market capitalizations less than $136 million;

4. Industry premium. Ibbotson has developed an industry premium methodology that appraisers can reference and cite in their appraisal reports. Table 3.5 *Ibbotson SSBI 2009 Valuation* Yearbook reports the premiums by industry;

5. A premium for the emergence from bankruptcy. In valuation disputes, bankruptcy courts have often accepted an additional emergence risk premium because a company is in bankruptcy.

Capital Asset Pricing Model (CAPM)

The CAPM model is another method widely used to estimate the cost of equity. The CAPM model uses three variables to determine a stock's expected return: the risk-free rate, the market risk premium, and a stock's Beta.

Chapter 3: Enterprise Value

The market risk premium is the difference between the long-term return for the stock market and the risk-free rate. The proxy for the stock market return is generally the S&P 500 index.

Beta is the relationship between the movement in the price of the market and the price of the company's stock. An adjusted CAPM model adds a premium for the size of the firm because research shows that small stocks outperform large stocks and the Beta does not fully account for all of the risk of small compaines. The adjusted CAPM model is:

Equity Cost = risk free rate + [beta x (expected market return equities − risk-free rate)] + size premium

Commercial firms such as Bloomberg, Capital IQ, Value Line, and Ibbotson provide Beta estimates for companies. The Beta of a stock can also be estimated by performing a regression analysis on five years of the monthly closing prices of the company's stock against the S&P 500 index. When the Beta of a company is measured, it is called a levered or equity Beta because it reflects the debt in a company's capital structure. The Beta for a company will increase as a company increases the percentage of debt in its capital structure.

The impact of debt leverage on the Beta can be removed to obtain an unlevered Beta. Using the unlevered Beta, the Beta for a firm can be relevered for a target debt to equity ratio. This technique can be used to determine the levered Beta for a reorganized debtor based on the the pro-forma debt that has been modeled for the reorganized debtor.

A company with a Beta of 1.0 has the same systematic risk as the market. A company with a Beta of 2.0 will under or outpeform the market by a factor of 2x. Beta is only the measurement of the movement of the price of a company's stock to the price movement of the S&P 500 index (the general market).

A stock with a low Beta does not necessarily imply lower risk. An investment in a stock whose principal business is attempting to win money by gambling against the Las Vegas casinos is predicted to have Beta close to zero. The winnings and losses of the gambling company should not have a correlation with the movement in the price of the S&P 500 index. Nevertheless, the investment in the gambling company stock is a very risky investment.

A high Beta is expected for an auto company because its sales are senstive to economic condtions and the industry has high fixed costs. A low Beta is expected for a water company because its sales are not senstive to economic conditions.

A company Betas can also shift over time. In addition, a Beta cannot be measured if a company's stock does not trade on an exchange. An industry Beta can be used as a proxy for a company Beta, but care must be exercised to make

Part II: Estimating Enterprise Value

sure the industry Beta is appropriate for the company. Many valuation experts believe an industry Beta can produce superior results.

A company's Beta should be closely tied to the movement in its earnings or EBITDA as compared to the general market. If a company's stock is not traded, some experts have recommended estimating a proxy for the company's Beta by performing a regression on the company's EBITDA or earnings against the S&P 500 index.

The movement in a company's earnings will generally be a function of the senstivitiy of a company's sales to the economy, the cost structure of the company, and the debt leverage of the firm. Therefore, when selecting an industry Beta or comparable company Beta, the cost structure of the company should be comparable to the cost structure of the industry or comparable company.

Hotchkiss and Altman reported in *Corporate Financial Distress and Bankruptcy* (2006) that historical stock returns for a company heading into distress bear little resemblance to the return stockhlders expect from a successfully reorganized debtor. In valuing a distressed company, they believe a preferable alternative is to use the Beta of a comparable firm. If a company operates in several different industries, the Beta can be weighted for the industries based on the relative sales contribution from each industry.

The levered Beta or equity Beta reflects both operating risk and financial risk (the leverage of the firm). As previously discussed, if a company's Beta is observed, then the Beta includes the amount of debt leverage in the firm. Likewise, if an industry Beta is observed, it includes the debt leverage of those firms. In valuing a company as a reorganized debtor, the Beta should be based upon the target leverage that is planned for the reorganized firm. Therefore, the comparable company or industry Beta needs to be unlevered and then relevered for the target debt to equity ratio for the reorganized firm.

A levered Beta can be unlevered and relevered using the following formulas:

Beta unlevered = Beta levered / [1 + debt/equity ratio x   (1- tax rate)]

Beta levered =   Beta unlevered   x   [1 + (1 − tax rate) x debt/equity]

If possible, the debt and the equity in the equation should be the market value of the debt and equity. It may be difficult to observe the trading market value of the debt for a company or for the industry.

The matrix in the Table 3.0 shows the calculated levered Betas based on various combinations of unlevered Betas and debt to equity ratios. The analysis assumes a 40% marginal tax rate. The blue cells in Table 3.0 represent the

Chapter 3: Enterprise Value

levered Beta based on the various combinations of Beta and debt to equity ratios.

Table 3.0—Matrix Calculating Levered Beta, assuming Various Combinations of Unlevered Betas and Debt/Equity Ratios

Debt to Equity Ratio	Beta Unlevered						
	0.00	0.10	0.50	1.00	1.50	2.00	2.50
0	0.00	0.10	0.50	1.00	1.50	2.00	2.50
0.10	0.00	0.11	0.53	1.06	1.59	2.12	2.65
0.50	0.00	0.13	0.65	1.30	1.95	2.60	3.25
1.00	0.00	0.16	0.80	1.60	2.40	3.20	4.00
1.50	0.00	0.19	0.95	1.90	2.85	3.80	4.75
2.00	0.00	0.22	1.10	2.20	3.30	4.40	5.50
2.50	0.00	0.25	1.25	2.50	3.75	5.00	6.25
3.00	0.00	0.28	1.40	2.80	4.20	5.60	7.00
3.50	0.00	0.31	1.55	3.10	4.65	6.20	7.75
4.00	0.00	0.34	1.70	3.40	5.10	6.80	8.50
5.00	0.00	0.40	2.00	4.00	6.00	8.00	10.00
5.50	0.00	0.43	2.15	4.30	6.45	8.60	10.75
6.00	0.00	0.46	2.30	4.60	6.90	9.20	11.50

In the capital asset pricing model, the equity risk premium for a company is the levered Beta times the equity risk premium assumed for the market. The matrix in the Table 3.1 shows the impact on the required equity risk premium for a company based on various combinatons of the assumed market equity risk premium and levered Betas. The blue cells in Table 3.1 represent the equity risk premium for the company based on the various combinations of the levered Beta and assumed market equity risk premium.

Table 3.1—Matrix Calculating a Firms Equity Risk Premium, Using Various Combinations of Levered Betas & Market Equity Risk Premiums

Equity Premium	Beta Levered						
	0.00	0.10	0.50	1.00	1.50	2.00	2.50
3%	0.0%	0.3%	1.5%	3.0%	4.5%	6.0%	7.50%
4%	0.0%	0.4%	2.0%	4.0%	6.0%	8.0%	10.0%
5%	0.0%	0.5%	2.5%	5.0%	7.5%	10.0%	12.5%
6%	0.0%	0.6%	3.0%	6.0%	9.0%	12.0%	15.0%
7%	0.0%	0.7%	3.5%	7.0%	10.5%	14.0%	17.5%
8%	0.0%	0.8%	4.0%	8.0%	12.0%	16.0%	20.0%

Part II: Estimating Enterprise Value

The data in Tables 3.0 and 3.1 are important because the Enterprise Value of a company is extremely senstive to the assumed variables in the valuation models. As previously noted, decreasing the discount rate from 9% to 11% increases the Enterprise Value by 22.2%.

Average Leverage Ratios and Other Key Financial Metrics for U.S. Exchange Traded Non-Financial Companies Based in the U.S.

When valuing a firm, it is important to measure key profitability and asset turnover assumptions for the firm against the general market and industry. The projected EBITDA to sales ratio and asset turnover ratios for the reorganized firm can be compared to the industry and general market to test for reasonableness. For future reference in the Pierre's Foods case analysis, Table 3.2 shows key ratios for leverage, profitablity, and asset turnover for all U.S. non-financial exchange traded firms in the U.S. with sales over $25 million.

Table 3.2—Key Financial Metrics for All Non-Financial U.S. Exchange Traded Firms in U.S. with Revenue Greater than $25 million

	Average	Median
Sales	$3.9 billion	$618 million
Total Assets	$4.1 billion	$628 million
Ratios:		
Debt to equity	0.76x	0.42x
Net debt to equity	0.51x	0.08x
Debt to market value stock	0.34x	0.25x
Net debt to market value stock	0.23x	0.04x
Debt to EBITDA	1.80x	1.37x
Net debt to EBITDA	1.23x	0.25x
Enterprise Value to EBITDA	7.03x	6.93x
Net Enterprise Value to EBITDA	6.45x	5.81x
EBITDA to Interest Expense	10.0x	10.4x
Gross profit percentage	31.5%	32.8%
Operating Income to Sales	10.8%	6.5%
EBITDA to Sales %	15.8%	12.1%
Sales to Total Assets	0.98x	0.98x

Source: Custom data screen developed through Capital IQ screening by the author. Capital IQ is not responsible for the actual data results returned in the screening or in the table.
Notes: All U.S. exchange traded firms based in U.S. with revenue over $25 million, excluding financial firms and government sponsored agencies. The screening returned 2,580 companies. Ratios based on the most recent annual financial statements as of June 1, 2009. The market value of stock is as of June 1, 2009. Net debt and net Enterprise Value is net of cash & equivalents, short term investments, and trading asset securities.

Chapter 3: Enterprise Value

The Equity Risk Premium Debate

There is widespread debate among scholars over the appropriate historical equity risk premium for the market. The debate is primarily based on the time period over which the returns are measured and on which market to measure. The *Ibbotson SSBI 2009 Valuation Yearbook* only measures data after 1926 because of concern with the intergrity of the data prior to 1926.

There is futher debate among the experts over whether the historical long-term equity premium should be used for forward equity risk premiums.

Corporate Finance and Valuation (Ryan, 2007) believes a 4.1% forward equity risk premium is appropriate.

Valuation: Measuring and Managing the Value of Companies (Koller, Gooedhart, Wessels, 2005) recommends a 4.5% to 5.5% equity risk premium. The authors argue: "historical estimates found in most textbooks (and locked in the minds of many), which often report equity premiums of near 8 percent, are too high for valuation purposes because they compare the market risk premium versus short-term bonds, use only 75 years of data, and are biased by the historical strength of the U.S. market."

The *2009 Global Investment Returns Yearbook* (Dimson, Marsh, Staunton, Wilmot, 2009) is a comprehensive analysis of equity returns since 1900 for 17 national stock markets, including markets in Europe, North America, Asia, and Africa. The *2009 Global Invesment Returns Yearbook* reported an equity return premium of 3.4% over bonds for global investors (3.8% equity premium for the U.S.). They believe the equity premiums they report in the *2009 Global Investment Yearbook* are lower because of the global focus and longer time frame. Moreover, they believe investors were "spoiled by the high returns of the 1980s and 1990s; and, even though many investment books still cite stock returns of 7%, investors are likely to be disappointed. The authors believe their data captures a longer period as it dates from 1900 and also measures the worldwide market. They argue the historical Ibbotson U.S. equity premium captures a success bias because in the 20th century the U.S. was rapidly became the world's foremost political, military, and eonomic power. They believe the forward investor equity risk premium should be 3.0% to 3.5% over short-term government bills (2.2% to 2.7% over bonds).

The annual *Ibbotson SSBI (Stocks, Bonds, Bills, and Inflation) Yearbook* provides U.S. market returns from 1926 through the end of each year for stocks and bonds. Ibbotson is widely used by U.S. valuation practitioners. Ibbotson begins with data from 1926 in measuring returns because they believe that it was around that time that quality finanical data became available and as the data includes one full business cyle before the market crash of 1929. From 1926 to

Part II: Estimating Enterprise Value

the end of 2008, the *2009 SSBI Yearbook* reported the S&P 500 had an average equity risk premium of 6.50% over the risk-free rate.

Table 3.3 summarizes the market equity returns for stocks based on the various experts previously cited

Table 3.3—Summary of U.S. Equity Risk Premium Estimates Recommended by Experts

Ibbotson	Ryan	Dimson, Marsh, Staunton	Koller, Goedhart, Wessels
6.50% historical	4.1% forward	2.2% to 2.7% forward 3.8% historical	4.5% to 5.5% forward

The range of the equity premium in Table 3.3 is between 2.2% and 6.47%, a spread of 4.27%. A 2% variance in the equity risk premium changes the Enteprise Value of a firm by 22.2%. A 4% variance changes the valuaton by 55.5%. It is critical for the debtor's reorganization plan to fully disclose and rationalize all of the assumptions in the valuation model used to estimate the debtor's Enterprise Value.

Equity Premium for Firm Size

It has been recognized by experts that an additonal equity risk premium is required for smaller capitalizaton firms.

The University of Chicago's Center for Research in Security Prices has reported (Dimson, et al., 2009) a 1.4% premium for low capitalization stocks over the return for the U.S. market from 1926 to 2008.

Ibbotson divides the S&P 500 stock returns into deciles to determine size premium based on the market capitalization of a company. The *Ibbotson 2009 SSBI Yearbook* reported the size premium has ranged between -0.36% for the top decile capitalization companies (market cap above $465.6 billion) to 5.81% for the tenth decile (market cap less than $453.3 million). Ibbotson provides a further breakout for firms in the tenth decile. The size premium is 4.11% for firms with a market cap between $136.6 million and $218.5 million and 9.53% for firms with a market cap below $136.5 million. The 4.11% size premium will be used in the estimate of Pierre's Alternative Enterprise Value (Chapter 24).

Industry Premium

Ibbotson has developed an industry premium method that appraisers can reference and cite in their appraisal reports. The Ibbotson industry risk premium relies on an estimation of Beta developed by Ibbotson.

Chapter 3: Enterprise Value

Bankruptcy Emergence Premium

The Delaware Bankruptcy Court, in the cases of Nellson Nutraceutical (2007) and Exide Technologies (2003), accepted an additional premium for the risk associated with a company emerging from bankruptcy. The Delaware Court held that the Consolidated Rock case justified the basis for the existence of a bankruptcy emergence premium. In Nellson Nutraceutical, the risk premium assigned by three different valuation experts was 0.0%, 2.05%, and 6.0%, but the Court's opinion was that the premium in the case should not exceed 4.0%.

Careful qualitative analysis must be performed for each bankruptcy case to determine the need for a bankruptcy emergence premium. The industry, the competition, and the company's growth prospects can make a difference. In the early 1930s, the industry outlook for firms operating in the horse and buggy industry differed from those in the auto industry. The reason(s) a firm has filed for bankruptcy is important in evaluating the need for a bankruptcy emergence premium.

Estimating the Cost of Debt as a Component of the Cost of Capital

The prior discussion focused on estimating the cost of equity as a component of the cost of capital. The other component in the cost of capital is the cost of debt.

As of December 2008, the *JPMorgan Daily High Yield Update* (Acciavatti, Linares, Nelson, 2008) reported high-yield unsecured bond spreads were 18.80% over comparable term U.S. Treasuries. The prior record spread was 11.26% in October 2002.

For secured leveraged loans, assuming a four-year repayment, the average spread was LIBOR plus 14.98%, almost triple the peak rate spread from the prior credit cycle.

The December 2008 record spreads over the long-term historical spread was because of the 2008/2009 worldwide financial and economic crisis. Valuation experts all agree that the equity premium should be based on the long-term equity and risk-free returns in the market. On the other hand, many experts advise that the cost of a firm's debt should be based on the current market pricing of debt.

Few experts would recommend using the negative 38.5% return for the S&P 500 in 2008 to determine the cost of equity. If the December 2008 bond and leveraged loan yields are used in the valuation model, debt which is protected by assets and income over equity, would actually have a higher cost of capital than the long-term equity risk premiums in the valuation model.

Part II: Estimating Enterprise Value

Markets were not stable in the 2008/2009 worldwide financial and economic crisis and they did not reflect the historical long-term average cost of debt. The cost of debt should be based on the historical long-term yield spread over comparable term U.S. Treasury securities. The interest rate for the company's cost of captial should also be based on the company's debt structure and its credit risk profile/credit rating. In the case of Pierre Foods, Chapter 24 and Chapter 25 will target a credit rating for Pierre that is comparable to an S&P B rated credit.

The *JP Morgan 2008 High-Yield Annual Review* (Acciavatti, et al., 2008) reported the following historical spreads for secured and unsecured debt

- For high-yield unsecured bonds with an S&P credit rating of B, spreads averaged approximately 5.66% over comparable term U.S. Treasury securities from 1987 to 2008;
- Leveraged secured loans spreads averaged approximately 2.5% over comparable term U.S. securities from 1987 to 2008.

Comparable Company Method of Valuing a Company

The comparable company method typically uses valuation multiples based ratios of Enterprise Value to earnings, Enterprise Value to EBITDA, Enterprise Value to sales, and other key financial ratios.

Many analysts and valuation experts use the ratio of Enterprise Value to EBITDA as a key metric for a quick assessment of the fairness of a company's Enterprise Value. Although the Enterprise Value to EBITDA method is appealing because of its simplicity, it is difficult to find a truly comparable company. The multiples used to value a company should take into account differences in growth, risk, asset turnover, cost structure, competitive advantage, management talent, firm size, time in business, and other significant factors.

In the initial stages of reviewing a bankruptcy case, the analyst can use the Enterprise Value to EBITDA method for a quick estimate of the fair market value of the debtor's business. The debtor's Enterprise Value should be based on a normalized pro-forma EBITDA. The bankruptcy will allow the debtor to rationalize business operations and reduce costs for labor, leases, and executory contracts. The debtor will often eliminate unprofitable segments of the business.

Comparable Transactions Method of Valuing a Company

The comparative transaction method values a company using the same financial metrics as used in the comparable company method. The difference is that the comparable transaction financial valuation ratios are validated by an

Chapter 3: Enterprise Value

actual acquisition transaction. The buyer contributes cash equity and borrows capital for the acquisition. The difficulty with the comparable transaction method is finding a company that has been recently purchased that is truly comparable to the company being valued.

At the top of the year 2000 technology stock market bubble, many companies were extremely overvalued but their prices seemed fair on a comparative basis.

Regardless of the model used to determine Enterprise Value, financial and credit analysis is required to validate the company's Enterprise Value. The credit and financial analysis should analyze company history, ownership/sponsors, management, business operations, products, the industry, competition, firm distinctive advantage, cost structures, operating results, capital structure, liquidity, and cash flow.

Part III

Strategic Guide to Chapter 11 Case Analysis

"We, members of the human variety of Primates, have a hunger for rules because we need to reduce the dimension of matters so they can get into our heads. Or, rather, sadly, we can squeeze them into our heads. The more random information is, the greater the dimensionality, and thus the more difficult to summarize. The more you summarize, the more order you put in, the less randomness. Hence the same condition that makes us simplify pushes us to think that the world is less random than it actually is."
Nicholas Taleb, The Black Swan, New York, Random House, 2007, Chapter Six

Chapter 4

30 Point Checklist & Reminders for Case Analysis

1. Perform a complete credit and financial analysis on the debtor and its industry. It is critical to understand why a company filed bankruptcy. Texaco filed for bankruptcy in 1987 following a $10.5 billion court judgment. Texaco had a sound business model and filed bankruptcy only because of the judgment.

Moody's (Mulvaney, Fahy, Gates, 2009) developed a useful model for characterizing the future prospects for a company in bankruptcy. The author of this book has used some of the information from the Moody's model to develop a modified classification scheme for the evaluation of the future prospects of a company in bankruptcy:

- The bankruptcy was due to a specific event, such as, an unusual period of rapidly rising costs, a legal judgment, or rapid growth causing a liquidity crisis. The event was controllable or is not expected to re-occur in the future. The debtor's business model remains strong and products are in demand.
- The bankruptcy was due to high debt and the company was unable to service the debt because of a cyclical downturn. The business is expected to recover as the economy or industry cycles to a recovery stage. The business model remains sound.
- The bankruptcy was due to high debt and the company was unable to service the debt. The business model requires adjustment or the industry that has had a history of poor performance. The company has significant market share or some distinctive competitive advantage. The size of the company's operations may allow the company to right size the business.
- The bankruptcy was because of a failing business model. Substantial restructuring is required for debt and business operations. A large amount of new capital may be required to improve the business.
- The bankruptcy was due to a flawed business model. A compromise of debt and financial obligations will not result in positive cash flow.

Part III: Strategic Guide to Chapter 11 Case Analysis

2. On a monthly basis, track the debtor's cash and bank revolver availability (the "liquidity"). Track the liquidity burn rate by dividing the debtor's liquidity by the monthly cash flow shortfall.

3. Track EBITDA on a monthly basis, excluding professional fees and other non-recurring costs. Cash flow and liquidity should improve from the rejection of executory contracts and non-payment of interest on unsecured or undersecured debt.

If the elimination of interest on unsecured debt and rejection of executory contracts allows the debtor's cash flow to service the remaining prepetition debt, then a successful reorganization is likely. In this case, the impaired unsecured creditors may be in a better position to exert greater influence over the debtor in the formulation of a reorganization plan.

If secured debt requires compromising to achieve positive cash flow, a successful reorganization remains likely. The impaired secured creditors will be in position to exert greater influence over the debtor in the formulation of a reorganization plan.

If the business does not have positive cash flow after the compromise of debt and rejection of executory contracts, a successful reorganization is less likely.

4. Review covenants in the DIP loan agreement. Look for case milestone covenants and a covenant that requires the debtor to submit a plan by a deadline. Read and analyze key terms and conditions in prepetition credit agreements, the DIP credit agreement, and the debtor's court motions for the DIP facility and use of cash collateral.

For each class of debt, identify the collateral security, the maturity date, the interest rate, default interest rate, key financial covenants, affirmative/negative loan covenants, and change of control provisions.

5. The creditor's committee should retain an expert to value the debtor's assets. Request a copy of the liquidation analysis. Based on the asset valuation, analyze the cost and benefit of the creditors committee filing a motion to bifurcate an undersecured creditor's claim into a secured and unsecured claim.

6. If a creditor with collateral is undersecured, the creditor should evaluate the option of electing Section 1111(b) treatment for its claim.

Chapter 4: 30 Point Checklist & Reminders for Case Analysis

7. Carefully review off-balance sheet financial obligations. Review health-care, pension, and environmental obligations because they can represent potential significant claims for some debtors. How will these obligations affect claims in the cases of liquidation and reorganization? The claims for rejected executory contracts will be higher in the event of liquidation.

8. If the debtor is requesting use of cash collateral or a DIP priming lien, carefully evaluate the DIP loan terms and the adequate protection granted to the prepetition lender because the form of the protection can give the creditor strong rights in negotiating a reorganization plan.

9. Review for disgorgement of preference payments and fraudulent transfers. Compare the debtor's balance sheet accounts at the petition date to the debtor's monthly or quarterly financial statements for all reporting periods up to one year prior to the petition date. Review for any significant change in accounts payables, accruals, debt, inventory, prepaid items or deposits. The debtor's Schedule of Financial Affairs filed with the bankruptcy court discloses all payments to creditors 90 days to bankruptcy and payments to insiders one year prior to bankruptcy. Review the payments for any creditor improving its position 90 days prior to bankruptcy (including vendor advance payments) and for any insider improving its position one year prior to bankruptcy. Review the same with respect to transfers of property or grants of security interest to creditors or insiders.

10. If the debtor has significant operating leases, review the leases for re-characterization as debt.

11. The estimate of Enterprise Value is critical. Develop an independent estimate of Enterprise Value, factoring in savings from rejected executory contracts and other projected cost savings.

Request that the creditors committee retain experts for an estimate of Enterprise Value. The Bankruptcy Code gives the creditors committee the right to retain professional experts and, subject to court approval, the debtor is required to pay the expenses.

12. If the debtor's management and directors' own a significant amount of prepetition stock, management has more incentive to structure a feasible plan that offers a greater recovery for all claims.

Part III: Strategic Guide to Chapter 11 Case Analysis

If the prepetition stock ownership is not significant, management may have more incentive to recommend a conservative capital structure that does not provide for the maximum recovery for all claims. The debtor has a better opportunity to survive with less debt in the capital structure. Management and employees benefit by retaining jobs. Executives may also benefit from an executive bonus and stock compensation plan.

13. A trade vendor prefers a quick bankruptcy. A trade vendor has an average gross profit margin of 31.5% and turns sales many times a year. A trade vendor's future sales to the debtor can quickly make up for the 100% loss of its prepetition claim.

An unsecured debt holder seeks to maximize its recovery through a feasible plan based on the highest possible Enterprise Value of the reorganized debtor.

Analyze the makeup of the creditors committee. The debtor and the bankruptcy court value the opinion of the creditors committee. A member of the creditors committee has a fiduciary duty to act in the best interest of all unsecured creditors. The debtor is required to pay for the creditors committee's reasonable expenses for professionals. Buy an unsecured claim and work through the creditors committee.

14. Analyze the dollar amount of the claims for each class and the major holders of claims. Commercial bank lenders prefer debt rather than stock. A distressed debt investor may negotiate hard for recovery in both debt and stock ownership. The price a claim holder paid for its claim will have a bearing on the settlement the holder is willing to accept.

15. Institutional holders typically underwrite unsecured debt on the strength of cash flow, credit agency ratings, and the trading liquidity of the debt in institutional markets. If a debtor experiences signs of cash flow distress or a credit downgrade, the institutional unsecured debt holders are more likely to sell their position to distressed investors at a discount.

16. The form of the debt or security offered to class of claims under a plan can be as important as the recovery amount. Commercial banks are required to hold debt instruments. Use the internet and/or Capital IQ for background research on holders of large claims, including their stated investment objectives and the type of investments they hold.

Chapter 4: 30 Point Checklist & Reminders for Case Analysis

17. Attempt to structure a feasible plan that does not impair creditors, beginning with the most senior creditors and working down the capital structure. No class of unimpaired claims is entitled to a recovery that is more than the value of its claim, subject to the test of a plan being feasible. If a creditor receives stock in a plan, the only way to know that the creditor is not receiving value that is greater than its claim is through a valuation of the business.

18. Best Interest of Creditors Test: A claim holder has the right to receive an amount that is not less than it would receive in a liquidation of the business. This holds true even if the creditor's class votes to approve a plan.

Estimate the recovery value of hard assets, assuming distress liquidation, orderly liquidation, and fair market value. From the net proceeds of the assumed asset recovery, subtract superpriority expenses, administrative expenses, wind-down costs, and a trustee liquidation fee.

Professional fees can consume 5% to 15% of a debtor's assets. If the debtor is liquidated, the liquidating Trustee will receive a 3% fee and wind-down costs can be significant. The wind down-costs for Pierre Foods were estimated at 15% of tangible assets in Pierre's Plan. Analyze the liquidation analysis in the plan, including the reasonableness of the assumptions. The debtor may attempt to over estimate wind-down costs. If the debtor can present a case for high wind-down costs, then the debtor's plan recovery will look more favorable as compared to the liquidation analysis recovery.

Use Table 4.0 for a quick initial estimate of the recovery value of assets for the different valuation assumptions set forth in Table 4.0

Table 4.0—Table to Estimate Asset Values

Asset Book Value	Quick Liquidation	Orderly Liquidation	Fair Market Value (Excludes goodwill)	Fair Market Value Enterprise Value Basis (Includes goodwill)
Cash	100%	100%	100%	100%
Receivables	75%	85%	100%	100%
Inventory	50%	70%	100%	100%
Equipment	25%	50%	100%	100%
Real Estate	50%	75%	100%	100%
Goodwill	0%	0%	0%	Estimate
Less expenses:				
Trustee fee	3% of assets	3% of assets	N/A	N/A
Professional fees	7% of assets [a]	7% of assets [a]	7% of assets	7% of assets
Wind-down costs	10% of assets [b]	10% to 15% of assets [b]	N/A	N/A
Net Proceeds	$	$	$	$

(a) In Pierre's 5.5 months in bankruptcy, professional fees were 8.3% of the net book value of Pierre's hard assets.
(b) Wind-down costs are typically estimated by the debtor in its liquidation analysis. The debtor's assumptions should be carefully evaluated for reasonableness. Pierre's Reorganization Plan estimated wind-down costs equal to 15% of its tangible assets for a 12-month period.

Part III: Strategic Guide to Chapter 11 Case Analysis

19. Prepare a table showing recovery for each class of claims based on valuations in Table 4.1. Evaluate holding, buying, or selling claims based on the recovery matrix. A cost of holding a claim includes the opportunity cost of lost income from alternative investments, and the cost of legal/professional fees related to the bankruptcy.

Table 4.1—Table to Estimate Recoveries

Class	Claim	Quick Liquidation of Assets	Orderly Liquidation of Assets	Fair Market Value of Assets	Enterprise Value of Reorganized Debtor	Recovery Debtor's Plan
Secured debt	$	Recovery %	Recovery %	Recovery %	Recovery %	Recovery %
Unsecured debt	$	Recovery %	Recovery %	Recovery %	Recovery %	Recovery %
Unsecured other	$	Recovery %	Recovery %	Recovery %	Recovery %	Recovery %
Other claims	$	Recovery %	Recovery %	Recovery %	Recovery %	Recovery %
Equity	$	Recovery %	Recovery %	Recovery %	Recovery %	Recovery %

20. Estimate the amount of pro-forma debt the debtor can cash flow based on pro-forma normalized EBITDA. Include projected cost savings from rejected executory contract and other expense reductions. Estimate pro-forma interest expense based on reasonable historical interest rate spreads for a firm with a comparable credit profile, similar collateral, and a comparable transaction structure.

The reorganization plan must be feasible. Use structured credit analysis to establish key credit ratios to qualify the debtor for a credit rating comparable to a company rated B- by S&P and B3 by Moody's.

For an initial estimate of the amount of pro-forma debt and debt service, use the following targeted ratios:

- Pro-forma EBITDA to interest coverage > 1.80:1;
- Pro-forma EBITDAR to fixed charge coverage > 1.10:1;
- Secured debt to EBITDA ratio < 3.5:1;
- Debt to EBITDA ratio < 5.0:1;
- Minimum liquidity equal to one year of interest on pro-forma debt.

Allocate pro-forma debt to secured creditors in an amount up to their claims and then any excess to junior classes.

21. The difference between the Enterprise Value and the pro-forma debt is the amount of equity available to classes of claims receiving less than a 100% recovery in the form of debt and/or cash payment at plan exit.

Chapter 4: 30 Point Checklist & Reminders for Case Analysis

22. Subject to the best interest of creditors test, a class can vote to agree (75% in dollar and more than 50% in number) to accept any treatment for its claim in a plan, including approval of a recovery for junior creditors. The best interest of creditors rule provides each claim holder has a right to a recovery that is at least equal to what it would receive in a liquidation of the debtor.

23. If a voting class of claims does not accept the plan and it receives less than its claim under the plan, then the bankruptcy court cannot approve the plan unless a hearing is held to determine that the treatment is fair and equitable to the class. The definition of fair and equitable is different for a secured claim and an unsecured claim. With respect to any junior dissenting class impaired class, no senior class is entitled to receive a distribution more than its claim. An estimate Enterprise Value is required to determine fair and equitable test and to ensure a claim receives no more than a 100% recovery of its claim.

24. If a secured class does not accept the plan and the class receives less than its claim under the plan, the court cannot approve the plan unless the secured creditor:
- returns the collateral to the creditor, or
- allows the creditor to retain its lien, and
- Receives future payments that have value at least equal to the amount of the claim and the payments must also have a net present value at least equal to the fair market value of the collateral.

The interest rate used to discount the payment to the present value should be comparable to the historical interest rate spread for a comparable risk debt.

25. The court cannot approve a plan over a class of impaired claims unless one other impaired class has accepted the plan. Holders of claims in a class may try to accumulate 25% of the dollar amount of the claims in a class as a strategy to block the plan approval.

26. The court cannot confirm a plan unless the plan is not likely to be followed by the debtor's liquidation or need for further financial reorganization. The projected plan EBITDA, debt structure, debt service, projected cash flows, and projected liquidity are important determinants of the feasibility of the plan.

Cash flows in a plan can be improved by compromising debt, lowering the interest rates, stretching the debt amortization, use of payment-in-kind debt structures, and issuance of equity.

Part III: Strategic Guide to Chapter 11 Case Analysis

Liquidity can be improved by lowering cash payouts, increasing the exit line of credit, selling assets/divisions, and issuing equity.

27. There is greater credit and investment risk in bankruptcy because of the uncertainty of legal outcomes.

A trend has been the greater use of 363 sales to reorganize to speed up and control the reorganization process. The approval of Chrysler's 363 sale increases the risk that debtors will attempt to follow the Chrysler 363 sale example and circumvent creditor rights in a plan of reorganization. The larger a debtor relative to the economy and its industry, the greater the political risk of a bankruptcy court decision that impairs the rights of creditors.

28. Super-priority and administrative claims have the right to receive cash payment when a debtor emerges from Chapter 11. Professional fees will increase as a debtor lingers in bankruptcy. The payment of professional fees is a permanent cash outflow to the debtor. Pierre Foods was in bankruptcy for 5 months. Pierre had tangible assets of $193 million as of its bankruptcy filing date. The professional fees were 8.3% of Pierre's tangible assets for the 5-month bankruptcy.

A trade vendor is also entitled to receive cash payment for the essential goods it provides to the debtor during bankruptcy. After bankruptcy, a vendor will most likely continue to sell goods/services to the debtor and extend credit terms, providing a source of financing for the debtor.

29. The bankruptcy court filings will contain names, addresses, and contact information for all creditors. Call and network. Ask for the opinion of the creditors committee and other creditors.

30. Seek the advice of bankruptcy counsel and other professionals skilled in distressed credit and financial analysis. The bankruptcy court, judge, and the particulars of a case are always of significance.

Part IV

Case Analysis of Pierre Foods

Studies have shown that people believe they can roll a higher number in craps by rolling the dice harder and a lower number by rolling the dice softer (Ellen Langer Studies, 1975).

Chapters 5 through 26 are the full case study of Pierre, its Plan, and the presentation of the Alternative Plan.

Chapter 5

Bankruptcy Filing Information & Parties

The purpose of Chapter 5 is to identify Pierre's basic bankruptcy filing information, the parties of interest, and the outside professional firms and their fees in the case.

Debtor: Pierre Foods, Inc. and subsidiaries, a North Carolina corporation with its primary headquarters in Cincinnati, Ohio, hereinafter collectively referred to as Pierre.

Chapter 11 Date: Filed July 15, 2008 in Delaware

Case Number: 08-11480

Debtor's Plan: Second Amended Plan filed October 29, 2008

Plan Approval: December 10, 2008

Exit Chapter 11: December 12, 2008

Bankruptcy Judge: Kevin Gross

U.S. Trustee: Joseph McMahon

Organization Chart:

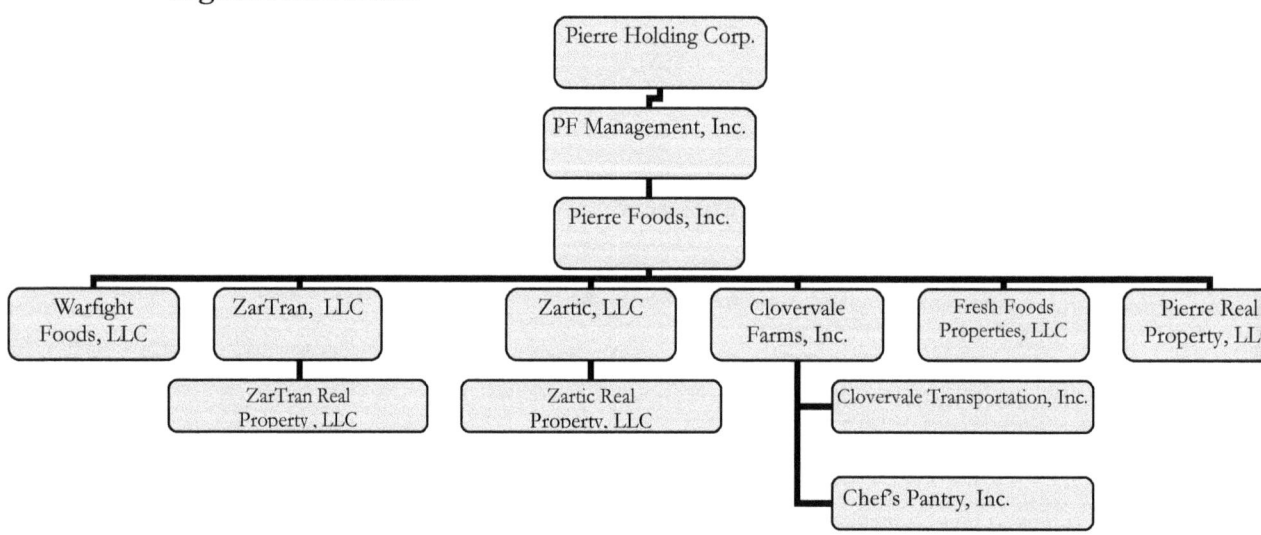

Chapter 5: Bankruptcy Filing Information & Parties

Subsidiaries:

Chef's Pantry, Inc.
Clovervale Farms, Inc.
Clovervale Transportation, Inc.
Fresh Foods Properties, LLC
PF Management, Inc.
Pierre Holding Corp.
Pierre Real Property, LLC
Zar Tran, LLC
Zar Tran Real Property, LLC
Zartic, LLC
Zartic Real Property, LLC
Warfighter Foods, LLC

Corporate Structure at Petition Date

Madison Dearborn Capital Partners IV. L.P. owned 96.27% of the preferred stock of Pierre Holding Corp. and 90.24% of the common stock.

The only asset owned by Pierre Holding Corp. was 100% of the stock of PF Management, Inc.

The sole asset owned by PF Management, Inc. was 100% of the stock in Pierre Foods, Inc.

Pierre Holding Corp. and PF Management, Inc. did not have any direct liabilities, but both entities guaranteed the debt of Pierre Foods, Inc. The debt consisted of a $252.7 million Wachovia secured Credit Facility and $125 million of unsecured Senior Notes.

Debtor's Professionals and Fees

Table 5.0—Debtor's Professionals and Fees During Bankruptcy

Function	Firm	7–15–08 to 12–27–08
Lead counsel	Kirkland & Ellis	$4,350,000
Investment banker	Perella Weinberg Partners	$ 900,000
Restructuring & crisis management	Alvarez and Marsal	$2,203,000
Other legal	Thompson Hine	$ 725,000
Other professionals	All other firms	$5,734,717
Contingency accrual	Perella Weinberg success fee	$2,000,000
Local & conflicts counsel	Richards, Layton & Finger	in other above
General tax advisor	Battelle & Battelle	in other above
	Total professional fees	$15,912,717

Source: Pierre's December 27, 2008 Operating Report filed in Bankruptcy Court.

Professional fees in the case were $15.9 million, representing 8.3% of Pierre's tangible assets. The debtor's investment banker, Perella Weinberg Partners, was paid a $2 million restructuring fee for the completion of the

Part IV: Case Analysis of Pierre Foods

reorganization. The Creditors Committee's financial advisor, Imperial Capital, was paid $1 million, with $500,000 of the amount paid as a success fee for the completion of the reorganization.

Prior to filing for bankruptcy, Pierre paid $1.8 million in deposits to professional firms for retainers. Professional firms also held $2.5 million in letters of credits to cover expenses.

Unsecured Creditors Committee Members

Table 5.1—Unsecured Creditors Committee Members

Credit Committee Member	Unsecured Claim Type
Genpak	Vendor - $218,916 claim
Skidmore Sales & Distributing	Vendor - $174,592 claim
Americraft Carton	Vendor - $236,060 claim
U.S. National Bank	Indenture Trustee for 9.875% $125 million Senior Note
Federated High Income Bond Fund	Held position in 9.875% $125 million Senior Note
Fidelity Puritan Fund	Held position in 9.875% $125 million Senior Note
Ares	Held position in 9.875% $125 million Senior Note

Fidelity Investment entities held $13.4 million (11%) of the unsecured Senior Notes—the Fidelity Puritan Fund held $11.1 million and other Fidelity entities held $2.3 million.

On March 31, 2008, the Fidelity Central Investment Portfolio held $5.9 million (2.4%) of the Wachovia secured Credit Facility, but sold the position by June 30, 2008.

Federated Investment entities held $11.2 million (8.7%) of the unsecured Senior Notes—the Federated High Income Bond Fund held $4.1 million and other Federated entities held $7.1 million.

Trade Creditors Unsecured Claims vs. Unsecured Debt

On the day of bankruptcy, Pierre owed trade creditors $15.2 million. The balance on the $125 million of unsecured Senior Notes was $131.1 million including interest. The $15.2 million of unsecured trade debt was 11% of total unsecured debt. A creditors committee representing the balanced interests of the unsecured claims should have included one vendor and six Senior Note holders. The Bankruptcy Trustee appointed three trade vendors and four Senior Note holders to the creditors committee.

Trade vendors were able to achieve a substantial reduction in their claims in the 90 days prior to bankruptcy. Trade payables decreased by $7.7 million from March 1, 2008 to July 15, 2008 as compared to only a $1.6 million decrease in

Chapter 5: Bankruptcy Filing Information & Parties

inventories over the same time. Moreover, Pierre carried a $7.5 million prepaid asset for prepayments to trade vendors at the petition date compared to a zero prepayments on the March 1, 2008 balance sheet. Furthermore, in first-day bankruptcy orders, the Bankruptcy Court approved the payment of prepetition vendor claims of up to $6.4 million for critical vendors, $2.6 million for potential warehouse/materialmens' liens, and $0.4 million for other vendor claims with statutory lien priority.

Creditors Committee Professionals

Table 5.2—Creditors Committee Professionals

Function	Firm
Lead counsel	Akin, Gump, Strauss, Hauer, & Feld
Local & conflicts counsel	Young, Conaway, Stargatt & Taylor
Financial advisor	Imperial Capital

Sponsor of the Plan for Pierre's Reorganization

Oaktree Capital Management L.P. is a part of Oaktree Capital Management (Oaktree Capital), an investment firm specializing in securities and private investments. The firm manages over $51 billion of investment funds. Oaktree Capital's investments include high-yield debt, convertible debt, distressed debt, private equity, real estate, and listed equities. The firm typically seeks to have a seat on the Board of Directors or observation rights in its portfolio of companies. Oaktree Capital's stock does not trade on a public exchange and Oaktree Capital is not required to report under the Securities Exchange Act of 1934. Oaktree Capital's Class A shares trade under the ticker symbol OAKTRZ on the Goldman Sachs Tradable Unregistered Equities over-the-counter marketplace. As of March 9, 2009, Oaktree Capital's market capitalization was approximately $4.1 billon.

Oaktree Capital describes the types of investments it seeks as including distressed debt and distressed opportunites. The Company's website dicloses the following investment strategy:

> "Investment opportunities in distressed debt typically arise as a result of lowered credit standards and the unwise extension of credit, followed by the onset of economic weakness or some other igniter. When both elements are in place, distressed debt can be the market in which negativism is most crystallized and concentrated, giving us unusual opportunities for bargain purchases. Directed by the same management since the strategy's inception 19 years ago, Oaktree

Part IV: Case Analysis of Pierre Foods

Capital's industry leading distressed debt team has invested successfully through several full cycles in the distressed debt market. The team is comprised of professionals with diverse backgrounds in portfolio management, law, accounting, valuation and banking. They combine extensive experience in distressed bank debt, defaulted securities and bankruptcy situations with proven expertise in valuing companies and assets, negotiation and restructuring. The team benefits from a large and expert staff, from Oaktree's proprietary analytical capability, and from a unique and superior access to deal flow. We favor large, fundamentally sound companies that are overleveraged, says Bruce Karsh, who serves as portfolio manager. Oaktree Capital often assumes a leadership role in the financial restructuring process, investing at every level of the capital structure, in foreign or domestic securities, in companies or hard assets, in stressed securities and in unusual instruments and special situations. Oaktree Capital seeks to avoid losses through an emphasis on secured or senior debt, a mix of public and private debt, an insistence on protection from underlying asset values or franchise value, and limited concentrations of positions."

In June 2009, Oaktree Capital raised an additional $10.9 billion for investing in distressed opportunities.

Legal Counsel for Oaktree Capital
Skadden, Arps, Slate, Meagher & Flom.

Chapter 6

Pierre's Business & History

"An ignorant person is one who doesn't know what you just found out."
Will Rogers

Pierre's Business

Pierre Foods is engaged in the manufacture, marketing, and distribution of processed food solutions, with a focus on formed, pre-cooked, ready-to-cook products, compartmentalized meals, and hand-held convenience sandwiches. Its products include beef, pork, poultry, bakery items, vegetables, fruits, cobblers, and peanut butter and jelly bars, as well as sandwiches and cups.

The Company's pre-cooked and ready-to-cook proteins include hamburgers, meatloaf, chicken strips, and barbecued pork rib products.

Pierre markets its products under various brand names, such as Pierre, Zartic, Z-Bird, Circle Z, Jim's Country Mill Sausage, Clovervale Farms, Chef's Pantry, Fast Choice, Rib-B-Q, Blue Stone Grill, Hot 'n' Ready, Big AZ, Chicken FryZ, Smokie Grill, and Chop House.

Pierre has licenses to sell sandwiches using Checkers, Rally's, Krystal, Tony Roma's, and Nathan's Famous brand names.

Part IV: Case Analysis of Pierre Foods

Leading Market Share

Management of Pierre believes they have the number one market position in the United States in the packaged sandwich segment. Microwavable packaged sandwiches account for 38% of Pierre's sales and cooked protein products account for 56% of sales. Pre-cooked proteins include hamburgers, meatloaf, chicken strips, and barbecued pork rib products.

Diverse Product Lines and End Markets

Pierre's product line consists of approximately 800 stock-keeping units (SKUs), including a wide variety of cooked beef, poultry and pork products, hand-held convenience sandwiches, and value-added bakery products. The Company targets a broad array of customers in six distinct and growing end markets. Pierre has had a history of growing sales at rates in excess of the market growth rate in each of its end markets.

Pierre's End Markets

Vending Sales

Pierre is a leading supplier of packaged sandwiches to the U.S. vending market. Pierre is the only significant sandwich supplier to Canteen, the largest vending operator in the United States. Other key customers in the vending end market include VSA, Market Day, Continental Airlines, and Superior Meats.

Convenience Stores

Pierre sells a variety of innovative packaged sandwiches to many of the top convenience store chains, such as 7-Eleven, Circle K, Quik-Trip and other national and regional convenience store chains, as well as thousands of individual unit locations across the United States.

Warehouse Clubs/Grocery Stores

Pierre produces "club packs" of packaged sandwiches for many long-term customers, including Sam's, Costco, BJ's, Smart & Final, and other warehouse club chains. Other customers in this end market include traditional grocery store chains such as Food Lion and Bi-Lo.

Schools

Pierre is one of the leading suppliers of pre-cooked beef and pork products to school cafeterias in the United States, selling product to school systems in 49 states, including 94 of the 100 largest school districts in the United States. Pierre sells a full line of food products to more than 50% of all U.S. public primary and

Chapter 6: Pierre's Business & History

secondary school systems. Sales to schools accounted for 25% of Pierre's fiscal March 2008 sales.

Approximately 8%, or $52.7 million, of Pierre's fiscal 2008 sales were products sold to schools through programs with the United States Department of Agriculture (USDA).

Foodservice

Pierre believes it has been an innovator in providing pre-cooked proteins and packaged sandwiches to the foodservice end market. Pierre's customers in this end market represent a broad range of industries in healthcare, recreation, airlines, military, and restaurants. Key customers include SYSCO, U.S. Foodservice, Schwan's and Subway.

Sales & Marketing

Pierre markets its products through its direct sales force and a network of independent food brokers to a range of customers, including restaurant chains, schools, military and other food service providers. The sales department is organized predominantly by sales channel. In addition to its direct sales force, the Company utilizes a nationwide network of over 130 independent food brokers compensated on a commission basis.

Product Research and Development

Pierre employs 14 food scientists and culinary experts in the product and process development department. Ongoing food production research and development activities include development of new products, improvement of existing products, and refinement of food production processes. These activities resulted in the launch of 628 new SKUs in fiscal March 2008. Thirty-two percent of the of Pierre's fiscal March 2008 revenues were derived from product SKUs developed in the prior two years. Pierre spent $1.8 million on product development programs in each of the prior two years.

Customer Concentration

In FYE March 2008, Pierre's top ten customers accounted for 46% of total sales. Sales to CKE Restaurants, Inc., who had a Standard & Poor's (S&P) corporate credit rating of BB-, accounted for 11%, 14%, and 21% of sales in fiscal 2008, 2007, and 2006, respectively. Pierre's contract with CKE Restaurants, Inc. is for the Hardee's and Carl's Jr. fast-food restaurants.

No other customer accounted for more than 10% of Pierre's sales in each of the most recent three fiscal years.

Part IV: Case Analysis of Pierre Foods

USDA Program Requirements

The USDA program requires Pierre to provide either: (1) a performance bond, (2) an irrevocable letter of credit, or (3) an escrow account to cover the amount of inventory on hand and on order.

In fiscal March 2008, Pierre provided $5.7 million of letters of credit to its insurance company to secure the USDA Programs performance bonds. The letters of credit were issued under the Wachovia secured Credit Facility.

Because of Pierre's deteriorating financial condition in 2008, the USDA required Pierre to increase the performance bonds to $8.0 million for fiscal March 2009. Pierre used the $35 million DIP loan approved in bankruptcy to issue $8.0 million letters of credit to secure USDA performance obligations. As a result, the $5.7 million in letters of credit issued under the prepetition Wachovia Credit Facility terminated on August 29, 2008.

Manufacturing Facilities

Pierre manufactures products in five plants located throughout the Midwestern and Southeastern United States. The Company cooks and prepares food in plants located in Cincinnati, Ohio and Rome, Georgia.

Pierre ships frozen products to customers or to one of its sandwich assembly and entrée assembly plants located in: (1) Claremont, North Carolina, housing high-speed baking and sandwich assembly lines, or (2) Amherst, Ohio or Easley, South Carolina to assemble and package a variety of sandwiches and meal components.

In July 2007, the Zartic meat processing plant in Alabama was destroyed by fire and the plant was deemed a complete loss. Pierre received $2 million of casualty insurance proceeds in 2008.

On February 8, 2008, Pierre announced it would close the Cedartown, Georgia manufacturing facility as part of a strategic restructuring. In November 2008, Pierre signed an agreement to sell certain equipment in the plant for $1.1 million.

Raw Materials

The primary raw materials used in Pierre's food processing operations are boneless beef, chicken, pork, flour, cheese, yeast, breading, soy proteins, seasonings, peanut butter, and packaging supplies. Beef and chicken are the primary raw material costs, accounting for 51% and 10%, respectively of raw material costs.

Pierre typically purchases meat products under seven-day payment terms, with the exception of a few meats that require payment at the time the product

Chapter 6: Pierre's Business & History

is shipped. Historically, Pierre has not hedged in the futures markets. Pierre's raw material costs have fluctuated with the movement in the relevant commodity markets. The Company has attempted to manage raw material fluctuations through purchase orders, market-related customer pricing contracts, fixed-price customer contracts, and by passing on such cost increases to customers.

Pierre purchases all of its raw materials from outside sources. Pierre does not depend on a single source for any significant item. Pierre's FYE March 1, 2008 audited financial statements, released on June 6, 2008, contained a statement warning that Pierre's vendors and supplies could terminate their relationship with Pierre because of the Company's financial condition.

Industry

Pierre operates in the packaged foods and meats industry. Publicly traded firms in the industry have combined annual sales of over $1.1 trillion. The packaged foods and meats industry falls broadly under the consumer staples industry classification. Sub-sectors of the packaged foods and meats industry include the following industry classifications:

- Breads and bakery products;
- Meats, meat processing, and meat related products;
- Prepared and preserved foods, including sub-sectors of peanut butter and preserves, jams/jellies, and sandwiches and filled rolls.

Grant Thornton estimated Pierre's Enterprise Value in connection with the sale of the business to Madison Dearborn in 2004. Grant Thornton classified Pierre's business in the following Standard Industrial Classifications (SIC):

SIC Code	Industry
2011	Meat Packing Plants
2013	Sausages & Other Prepared Meats
2050	Bakery Products
2051	Bread & Other Bakery Products.

An SIC code exists for "Sandwiches, Assembled and Packaged for the Wholesale Market" (SIC code 20990706). Limited public data is available on companies in SIC code 20990706.

Part IV: Case Analysis of Pierre Foods

Sandwich Market

In 2006, the sandwich market was $121 billion with room to grow, according to U.S. Foodservice and Retail Market and Trends from Packaged Facts (QSR, 2006). Sandwich sales account for 25% of U.S food service sales. Sandwiches are sold to warehouse clubs, convenience stores, restaurants, and in various other institutions. Hamburger sales accounted for 45% of the sandwich market while sandwich chains were the fast growing segment of the market.

Packaged Sandwiches to Convenience Store Market

According to a report by NPD Group in 2005, Foodservice sales' at convenience stores is an $18 billion market, with $16 billion of on-site prepared food sales and $2 billion of packaged sandwich sales. Pierre had annual sales of $643 million in 2008.

Competition

The convenience food business is highly competitive. Sales are affected by changes in tastes, eating habits, economic conditions, and demographic factors. Pierre competes with manufacturers and distributors of value-added meat products, compartmentalized meals, and packaged sandwich suppliers. Some of Pierre's competitors have substantially greater financial resources, name recognition, research and development, marketing, and human resources.

Meat Processing Competition

Pierre faces competition from a variety of meat processing companies, including:

- Advance Food Company, who grew from $20 million in sales in 1990 to $600 million in 2008. Advance Food had a S&P credit rating of B;
- Tyson. $26.8 billion of annual sales and an S&P credit rating of BB;
- King's Command Foods. $29.9 million of annual sales;
- JTM Food Group. Estimated annual sales of $9.8 million;
- Don Lee Farms with unknown sales;
- Many other smaller local and regional operations.

Sandwich Competition

The sandwich industry is extremely fragmented and there are only a few large direct competitors to Pierre. The industry could be a candidate for consolidation.

Chapter 6: Pierre's Business & History

Pierre's competitors in the sandwich industry include:
- Sara Lee/Jimmy Dean Foods. $13 billion of annual sales. S&P credit rating of BBB+;
- Bridgford Foods. $121 million of annual sales;
- E. A. Sween Deli Express. $79 million of estimated annual sales;
- Landshire. $18 million of estimated annual sales.

Biscuit and Yeast Roll Competition

In sales of biscuit and yeast roll products, Pierre competes with a number of large bakeries in various parts of the country. The percentage of Pierre's sales from biscuit and yeast roll sales has not been disclosed by Pierre, but it is estimated they account for less than 8% of sales.

Seasonality

Pierre derives 25% of its total sales from schools. Due to the seasonality of sales to schools, Pierre's overall sales tend to be lower during the summer months and lower in November and December.

Employees

On March 1, 2008, Pierre had 2,629 employees.

History of Pierre's Ownership
- In 1990 Pierre was acquired by Hudson Foods;
- In 1998 Hudson Foods was acquired by Tyson Foods;
- In 1998 Tyson Foods sold Pierre for $122 million to WSMP (NASDAQ listed) and to certain management members of Pierre. WSMP changed its name to Fresh Foods;
- In 2000 Fresh Foods changed its name to Pierre Foods, Inc.;
- In 2001 PF Management acquired Pierre. PF Management was 88% owned by James Richardson, Jr. and David Clark, Pierre's Chairman and Vice-Chairman, respectively. PF Management also owned 100% of PF Purchasing (PFP). PFP paid Pierre $100,000 a quarter to serve as Pierre's exclusive purchasing agent. PFP received all rebates and discounts due from Pierre's suppliers. For FYE March 2004 and 2003, PFP received payments from suppliers of $2,122,000 and $3,960,000, respectively.
In FYE March 2004, Pierre paid Mr. Richardson and Mr. Clark $2.2 million (combined) for their service as Chairman and Vice-Chairman;

Part IV: Case Analysis of Pierre Foods

- In June 2004, PF Management sold Pierre to Madison Dearborn Capital Partners, LLC (Madison Dearborn). Madison Dearborn owned 96.3% of Pierre's stock on a post-closing basis and owned 89.6% of the stock on March 1, 2008. Pierre's President, Norbert Woodhams, owned 2.1% on a post-closing basis and owned 2.6% of the stock on March 1, 2008.

Background on James C. Richardson Jr. and David R. Clark
James C. Richardson, Jr., age 55.
- Retired from Pierre after Madison Dearborn acquired Pierre;
- Director of Pierre—1987 to June 2004;
- Pierre's Chief Executive Officer—1993 to 1996;
- Became an executive officer of Pierre in 1987.

David R. Clark, age 47.
- Retired from Pierre after Madison Dearborn acquired Pierre;
- Director of Pierre from 1996 to the June 2004;
- Pierre's President from 1996 to the June 2004;
- Previously Executive V.P. of Granite Bank—1994 to 1996;
- President of BB&T Bank 1993 to 1994. 13 year career at BB&T.

Management of Pierre at Date of the Bankruptcy Filing
Norbert Woodhams, age 62.
- President of Pierre on the day of Pierre's bankruptcy filing;
- Became President of Pierre in December 1998;
- President of Hudson Specialty Foods—1994 to 1998;
- Appointed Pierre's President after Hudson acquired Tyson in 1998;
- Group V.P. for Tyson's Pork and Beef Division—1990 to 1994;
- President of Henry House/Holly Farms—1987 to 1990.

Cynthia Hughes, age 55.
- Appointed Pierre's Chief Financial Officer in February 2008;
- Previously Chief Financial Officer of Effox, a division of CECO Environmental Corporation, serving in that position beginning in 2003;
- Prior to 2003, Chief Financial Officer of Klosterman Baking, one of the largest family-owned bakeries in the Midwest;
- Prior to that, she held various positions at Pierre and its predecessors.

Chapter 6: Pierre's Business & History

Joseph Meyers, age 41.
- Chief Financial Officer from June 2004 to June 20, 2008;
- On June 20, 2008, Pierre terminated his employment without cause;
- Pamela Witters, Pierre's CFO, left Pierre after Madison Dearborn acquired Pierre. Mr. Meyers became the new CFO after she left Pierre;
- Pierre's Vice-President Finance—February 2003 to June 20, 2008;
- He had held various high-level accounting and finance positions with Pierre dating back to 1996;
- From 1991–1996 he was General Accounting Manager at OhSe Foods, subsidiary of Hudson Foods;
- Previously he was a staff accountant at PGT Trucking.

Robert Naylor served as Pierre's Senior V.P. Sales and Marketing from 1998 to October 2007. He had served in various sales positions with Pierre from 1997. In October 2007, at the age of 55, Pierre issued a press release announcing his retirement. A subsequent SEC 8-K filed by Pierre showed that Mr. Naylor and Pierre executed a termination and severance agreement. Pierre's July 15, 2008 Schedule of Assets/Liabilities reported a $138,000 severance payment claim for Mr. Naylor. Mr. Naylor also filed a $1 million unsecured deferred compensation claim.

Anthony Schroder, age 41.
- Appointed Senior V.P. of Sales in November 2007;.
- Previously Pierre's V.P. Vending, Convenience Store, and Warehouse Club/Retail Divisions, beginning December 2006;
- Previously held various sales management positions at Pierre;
- Began working for Pierre in 1990 as a Production Supervisor.

Pierre's Board of Directors at Date of Bankruptcy

Madison Dearborn appointed new Board Directors after its June 2004 acquisition of Pierre. Norbert Woodhams became Chairman of the Board. Three of Pierre's five Board Directors were also Directors at Madison Dearborn. Excluding Norbert Williams, the average age of Pierre's Board of Directors was 41.5 years in 2004.

86
Part IV: Case Analysis of Pierre Foods

The Board members were:

Robin P. Selati, age 41 when appointed as Director of Pierre.
- Managing Director of Madison Dearborn;
- Joined Madison Dearborn in 1993;
- Prior to joining Madison Dearborn, Mr. Selati was associated with Alex Brown & Sons in the retail investment banking group;
- Served on the Board of Directors of Carrols Restaurant Group, Tuesday Morning Corporation, Cinemark, Ruth's Chris Steak House, and Yankee Candle.

Nicholas W. Alexos, age 43 when appointed as Director of Pierre.
- Co-founded Madison Dearborn in 1993;
- Director of Madison Dearborn;
- Previously with First Chicago Venture Capital for four years;
- Served on the Board of Directors of National Mentor and Sirona Holdings Luxco.

George A. Peinado, age 37 when he was appointed as a Director of Pierre.
- Board Director at Madison Dearborn;
- Joined Madison Dearborn in 2004;.
- Previously with DLJ Merchant Banking Partners and Morgan Stanley;
- Served on the Board of Directors of Yankee Candle.

Scott W. Meader, age 45 when he was appointed as a Director of Pierre.
- Formerly President of Milnot Holding Corp. from 1997 to 2006;
- Previously held various positions with Burns Philps Foods, Pet Incorporated, A.T. Kearney and Quaker Oats.

Compensation of Pierre's Top Officers

Table 6.0—Pierre's Top Executive Officer Compensation
(in dollars)

Officer	Salary	Severance	Insurance Premiums	Other [a]	Total Compensation
President, Woodhams	398,607		109,831	44,957	553,395
Former VP Sales, Naylor	193,479	138,000	113,287	22,807	467,573
Former CFO, Meyers	230,000 [b]				230,000 [b]
New VP Sales, Schroder	150,796 [c]				150,796 [c]
New CFO, Hughes	(d)				(d)
Total	972,882	138,000	223,118	67,764	1,401,764

Source: Pierre's U.S. SEC Edgar filings.

(a) Includes auto lease, 401(k) matching contribution, and disability insurance premiums.
(b) Employment terminated without cause on June 20, 2008.
(c) Salary increased to $180,000 in 2009 due to promotion to Vice-President Sales.
(d) Appointed to Chief Financial Officer in February 2008. Base salary of $180,000 year for 2009.

Chapter 7

- **Acquisitions**
- **Fairness of Price/Debt Leverage**

"Two things are infinite: the universe and human stupidity; and I am not sure about the universe"—Albert Einstein

Background on Private Equity Firm Madison Dearborn

Madison Dearborn, a leading private equity investment firm based in Chicago, Illinois, had $8 billion of investments under management when it acquired Pierre Foods in June 2004.

Madison Dearborn focused on investments in basic industries, in areas that included communications, consumer goods, financial services, and health care. Madison Dearborn's objective was to invest in companies with strong competitive characteristics that it believed had the potential for significant long-term equity appreciation.

John Canning, Jr. founded Madison Dearborn in 1992. Mr. Canning had previously operated the leveraged buyout and the venture capital equity investments for First Bank of Chicago. Mr. Canning and other top executives left First Bank of Chicago in 1992 to form Madison Dearborn. Mr. Canning was also a minority owner of the Milwaukee Brewers baseball team.

Part IV: Case Analysis of Pierre Foods

Madison Dearborn had previously completed a number of leveraged buyout transactions. In June 2007, Madison Dearborn participated in the $51.7 billion buyout of Bell Canada.

Madison Dearborn managed investments through a series of private limited partnerships and its investors included a variety of pension funds, endowments, and other institutional investors.

Madison Dearborn managed the five following funds:

Opened	Fund Name	Amount
1993	Madison Dearborn Capital	$550 million
1997	Fund II	$925 million
1999	Fund III	$2.2 billion
2000	Fund IV	$4.1 billion
2006	Fund V	$6.5 billion

Madison Dearborn's objective was to invest in companies with outstanding management teams to achieve significant long-term appreciation in value. Madison Dearborn sought to invest $100 million to $600 million of equity capital in a single transaction.

Madison Dearborn's Acquisition of Pierre in June 2004

Madison Dearborn acquired Pierre Foods in June 2004 for $422 million, contributing $142.5 million of cash equity. Table 7.0 shows the complete sources and uses of funds for the acquisition. Table 7.1 shows the pre and post closing balance sheets.

Pierre's selling stockholders, primarily James Richardson and David Clark (88% owners), received $211 million in cash from the sale of their stock in Pierre. Pierre paid Madison Dearborn an arrangement fee of $5.0 million. Pierre also paid Madison Dearborn's expenses in connection with the acquisition.

The acquisition increased Pierre's debt from $163 million to $275 million, an increase of $112 million.

The excess of the acquisition price over the fair market value of the assets acquired was allocated to goodwill and intangibles—$175 million for goodwill and $146 million for intangibles (trade names, customers, licenses, and formulas).

Chapter 7: Acquisitions/Fairness of Price/Debt Leverage

Table 7.0
Sources & Uses of Funds for Madison Dearborn's Acquisition of Pierre
($ millions)

Uses	
211.2	Cash paid to selling stockholders
2.0	Transaction expenses of selling stockholders
24.2	Bonus payments to management
116.4	Payoff unsecured Notes
21.4	Payoff revolving line of credit
9.0	Payoff term loan
5.5	Payoff airplane loan
14.3	Payoff subordinated debt
18.3	Fees: commitment, placement, advisory, legal, & professional
0.2	Non-compete fee
422.4	Total uses of funds

Sources	
142.0	Cash contributed by Madison Dearborn
0.5	Cash contributed by management of Pierre
4.9	Management contribution from deferred compensation plan
125.0	Senior unsecured Notes (9.875%) due July 2012
150.0	Wachovia Term Loan
0.0	Opening balance on Wachovia $40 million Term Loan
422.4	Total sources of funds

Source: Pierre's U.S. SEC Edgar filing.

Part IV: Case Analysis of Pierre Foods

Table 7.1—Balance Sheet: Pre & Post Madison Dearborn Acquisition

($ millions)	6/5/2004 Pre	Purchase Adjustment	Notes	6/5/2004 Post
Cash	1.3	(1.2)		0.1
Accounts receivable	22.2	0		22.2
Inventory	42.2	2.0	(a)	44.2
Other current assets	6.6	0.0		6.6
Property, plant, equipment	60.9	(4.3)	(a)	56.6
Goodwill	-0-	174.9	(a)	174.9
Intangible assets	38.8	145.8	(a)	184.6
Other assets	10.1	0		10.1
Total assets	182.1	317.2		499.3
CMLTD	5.1	(3.5)		1.6
Payables/accruals	17.9	(0.8)		17.1
Long term debt	157.8	115.8		273.6
Deferred tax	0.0	57.0	(a)	57.0
Other liabilities	0.5	7.1		7.6
Total liabilities	181.3	175.6		356.9
Stockholders equity	0.8	141.7	(b)	142.5
Total liabilities & equity	182.1	317.3		499.4

Source: Pierre's U.S. SEC Edgar filing.

(a) The acquisition was accounted for as a purchase in accordance with Statement of Financial Accounting Standards No. 141, "Business Combinations" as follows:

    414.5   Purchase price
    (105.5) Less book value of net assets acquired
    309.0   Excess of purchase price over book value of net assets acquired

The excess of the purchase price over the net book value of net assets acquired was allocated as follows:

    2.0   Inventory mark-up to fair market value (FMV)
    4.3   Property, plant and equipment mark-up to FMV
    184.6 Intangibles allocated to formulas, customer relationships, license agreements, and trade names
    174.9 Goodwill
    (57.0) Deferred tax
    309.0

(b) To reflect the impact on shareholders equity of the acquisition:

    142.5   Cash equity contributed by buyer Madison Dearborn
    (236.0) Payment to selling stockholders
    270.2   Excess of purchase price over book value of net assets acquired
    (10.5)   Fees & expenses
    (15.1)   Net assets retained by selling stockholders
    (4.9)   Deferred compensation plan
    (4.6)   Write-off deferred financing fees on debt paid off
    141.7   Total adjustment to stockholders equity

New Secured Loan From Wachovia Bank

On June 30, 2004, Pierre opened a $190 million Wachovia Credit Facility, consisting of a $150 million Term Loan and a $40 million Revolver. The proceeds of the $150 million Term Loan completed the Madison Dearborn

Chapter 7: Acquisitions/Fairness of Price/Debt Leverage

acquisition price. The $40 million Revolver was for future working capital needs. The post closing borrowing availability on the Revolver was $36.2 million (net of a $3.8 million reserve for letters of credit). The collateral securing the Wachovia Credit Facility was a first-lien on all of Pierre's assets.

Analysis of Madison Dearborn's Acquisition Price

For a quick analysis of the fairness of the Madison Dearborn acquisition price, the acquisition price will be compared to earnings before interest, taxes, deprecation, and amortization (EBITDA). The $422 million acquisition price was 16.8 times Pierre's $25 million EBITDA in FYE March 2004 and 9.3 times Pierre's $45 million EBITDA in FYE March 2005.

After the acquisition, Pierre planned to eliminate $31.6 million of expenses, including annual distribution fees of $11.6 million to PF Distribution (see Table 7.2 for the SG&A expenses to be eliminated)

Pro-forma adjusted EBITDA was $56.6 million after the planned elimination of expenses. The $422 million purchase price was equal to 7.5 times the pro-forma adjusted EBITDA.

Pierre's EBITDA was $56 million in FYE March 2006 and $60 million in FYE March 2007. Therefore, it is concluded the Madison Dearborn acquisition multiple was 7.5x Pierre's EBITDA because the planned elimination of expenses was validated by the 2006 and 2007 actual EBITDA.

Table 7.2—Pro-Forma SG&A to be Eliminated (Post Madison Dearborn Acquisition)

(in $ millions)	FYE 3/4/2005	FYE 3/4/2006	Cumulative Annual Savings
Distribution expenses	11.6	0	11.6
Personal house payment for management	0.1	0	0.1
Compensation expense	2.8	1.2	4.0
Travel and entertainment	2.0	1.0	3.0
Office expense	0.6	0.2	0.8
Aircraft expense	1.5	0.8	2.3
Compass Outfitters	0.7	0.1	0.8
Professional fees	2.4	2.6	5.0
Previous shareholders other expenses	1.1	0.7	1.8
Previous shareholders transaction fees	0	1.0	1.0
Consulting services	0	0.8	0.8
Endorsement termination & Other	0	0.4	0.4
Total	$22.8	$8.8	$31.6

Source: Pierre's U.S. SEC Edgar filing.

Acquisition Enterprise Value to EBITDA Ratio Compared to Industry

Pierre's broad industry classification is in the packaged foods and meats industry. Table 7.3 shows the ratios of Enterprise Value to EBITDA and debt to EBITDA for Pierre and 16 U.S. exchange traded firms with market

Part IV: Case Analysis of Pierre Foods

capitalizations under $2 billion in the packaged food and meat industry ("Industry Peer").

The Industry Peer median Enterprise Value to EBITDA ratio was 7.29 times 2004 EBITDA and 6.52 times 2005 EBITDA. The Industry Peer multiple is comparable to Madison Dearborn's acquisition price of 7.5 times Pierre's pro-forma adjusted EBITDA. In summary, without factoring in a premium for Madison Dearborn's ownership control, Madison Dearborn paid a price that was comparable to the Industry Peer EBITDA multiple.

Table 7.3—Enterprise to EBITDA & Enterprise to Debt for Pierre & Packaged Foods/Meats Industry

(in $ millions)	Market Cap Jun-2004	Debt Jun-2004	Enterprise Value Jun-2004	Enterprise Value Jun 2004 to FYE 2004 EBITDA	Enterprise Value Jun 2004 to FYE 2005 EBITDA	Debt Jun 2004 to FYE 2004 EBITDA	Debt Jun 2004 to FYE 2005 EBITDA
Pierre's reported EBITDA	147[a]	274	422	16.8x	9.3x	11.4x	6.84x
Pierre pro-forma Adj. EBITDA				7.6x	7.5x		4.95x
Median of firms below				7.29x	6.52x	0.12x	0.12x
Average of firms below				7.75x	7.07x	1.95x	1.78x
Smithfield Foods.	3,230	1,963	5,194	9.51x	5.49x	3.59x	2.07x
J&J Smack Foods	170	no debt	170	2.90x	2.65x	no debt	no debt
B&G Foods	176[b]	0.4	177	2.85x	2.52x	0.01x	0.01x
American Italian Pasta	490	309	799	14.17x	13.25x	5.48x	5.13x
Seneca Foods	209	239	448	6.80x	7.17x	3.63x	3.83x
Diamond Foods, Inc.	321[c]	22[c]	343	1.84x	1.84x	0.12x	0.12x
Del Monte	2,169	1,456	3,625	8.33x	8.77x	3.34x	3.52x
Treehouse Foods	913[d]	7.9[d]	921	10.66x	16.10x	0.09x	0.14x
The Hain Celestial	623	105	728	13.10x	10.95x	1.88x	1.57x
Green Mountain Coffee	48	17	65	3.34x	2.96x	0.86x	0.76x
Lance Inc.	386	65	451	7.09x	7.29x	1.02x	1.05x
Lancaster Colony	1,251	no debt	1,251	7.96x	8.62x	no debt	no debt
Tootsie Roll Ind.	1,488	8	1,495	14.72x	13.87x	0.07x	0.07x
Sanderson Farms	885	16	901	5.10x	6.52x	0.09x	0.11x
Cal-Maine Foods	292	89	381	3.09x	92.87x	0.72x	21.61x
Bridgford	77	no debt	77	19.72x	38.45x	no debt	No debt

Source: Custom data screen developed through Capital IQ screening by the author. Capital IQ is not responsible for the actual data results returned in the screening or in the Table 7.3. The debt for the Industry Peers is as of June 2004. EBITDA is for fiscal years 2004 and 2005, a comparable time to Madison Dearborn's June 2004 acquisition of Pierre.
(a) Pierre's stock was not traded in June 2004. The proxy used for Pierre's market capitalization is the difference between the $422 million Madison Dearborn purchase price and its $275 million of post acquisition debt.
(b) Stock price as of May 23, 2007 (first-day of trading history).
(c) Stock price as of July 23, 2005 (first-day of trading history). Debt is as of October 2005.
(d) Stock price as of June 28, 2005 (first-day of trading history). Debt is as of June 2005.

Chapter 7: Acquisitions/Fairness of Price/Debt Leverage

Measurement of Cash Flow and Debt Leverage Risk for Lenders

Secured and unsecured lenders have moved increasingly towards relying on two key financial covenants in loan agreements for the control of risks relating to financial leverage and cash flow. The two key ratios are:

1. Maximum leverage in the form of a Debt to EBITDA ratio;
2. Minimum cash flow coverage, typically in the form of a minimum EBITDA to interest ratio and/or minimum EBITDAR to fixed charges ratio.

Analysis of Debt to EBITDA Ratio—Post Madison Dearborn Acquisition

Post acquisition, Pierre's debt was 4.9 times pro-forma adjusted EBITDA. Pierre's debt to EBITDA ratio was significantly higher than the Industry Peer debt to EBITDA ratio of 2.0:1 (average) and 0.12:1 (median).

Table 7.4 shows the median debt to EBITDA ratio for 1,077 industrial companies rated AAA to CCC by Standard and Poor's.

For the period 2003–2005, the typical industrial company rated B by S&P had a median debt to EBITDA ratio of 5.5:1, decreasing to 3.5:1 for BB rated firms. Pierre's post acquisition debt to EBITDA ratio of 4.9:1 was comparable to a credit rated B by S&P. Thirty-three percent of the 1,077 U.S. industrial companies rated by S&P had a B credit rating.

Table 7.4—S&P's Key U.S. Industrial Financial Ratios, Long-Term debt Three-year (2003 to 2005 averages)

	AAA	AA	A	BBB	BB	B	CCC
Oper. income/sales (%)	21.2	23.3	19.3	15.8	16.8	15.7	15.8
Free oper. cash flow /sales (%)	15.9	11.7	7.9	6.1	4.3	1.5	(3.0)
Return on capital (%)	24.3	27.5	17.4	14.0	11.8	9.5	5.4
EBIT interest coverage (x)	25.5	20.8	8.8	5.6	2.8	1.5	0.6
EBITDA/interest coverage (x)	29.3	22.9	11.6	7.3	4.0	2.3	1.3
EBITDA/total assets (%)	19.9	22.2	15.4	13.1	12.3	11.2	9.0
FFO/total debt (%)	175.9	83.3	45.2	33.6	22.5	11.1	5.6
Free oper. cash flow/total debt (%)	124.4	49.4	24.2	15.6	8.0	2.2	(3.0)
Disc. Cash flow/total debt (%)	92.5	28.0	16.5	11.9	6.7	0.7	(3.6)
Total debt/EBITDA (x)	0.5	1.0	1.7	2.4	3.5	5.5	7.1
Total debt/capital (%)	13.8	32.2	40.8	45.0	55.1	76.0	103.0
No. of companies	6	15	125	223	316	355	37

Source: Reprinted with permission from Standard & Poor's

Another measure of debt burden is the ratio of EBITDA to interest. A low interest rate on debt will allow a firm to carry more debt in its capital structure. Convertible debt will typically carry a lower interest rate in return for the convertible feature. In contrast, unsecured debt typically carries a higher interest

Part IV: Case Analysis of Pierre Foods

rate. Pierre's capital structure included $125 million of unsecured Notes with a 9.875% coupon.

Table 7.4 also shows the median EBITDA to interest ratio for 1,077 industrial companies rated from AAA to CCC by S&P. Table 7.5 shows Pierre's adjusted EBITDA to interest ratio over time.

Pierre's EBITDA to interest ratio was 2.55:1 in FYE March 2006 and 2.40:1 in FYE March 2007. The S&P median EBITDA to interest ratio for a B rated industrial company was 2.3:1 for the three years 2003–2005. Pierre's 2006 and 2007 EBITDA to interest ratio supported a credit rating comparable to credit rated B by S&P.

Table 7.5—Pierre's Adjusted EBITDA to Interest Coverage Ratio

	FYE 3/6/04	FYE 3/5/05	FYE 3/4/06	FYE 3/3/07
Adj. EBITDA to Interest	1.47x	1.73:1	2.55:1	2.40:1

Source: Table 8.0 in Chapter 8

Post Acquisition Debt Leverage: Secured Lender Risk vs. Unsecured Lender Risk

Even though a firm's capital structure may have a relatively high level of debt, a secured lender can mitigate its risk by the relative amount of secured debt versus unsecured debt in the capital structure and/or through the use of subordination. These structural enhancements will not necessarily mitigate the overall risk of borrower default because the total debt remains the same. In addition, an unsecured debt holder will often require a higher rate of interest to compensate for lack of collateral and/or subordination.

Unsecured and secured investors often have substantially different workout and exit scenarios in the event of distress. In bankruptcy, the debtor's cash flows will improve because the debtor is not required to pay interest on unsecured debt. A plan of reorganization will most likely compromise unsecured debt. In underwriting a highly leveraged credit, a secured lender should analyze its risk in the event of a bankruptcy by measuring the ratio of secured debt to EBITDA and the ratio of EBITDA to interest expense on secured debt.

Table 7.6 shows the ratio of Pierre's secured debt to EBITDA and total debt to EBITDA. Pierre's debt leverage was high based on the total debt to EBITDA ratio of 4.95:1, but much lower based the secured debt to EBTIDA ratio of 2.70:1.

The secured debt to EBITDA measures the margin of a safety for a secured lender relative to the price a buyer would pay for a company's EBITDA—a lender exit scenario assuming the sale of the company.

Chapter 7: Acquisitions/Fairness of Price/Debt Leverage

Lenders participating in the senior secured lending market would view Pierre's secured debt to EBITDA ratio of 2.70:1 as acceptable for a loan exit scenario based on a sale of the business. The secured debt to EBITDA ratio of 2.70:1 was substantially less than the Industry Peer Enterprise Value to EBITDA ratio of 6.52:1 in 2004 and 7.29:1 in 2005 (Table 7.3).

Table 7.6—Unsecured & Secured Debt to EBITDA ($ millions)	
EBITDA FYE March 2004	24.0
Pro-forma savings	31.6
Adjusted EBITDA FYE March 2004	55.6
Secured debt— June 30, 2004	150.2
Unsecured debt—June 30, 2004	125.0
Total debt	275.2
	Ratio
Secured debt to pro-forma Adjusted EBITDA	2.70:1
Total debt to pro-forma Adjusted EBITDA	4.95:1

Source: Pierre's U.S. SEC EDGAR filings.

Secured Credit Facility Financial Covenants

The Wachovia Credit Facility had covenants to protect against a decrease in cash flow and an increase in debt. The covenants included a minimum EBITDAR to Fixed Charges ratio and a Maximum Debt to EBTIDA ratio.

Table 7.7 shows the Wachovia Credit Facility covenants and the tightening of the ratio requirements in future reporting periods.

Table 7.7—Wachovia Credit Facility Financial Covenants		
Period	Debt to EBITDA Maximum Ratio	EBITDAR to FC Minimum Ratio
Acquisition date through September 3, 2005	6.25:1	n/a
December 3, 2005 through September 2, 2006	5.75:1	1.05:1
December 2, 2006 through September 1, 2007	5.25:1	1.10:1
December 1, 2007 through August 30, 2008	4.50:1	1.15:1
November 29, 2008 through August 29, 2009	4.00:1	1.20:1
After November 29, 2009	3.25:1	1.20:1

Source: Wachovia Credit Agreement filed in Pierre's U.S SEC EDGAR filings.

Part IV: Case Analysis of Pierre Foods

The secured Wachovia Credit Facility permitted Pierre to carry substantially more debt than the Industry Peer. The Wachovia covenants were set to maintain a credit rating comparable to a firm rated B by S&P.

The Wachovia Credit Facility had an aggressive debt to EBITDA ratio covenant for future periods. Pierre's FYE March 2005 debt to EBITDA ratio was 5.87:1 (Table 8.0 in Chapter 8) as compared to the Wachovia loan covenant of 6.25:1. Table 7.7 shows that the Wachovia debt to EBITDA ratio covenant gradually tightened each year. The covenant for debt to EBITDA ratio reached 3.25:1 by November 2009.

Acquisition of Clovervale Farms and Zartic

Prior to the acquisition of Clovervale (August 2006) and Zartic (December 2006), the Wachovia loan balance was $150 million and the Senior Note balance was $125 million. Wachovia agreed to increase the Credit Facility by $24 million in August 2006 to finance Pierre's $23 million acquisition price of Clovervale. Wachovia also agreed to increase the Credit Facility by an additional $100 million in December 2006 to finance Pierre's $94 million acquisition price of Zartic.

Pierre had sales of $432 million in FYE March 2006. On a pro-forma basis, the two acquisitions would increase Pierre's total sales by approximately $200 million (20%).

Clovervale had plants in Ohio and South Carolina and manufactured entrees, vegetables, fruits, cobblers, sandwiches, and other similar products. Clovervale sold it products to schools, the military, hospitals, and senior citizen meal programs. The facilities acquired in the acquisition of Clovervale employed 122 people.

Zartic manufactured packaged beef, poultry, pork, and veal products. Zartic manufactured products in plants located in: (1) Hamilton, Alabama, (2) Cedartown, Georgia, and (3) Rome, Georgia

Zartic employed 788 people at the main plant in Rome, Georgia. In July 2007, the Alabama plant was destroyed in a fire. In February 2008, Pierre closed the Cedartown plant to rationalize business operations.

The Impact of the Clovervale and Zartic Acquisitions

The Clovervale and Zartic acquisitions increased Pierre's debt from $238 million to $362 million. To maintain the 5.25:1 debt to EBITDA covenant required by the Wachovia Credit Facility for the period December 2006 to September 2007, Pierre's EBITDA would need to increase to $68.8 million, an increase of 23% from Pierre's EBTIDA of $56 million in FYE March 2006.

Chapter 7: Acquisitions/Fairness of Price/Debt Leverage

Secured Wachovia Credit Facility Lender Risk and Collateral Deficiency

Although Pierre's total debt to EBITDA was high, implying a higher risk of default, the Wachovia Credit Facility had a lower ratio of secured debt to EBITDA, protecting the lender if the exit scenario came from the sale of the business. If a borrower has high debt leverage and tight cash flow, a prudent secured lender attempts to offset the risk by requiring more collateral.

The Wachovia Credit Facility was undersecured based on the prudent lending standards of an asset-based lender. Table 7.8 compares the Wachovia loan balance to tangible collateral (cash, receivables, inventory, and PP&E).

After Wachovia financed the acquisitions of Clovervale and Zartic, the book value of Pierre's tangible assets was $10.7 million less than the Wachovia loan.

Most asset-based lenders customarily loan 70%–90% of eligible receivables, 30%–60% of eligible inventory, and up to 50% of the book value of PP&E. The prudent lender loan value against Pierre's tangible collateral was $105–$138 million as compared to the $240 million Wachovia loan. The Wachovia loan exceeded the prudent lender loan value by $102–135 million, implying a 44%–58% recovery in the event of default.

In Chapter 14, in an assumed liquidation of Pierre's business, the estimate of the recovery for the Wachovia loan ranges from 33% (Debtor's Plan) and 47% (independent estimate).

The market trading value for the Wachovia debt was 67%–83% of par in the months prior to Pierre's bankruptcy.

Table 7.8—Post Acquisition Debt Compared to Book Value of Tangible Assets

(in $ millions)	June 2004 Before Madison Purchase of Pierre	June 2004 After Madison Purchase of Pierre	June 2006 Before Clovervale Acquisition	Sept. 2006 After Clovervale Acquisition	June 2007 After Zartic Acquisition
Cash	1.3	0.1	0.0	0.2	0.2
Accounts receivable	22.2	22.2	24.4	32.1	45.5
Inventory	42.2	44.2	49.7	57.8	82.8
Net property, plant, equipment	60.9	56.6	56.3	69.5	97.5
Net tangible assets	126.6	123.1	130.4	159.6	226.0
Wachovia loan	41.9	150.0	107.8	142.0	236.7 [a]
Tangible assets less Wachovia loan	84.7	(26.9)	22.6	(17.6)	(10.7)
Unsecured Senior Notes	115.0	125.0	125.0	125.0	125.0
Book value goodwill/intangibles	359.4	320.7	316.3	322.1	350.9

Source: Pierre's U.S.SEC EDGAR filing.
(a) $240.2 includes the $3.5 million letters of credit exposure

Part IV: Case Analysis of Pierre Foods

Required Loan Amortization

On the petition date, Pierre's non-depreciating inventories and receivables were $66 million and $27 million, respectively. A prudent lender's loan value against the inventories and receivables would be $65 million. Pierre debt was $369 million on the petition date. Inventories and receivables are non-amortizing assets. Therefore, the $65 million loan value for inventories and receivables supports a $65 million non-amortizing loan. The remaining $304 million of Pierre's debt should amortize over a reasonable time because the debt is undersecured. Excluding inventories and receivables, Pierre's remaining tangible depreciating assets had a book value of $130 million on the petition date.

The Wachovia Facility Term Loan required quarterly payments of $375,000 with a balloon of $141.4 million due June 2010. Pierre was required to make additional annual principal payments on the Wachovia Credit Facility based on Pierre's annual debt to EBITDA ratio, as follows:

Debt to EBITDA Ratio	Annual Required Principal Payments
< 4.50:1	50% of annual net cash flow
4.50:1 or greater	75% of annual net cash flow

Pierre's actual principal payments on the Wachovia Term Note were as follows:

Fiscal Year	Principal Payments
March 2005	$16.2 million
March 2006	$17.8 million
March 2007	$14.7 million
March 2008	$ 3.5 million

As previously discussed, Pierre had $304 million of debt that should have been set up on an amortizing loan. The $304 million debt was amortizing over 19 years based on the $16 million of average annual principal payments Pierre made for the three years FYE 2005-2007. The value of Pierre's assets had a useful remaining life substantially less than 19 years.

Elimination of the $125 million unsecured Senior Notes could free up cash flow to amortize the Wachovia debt over a more reasonable time. The interest on the unsecured Senior Notes was $12.3 million a year. If the Senior Notes are eliminated, the debt requiring amortization decreases to $179 million. The amortization of the $179 million of remaining debt improves to 6.5 years if Pierre: (1) applies the $12.3 million interest on the Senior Notes to the Wachovia debt and (2) continues to pay $16 million a year principal payments.

Chapter 7: Acquisitions/Fairness of Price/Debt Leverage

Unsecured $125 million Senior Note: The Hope and Prayer Lenders

Pierre's high debt leverage was contributing to minimal excess cash flow for principal repayment on debt.

The source of funds to repay the unsecured $125 million Note would most likely be from:

- The issuance of equity to pay off debt;
- Refinancing the debt at maturity;
- A substantial improvement in business cash flows;
- The hope that the equity sponsor, Madison Dearborn, would contribute more capital;
- The sale of the business.

The $125 million unsecured Senior Note had minimal prospects for recovery in a liquidation of the business. The $125 million Note Lenders underwrote an unsecured and subordinated loan to a highly leveraged company. The unsecured Senior Note Lenders were enticed by the 9.875% interest rate and the B credit rating assigned by S&P. In the event of distress and default, the unsecured Notes were in an undesirable place in Pierre's capital structure. The Lenders were hoping and praying for a refinance, improved cash flows, equity issuance, or for Madison Dearborn to contribute capital in the event of distress.

The next Chapter will analyze the Pierre's historical financial performance prior to and during bankruptcy.

Chapter 8

Analysis of Pierre's Operating Results and Balance Sheet

"Not everything that can be counted counts, and not everything that counts can be counted." Albert Einstein

The purpose of Chapter 8 is to:
- Analyze operating results and cash flow prior to bankruptcy;
- Analyze sales and EBITDA during the five month bankruptcy;
- Compare Pierre's EBITDA as a percent of sales to the industy and to all U.S. exchange traded firms;
- Determine Pierre's normalized EBITDA;
- Analyze the balance sheet prior to bankruptcy.

Key Operating & Cash Flow Metrics FYE March 2004 to FYE March 2008

The last audited financial statement released by Pierre, prior to its July 15, 2008 bankruptcy filing was for fiscal year-end March 1, 2008, as filed with the SEC on June 16, 2008. Deloitte & Touche audited the financial statement with a clear audit opinion, except for a disclosure that Pierre was in default under the Wachovia Credit Facility. The auditor warned there could not be any assurance that Pierre could negotiate an amendment to cure the default or that the Company could continue to operate as a going-concern without a bankruptcy filing.

Chapter 8: Analysis of Pierre's Operating Results & Balance Sheet

Table 8.0 shows Pierre's key income statement and cash flow metrics for fiscal years March 2004–2008.

Table 8.0
Key Operating Metrics & Cash Flow Coverage Prior to July 15, 2008 Bankruptcy

(in $ millions)		Prior to Chapter 11				
Fiscal Year Ending		3/6/04	3/5/05	3/4/06	3/3/07	3/1/08
Sales		358	410	432	488	643
Gross margin		29%	25.8%	28.3%	29.5%	23%
SG&A		80	66	68	85	126
SGA %		22.3%	16.0%	15.7%	17.4%	19.6%
Depreciation/Amortization		5	26	32	32	39
Operating income		19 [a]	15 [b]	24	28	(17)
Charge off goodwill & asset impairment						229
Interest expense		17	26	22	25	42
Pre-tax income		2 [a]	(11) [b]	2	3	(288)
EBITDA		24 [a]	41 [b]	56	60	(207)
+ non-cash goodwill/impairment charge						229
+ non-cash loan fee write-off		1	4			
+ non-cash change in interest rate swap						7
= Adjusted EBITDA		25 [a]	45 [b]	56	60	29
EBITDA as Percent of Sales		**7.0%**	**11.0%**	**12.9%**	**12.2%**	**4.5%**
Less: Current maturity debt		1.6	0.4	0.3	1.6	367 [c]
Less: Interest expense		17	26	22	25	42
Less: CAPX (exclude Zartic/Clovervale)		10	6	7	9	8
= EBITDA less debt service & CAPX		(4)	13	27	24	(399)
Less: Purchase of Zartic & Clovervale		0	0	0	114	0
= EBITDA less debt service & all CAPX		(3)	13	25	(90)	(397)
Debt outstanding		144	264	245	359	368
Ratios:		Ratio	Ratio	Ratio	Ratio	Ratio
Adjusted EBITDA to interest ratio		1.47x	1.73x	2.55x	2.40x	0.69x
Adjusted EBITDA to debt service ratio		1.34x	1.70x	2.51x	2.26x	.07x
Debt to Adjusted EBITDA ratio		5.76x	5.87x	4.38x	5.98x	12.7x

Source: Pierre's U.S. SEC EDGAR filings.

(a) FYE March 2004 SG&A, operating income, pre-tax income, and EBITDA have not been adjusted upward for expenses that were to be eliminated after Madison Dearborn purchased Pierre in June 2004. $22.8 million of SG&A expenses incurred in FYE March 2004 (prior to the Madison Dearborn acquisition). Pierre planned to eliminate the $22.8 million in expense on a post-acquisition basis.

(b) FYE March 2005 SG&A, operating income, pre-tax income, and EBITDA have not been adjusted upward for expenses that were be eliminated after Madison Dearborn purchased Pierre in June 2004. $8.8 million of SG&A expenses incurred in FYE March 2005. Pierre planned to eliminate the $8.8 million of expenses on a post-acquisition basis.

(c) At FYE 3/1/08, 100% of Pierre's debt was classified as current by the auditor due to debt defaults.

Part IV: Case Analysis of Pierre Foods

Analysis of FYE March 2006

Sales FYE March 2006

Sales in FYE March 2006 increased by $21.2 million (5.2%). The 5.2% change in sales was centered on: (1) growth in most market segments, (2) favorable pricing, and (3) lower sales from two large customers. The sales decrease for the two customers was because competitors offered promotions on products competing with sandwiches and because, to a lessor extent, higher gasoline prices decreased store traffic for national account customers.

Gross Profit FYE March 2006

Gross profit margin increased from 25.8% in FYE March 2005 to 28.3% in FYE 2006. The 2.5% increase in gross margin was centered on:

- 1.3% increase in margin from change in sales mix;
- 0.7% increase in margin as Pierre did not have start-up costs for a new customer as experienced in the prior year;
- 0.5% increase in margin from an accounting adjustment on inventory.

SG&A FYE March 2006

SG&A expenses increased by $1.6 million in FYE March 2006. As a percent of sales, SG&A decreased from 16% in FYE March 2005 to 15.7% in FYE March 2006. The $1.6 million increase in SG&A was centered on:

- $8.8 million decrease in acquisition fees in connection with Madison Dearborn's acquisition of Pierre in the prior year;
- $1.8 million increase in storage expense to maintain customer service levels and product line expansion;
- $2.1 million increase in freight expense due to higher fuel prices;
- $1.6 million increase in selling expenses to establish the new military selling channel, product line expansion, and an increase in demonstration expense related to growth in the warehouse club channel;
- $4.9 million increase in other general administrative costs.

Interest Expense FYE March 2006

Interest expense decreased $3.8 million in FYE March 2006, with $4.3 million of the decrease was due to the write-off of deferred loan origination fees in the prior year (the write-off was classified as interest expense on the FYE March 2005 income statement).

Chapter 8: Analysis of Pierre's Operating Results & Balance Sheet

Pre-Tax Income & Cash Flow Coverage FYE March 2006
- Pre-tax income $2 million;
- EBITDA to debt service (interest + CMLTD) ratio of 2.49:1 (vs. the Wachovia loan covenant of 1.05:1);
- Debt to EBITDA ratio of 4.36:1 (vs. Wachovia loan covenant of 5.75:1).

Free Cash Flow FYE March 2006

For FYE March 2006, EBITDA less debt service and CAPX was $25 million. Pierre made principal payments of $17.8 million on the Wachovia loan in FYE March 2006. Pierre's total debt was $244 million on March 4, 2006.

Analysis of FYE March 2007 Financial Results

Sales FYE March 2007

Sales in FYE March 2007 were $488 million, an increase of $56 million (11.4%) from the prior year. The sales increase was centered on:
- $54 million sales increase from the acquisition of Clovervale (acquired August 2006) and Zartic (acquired December 2006);
- $20 million sales increase from the Warehouse Club selling channel;
- $18 million sales decrease from two large restaurant chains. Pierre decreased promotional activity from the prior fiscal year.

Gross Profit FYE March 2007

Gross profit margin increased from 28.5% in FYE March 2006 to 29.5% in FYE March 2007. The 1.0% increase in gross margin was centered on:
- 2.4% increase in margin due to lower prices for raw material proteins;
- 1.0% increase in margin from change in product mix; partially offset by;
- 0.7% decrease in margin for due lower labor and overhead costs;
- 0.7% decrease in margin due to change in mix from increased volume from Zartic and Clovervale;
- 1.0% decrease in margin because of decreased efficiencies from lower sales to the national accounts and increases in utilities, insurance, maintenance, and property taxes.

Part IV: Case Analysis of Pierre Foods

In FYE March 2007, the prices Pierre paid for raw materials increased (decreased) as follows:

Beef	5.9%
Pork	4.6%
Cheese	11.2%
Chicken	(1.9%)
Aggregate change	6.9%

Pierre had some customer contracts that allowed for the immediate pass along of changes in commodity prices. Thirty-three percent of sales for the next fiscal year had provision to pass along changes in prices.

SG&A FYE March 2007

As a percent of sales, SG&A expenses increased from 15.7% in FYE March 2006 to 17.4% in FYE March 2007. The $17 million increase was centered on:

- $9.9 million increase due to higher sales volume from Clovervale and Zartic;
- $6.5 million increase in selling expenses, with $2.5 million due to the Zartic and Clovervale acquisitions;
- $9.8 million increase in distribution costs primarily due to increased fuel costs, higher storage costs to maintain customer service, and increased sales.

Pre-tax Income & Cash Flow Coverage FYE March 2007

- Pre-tax income of $3 million;
- EBITDA to debt service (interest + CMLTD) ratio of 2.23:1 (vs. 2.49:1 in the prior year). The Wachovia loan covenant ratio was 1.10:1;
- Debt to EBITDA ratio of 5.96:1 (vs. 4.36:1 in the prior year). The Wachovia loan covenant ratio was 5.25:1.

Pierre was able to comply with the Wachovia loan covenant debt to EBITDA requirement by adjusting EBITDA upward for pro-forma SG&A cost savings (as permitted by the terms of the Wachovia Credit Facility).

Free Cash Flow FYE March 2007

For FYE March 2007, EBITDA less debt service and CAPX was $24 million compared to $25 million in the prior year. Pierre paid principal payments of $14.7 million on the Wachovia loan in FYE March 2007.

Chapter 8: Analysis of Pierre's Operating Results & Balance Sheet

Pierre's 2006 acquisitions of Clovervale (August 2006) and Zartic (December 2006) was an opportunity to improve cash flow. The acquisitions were financed 100% by debt and Pierre's interest expense burden would increase in the future. Pierre would also be faced with the risks and challenges involved with integrating the Clovervale and Zartic acquisitions into Pierre's existing business.

Analysis of FYE March 2008 Operating Results

Sales FYE March 2008
FYE March 2008 sales increased by $155 million. The sales increase was centered on:
- A $146 million sales increase from acquisition of Clovervale and Zartic;
- $14.8 million sales increase from various end markets and changes in sales mix;
- $7.6 million sales decrease from two national account restaurant chains.

On October 22, 2007, Pierre announced the retirement of Robert Naylor, Senior Vice-President of Sales and Marketing. A subsequent SEC filing by Pierre disclosed a severance agreement between Pierre and Mr. Naylor.

Gross Profit Margin FYE March 2008
Gross profit margin decreased from 29% in FYE March 2007 to 23% in FYE March 2008. The 6% decrease margin was centered on:
- 3.9% margin decrease due to higher prices for raw material proteins;
- 1.0% margin decrease from volume growth and change in sales mix;
- 0.7% margin decrease from higher labor costs;
- 0.6% margin decrease from higher-cost products from the Zartic acquisition;
- 0.4% margin decrease from an inventory reduction initiative;
- 0.4% margin decrease from missed yields and inventory losses associated with the USDA Commodity Program;
- 0.3% margin decrease from an inventory obsolescence charge;
- 0.3% margin decrease related to product outsourcing due to the destruction of the Hamilton, Alabama facility;
- 0.3% margin decrease from the closure of the Cedartown, Georgia plant;

Part IV: Case Analysis of Pierre Foods

- 0.2% margin decrease from excessive equipment downtime on three fry lines in the Rome, Georgia facility, offset by;
- 1.0% margin increase from the decrease in other overhead costs.

In FYE March 2008, the prices Pierre paid for product raw material increased as follows:

Beef	1.5%
Pork	7.4%
Cheese	37.1%
Chicken	24.6%
Aggregate change	7.4%

Thirty-one percent of sales for the next fiscal year had provision to pass along changes in prices.

SG&A Expense FYE March 2008

As a percent of sales, SG&A expense increased from 17.4% in FYE March 2007 to 19.6% in FYE March 2008. The $41 million increase in SG&A was centered on:

- $27.7 million increase from higher sales volume in the connection with the acquisition of Clovervale and Zartic;
- $3.5 million increase from increased sales and mix shift across most end-markets;
- $3.4 million increase in selling expense related to higher promotional activity and demonstration expenses;
- $2.7 million of increased professional fees, including fees for the integration of Zartic and Clovervale and costs/fees related to the Wachovia Credit Facility;
- $2.1 million increase primarily due to bad debt associated with the bankruptcy of a customer and for increases in insurance, wages, and travel;
- $1.6 million increase in marketing expense from the implementation of an inventory reduction initiative;
- $1.3 million increase in freight, primarily from increased fuel surcharges;
- $1.4 million increase in costs in connection with the Zartic plant fire;
- $1.3 million decrease in other general costs.

Chapter 8: Analysis of Pierre's Operating Results & Balance Sheet

Plant Fire FYE 2008

In July 2007, the Zartic meat processing plant in Alabama was destroyed by fire and the facility was deemed a complete loss. Although Pierre implemented a disaster recovery plan to supply customers, the fire caused Pierre to incur $1.4 million in increased production costs.

Closure of Cedartown, Georgia Plant February 2008

On February 8, 2008, Pierre announced the closure of the Cedartown, Georgia plant. Pierre recognized a $1.5 million pre-tax charge in FYE March 2008 for the plant closure. Pierre planned to recognize the remaining cost in the first quarter of fiscal 2009.

Non-Cash Goodwill & Intangible Impairment Charges FYE March 2008

Pierre had a $228 million non-cash charge in the fourth quarter of FYE March 2008 for the impairment of goodwill and intangible assets.

Non-Cash Mark to Fair Market Value for Interest Rate Swap FYE March 2008

FYE March 2008 included a $7 million non-cash charge for marking the Wachovia loan interest rate swap to market value.

Operating Lease Payments FYE March 2008

Operating lease payments were $8.1 million in FYE March 2008, consisting of $0.3 million for real estate leases and $7.8 million for equipment lease payments. Operating lease payments due for FYE March 2009 were $5.4 million. Operating lease payments due after FYE 2009 were $1.9 million.

The present value of future rental payments were $6.9 million (discounted at a rate of 7%). The off-balance sheet lease obligations were not significant compared to Pierre's $368 million of debt.

Interest Expense FYE March 2008

Interest expense increased from $25 million in FYE March 2007 to $42 million in FYE 2008. This $17 million increase was centered on:

- $6.9 million of the interest expense was related to the change in the fair value of the interest rate swaps.

- Higher balance on the Wachovia Term Loan to finance the acquisition of Clovervale and Zartic. The Term Loan average loan balance increased

Part IV: Case Analysis of Pierre Foods

from $144 million in FYE March 2007 to $227 million in FYE March 2008;

- The average interest rate increased from 8.4% to 8.8%, primarily because of an increase in the rate in October 2007 in return for a waiver granted for non-compliance with the Wachovia Credit Facility covenant for the leverage ratio.

Change in Interest Rate FYE March 2008

On June 2, 2008, Pierre received a notice from Wachovia Bank that loan interest rate would increase to the default rate. The default rate was 2% higher than the non-default rate. Wachovia sent the notice after the Company advised Wachovia that Pierre would be delayed in delivering its year-end financial statement and would not able to meet the financial covenants for the quarter and year ending March 1, 2008.

Cash Flow FYE March 2008

EBITDA decreased to $20 million for FYE March 2008 (after adding back non-cash charges for asset impairment and goodwill). The $20 million of EBITDA was $22 million short of covering the $42 million of interest expense in FYE March 2008.

Pierre paid principal payments of $3.5 million on the Wachovia loan in FYE March 2008.

Change in Chief Financial Officer FYE March 2008

In February 2008, Pierre hired Cynthia S. Hughes to serve Pierre's Chief Financial Officer. On June 20, 2008, the employment of Joseph Meyers, CFO, was terminated without cause

Comparison of Pierre's EBITDA Margins to Packaged Foods & Meats Industry

Using Capital IQ, a screen has been performed as of June 1, 2009 all U.S. exchange traded companies in the packaged foods & meats industry who have a market capitalization less than $2 billion. Table 8.1 shows 21 companies from the screen most comparable to Pierre Foods.

For the 21 companies in Table 21, the average EBITDA to sales ratio was 11% from 2005–2007. Assuming the 11% industry EBITDA to sales ratio and Pierre's $643 million of sales, Pierre's would have annual pro forma EBITDA of $70.7 million. During the three years 2005–2007, Pierre's Adjusted EBITDA averaged $53.6 million or 8.3% of EBITDA.

Chapter 8: Analysis of Pierre's Operating Results & Balance Sheet

The estimate of Pierre's Alternative Enterprise Value in Chapter 24 assumes $53.6 million of EBITDA. The $53.6 million of EBITDA for Pierre is reasonable based on the the average EBITDA to sales ratio for industry peers.

Table— 8.1
EBITDA Margins for Firms in Packaged Foods & Meats Industry with Market Cap under $2 billion

($ millions)

Company	Business	Sales	EBITDA Margin
Del Monte Foods Co.	Food & pet products	3,244.1	14%
Lancaster Colony Corp.	Specialty Food, glassware, candles	904.8	13%
Tootsie Roll Industries Inc.	Candy	497.7	20%
The Hain Celestial Group, Inc.	Food & personal care products	973.8	11%
Seneca Foods Corp.	Vegetables, fruits, canned & frozen	1,047.3	8%
B&G Foods Inc.	Shelf grocery store food products	471.3	18%
J&J Snack Foods Corp.	Snacks	585.7	13%
Lance, Inc.	Snacks	762.7	9%
Treehouse Foods Inc.	Shelf grocery store food products	1,157.9	9%
John B Sanfilippo & Son Inc.	Nuts and peanuts	539.2	2%
Omega Protein Corp.	Fish meal and fish oil	157.1	17%
Overhill Farms Inc.	Frozen food products	208.9	8%
Tasty Baking Co.	Sweet baked goods	169.9	7%
Diamond Foods, Inc.	Snacks	527.8	4%
Cuisine Solutions Inc.	Fully cooked and prepared foods	84.1	6%
Monterey Gourmet Foods Inc.	Gourmet refrigerated foods	100.5	4%
Bridgford Foods Corp.	Frozen & refrigerated snack foods	124.1	2%
The Inventure Group Inc.	Snacks	90.9	3%
Vaughan Foods Inc.	Refrigerated foods	67.2	3%
Golden Enterprises Inc.	Snacks	112.3	3%
Armanino Foods of Distinction	Frozen & refrigerated foods	19.1	8%
Total		11,846	11% average

Source: Capital IQ screening performed by the author. Capital IQ is not responsible for the actual data results returned in the screening or in the table. Data as of as June 1, 2009.

Pierre's EBITDA Margin Compared to all U.S. Exchange Traded Non-Financial Firms

Table 8.2 shows ratios for EBITDA to sales and sales to assets for U.S. exchange traded and U.S. based non-financial firms. The firms in Table 8.2 have a median EBITDA to sales percentage of 12.1% based on their most recent year-end financial statement. Assuming the 12.1% EBITDA to sales ratio and Pierre's $643 million of sales, Pierre's woulld have annual pro forma EBITDA of $77.8 million.

The $53.6 million of EBITDA used for the estimate of Pierre's Alternative Enterprise Value in Chapter 24 is reasonable based on the the average EBITDA to sales ratio for U.S. non-financial exchange traded companies.

Part IV: Case Analysis of Pierre Foods

Asset Turnover

Prior to Pierre's charge off in goodwill and intangibles, Pierre had total assets of $600 million compared to sales of $643 million, for a sales to total asset turnover of 1.07x which compares favorably to the 0.98:1 sales to asset turnover ratio for the U.S. exchange traded firms in Table 8.2.

Table 8.2—EBITDA to Sales and Sales to Total Assets for U.S. Exchange Traded Firms

	Average	Median
EBITDA to sales ratio	15.8%	12.1%
Sales to total assets	0.98:1	0.98:1

Source: Table 3.2 in Chapter 3

Sales & EBTIDA Analysis in Bankruptcy

Table 8.3 shows Pierre's financial performance for each month during Pierre's stay in bankruptcy. The expenses exclude professional fees related to the bankruptcy and other non-recurring reorganization expenses. It is assumed the reorganization expenses will not be a future on-going expense after Pierre's emergence from Chapter 11.

For the 164 days in bankruptcy, Pierre had $292.6 million of sales and $18.2 million of EBTIDA—on an annualized basis, sales of $651 million and EBITDA of $40.5 million. The sales level in bankruptcy is comparable to FYE March 2008 sales of $643 million.

Pierre's annualized EBITDA is $44.4 million based on the level of EBITDA generated in October, November, and December 2008. As previously noted, Pierre's sales tend to be lower in the summer months and in November and December because of school sales.

Commodity prices in the United States decreased significantly in the fourth quarter of 2008 and into 2009. Pierre makes the following statement in its Reorganization Plan: "In early 2008, skyrocketing energy and industrial commodity costs combined with sharp increases in raw material pricing, translated into significant pricing pressure…these soaring prices contributed to a decline in the Debtor's margins and profitability in the months prior to the bankruptcy."

Pierre was forced into bankruptcy primarily due to an unusual period of rapidly rising costs for commodities and high debt leverage. Based on the substantial reduction in commodity prices in late 2008 and early 2009, Pierre's cost of goods sold should benefit in 2009 from the lower commodity costs.

The Alternative Enterprise Valuation analysis in Chapter 24 assumes $53.6 million of normalized annual EBITDA. The Alternative Plan will also present a distress analysis in Chapter 25 that assumes $40.5 million of annual EBITDA.

Chapter 8: Analysis of Pierre's Operating Results & Balance Sheet

The $40.5 million of EBITDA is equal to the annualized EBTIDA Pierre generated during the 164 days in bankruptcy.

Table—8.3
Pierre Food's Sales, Costs, & EBITDA During Bankruptcy on Accrual Basis of Accounting

($ millions)	7-15 to 8-31	Aug-08	Sep-08	Oct-08	Nov-08	Dec-08	7-15 to 12-27 164 days
Sales	34.0	52.8	52.2	64.9	47.1	41.6	292.6
Raw material	19.3	30.1	28.5	37.6	25.7	22.5	163.7
Labor	2.4	3.8	3.8	4.5	3.4	3.1	21.0
Overhead	4.8	7.3	7.3	7.5	6.4	5.3	38.8
Distribution	2.5	4.5	4.8	5.1	4.1	3.3	24.4
Selling	1.6	4.3	3.9	3.9	3.1	2.9	19.8
Administration	0.8	1.0	1.2	1.3	0.9	1.6	6.8
Total expenses	31.3	51.0	49.5	60.0	43.8	38.7	274.4
EBITDA	2.7	1.7	2.8	4.9	3.3	2.9	18.2
EBITDA %	7.8%	3.3%	5.3%	7.5%	7.1%	6.9%	6.2%

Source: Pierre's monthly Operating Statements in Bankruptcy. Excludes professional fees & reorganization expenses.

Balance Sheet Prior to Chapter 11

Table 8.4 shows Pierre's balance sheet for the most recent five fiscal years. Subsequent sections in this Chapter will analyze key balance sheet accounts.

Table 8.4—Balance Sheet Prior to Chapter 11
($ millions)

Fiscal Year Ending	3/6/04	3/5/05	3/4/06	3/3/07	3/1/08
Cash	0	0	2	0	6
Receivables	26	30	30	46	46
Tax refund receivable	0	3	2	5	7
Inventory	39	44	46	68	65
Plant, property & equipment	61	56	56	99	80
Goodwill & intangibles	39	352	330	358	112
Total assets	176	497	472	600	349
Payables & accruals	25	23	24	41	54
CMLTD	1.6	0.4	0.2	1.6	367 [a]
Wachovia Credit Facility	22	137	119	230	[b]
9.875% Senior Notes	115	125	125	125	[b]
Capital lease/other debt	5	$0	$0	4	$2
Total debt	144	263	245	359	368
Total liabilities	169	351	324	450	441
Stockholders equity	7	146	148	150	(92)
Total liabilities & equity	176	497	472	600	349

Source: Pierre's U.S. SEC Edgar Filings
(a) At 3/1/08, 100% of debt was classified as CMLTD because of debt defaults.
(b) $367 in CMLTD because of debt defaults. The March 1, 2008 balances on the Wachovia Credit Facility and Senior Notes were $241 million and $125 million, respectively.

Part IV: Case Analysis of Pierre Foods

Liquidity

On FYE March 1, 2008, Pierre had $6 million of cash and $19.6 million of borrowing availability on the $40 million Wachovia Revolver. On June 2, 2008, the agent for Wachovia Credit Facility notified Pierre of default under the Credit Facility and terminated Pierre's ability to draw any future amounts on the Revolver.

On the July 15, 2008 bankruptcy date, Pierre reported cash balances of $1.5 million and a $7 million tax refund receivable.

Substantial Decrease in Accounts Receivables Prior to Bankruptcy

Pierre reduced accounts receivables by $13.2 million (32.7%) from March 1, 2008 to July 15, 2008. Seasonality does not appear to be the reason for the decrease. Receivables decreased 6% from March 1, 2007 to June 1, 2007. (Pierre does not have a July 15, 2007 balance sheet for the exact prior year comparison).

Possible explanations for the $13.2 million decrease in receivables from March 1, 2008 to July 15, 2008 could be: (1) a large decrease in sales because of the financial distress in the period leading up to bankruptcy and/or (2) Pierre aggressively collected receivables to build cash in order to make payments to other parties prior to the bankruptcy.

After bankruptcy, receivables increased to $44.7 million on August 30, 2008 and $49.1 million on September 27, 2008.

Pierre may have offered its customers an additional early payment discount in the month prior to bankruptcy, allowing Pierre to use the cash to make payments to trade suppliers and employees.

Substantial Increase in Prepaid Amounts to Trade Vendors Prior to Bankruptcy

Pierre had $7.5 million in prepayments to vendors as an asset on the July 15, 2008 balance sheet. The March 1, 2008 balance sheet did show any vendor prepayments.

Substantial Decrease in Trade Vendor Payables Prior to Bankruptcy

Table 8.5 shows trade vendor payables decreased by $7.7 million from March 1, 2008 to July 15, 2008. This decrease was not consistent with changes in inventories. Pierre's inventories were $64.7 million on March 1, 2008 and $63.1 million on July 15, 2008.

In conclusion, Pierre reduced trade vendor payables by $7.7 million in the months before bankruptcy and Pierre paid $7.5 million to trade vendors in the form of prepayments in the months before bankruptcy.

Chapter 8: Analysis of Pierre's Operating Results & Balance Sheet

Table 8.5—Table of Pierre's Current Liabilities
($ millions)

	March 2007	March 2008	July 15, 2008
Trade payables	20.5	22.9	15.2 [a]
Accrued promotions	3.3	6.0	Undisclosed
Other accruals	3.1	6.6	Undisclosed
Accrued interest	5.6	2.4	10.4
Swap liability	0.0	6.9	3.6
Accrued payroll	7.1	7.9	1.1

Source: Pierre's U.S. SEC EDGAR filings and Pierre's July 15, 2008 Schedule of Assets & Liabilities filed with the Bankruptcy Court.

(a) Pierre's Schedule of Assets & Liabilities as of July 15, 2008 reported $15.2 million of prepetition trade vendor payables. In Pierre's first-day Bankruptcy Court motion for the payment of critical vendors, the company estimated $15 million of vendor payables as of July 15, 2008.

Analysis of Accrued Payroll

Accrued payroll decreased from $7.9 million on March 1, 2008 to $1.2 million on July 15, 2008. In Pierre's first-day Bankruptcy Court motion for the payment of wages, Pierre estimated $1.2 million of accrued wages as of July 15, 2008.

Debt Balances

On March 1, 2008, Pierre was in default of its maximum leverage ratio covenant on the Wachovia Credit Facility. As a result, most all of Pierre's debt was classified in current maturities of long-term debt.

Table 8.6 shows a $5.5 million reduction in the prepetition Wachovia Credit Facility obligation from March 1, 2008 to July 15, 2008 (136 days prior to bankruptcy).

Table 8.6—Change in Wachovia Loan Balance 136 days prior to Bankruptcy
(in $ millions)

	March 1, 2008	July 15, 2008	Variance
Loan balance	241.0	238.0	3.0
Interest	6.2	4.2	2.0
Swap Liability	4.0	3.6	0.4
Undrawn letters of credits	6.4	6.3	0.1
Totals	257.6	252.2	5.5

Source: Pierre's July 15, 2008 first-day Bankruptcy Court Orders and U.S. SEC EDGAR filings.

In Chapter 13 of this book, the payments to vendors and Wachovia will be reviewed for disgorgement.

On March 1, 2008, the 9.875% Senior Notes had a balance of $125 million. Interest payments of $6.2 million were due semi-annually, each January 15 and

Part IV: Case Analysis of Pierre Foods

July 15. Pierre's bankruptcy filing date coincided with the interest payment due on the unsecured Senior Notes.

Net Worth

Pierre's net worth decreased from $150 million on March 3, 2007 to a deficit $92 million on March 1, 2008. The decrease was primarily due to non-cash charges for goodwill and asset impairment. After the FYE March 2008 charge-off, Pierre continued to carry $44 million of goodwill and $68 million of intangibles as assets on the balance sheet.

Tax Loss Carry-forwards

On March 1, 2008, Pierre had $4.3 million of federal tax loss carry-forwards, with the tax losses expiring in 2022–2024. Pierre had $20.3 million of state operating loss carry-forwards expiring in 2025–2028.

Pierre had $18.2 million of EBITDA between the July 15, 2008 and December 27, 2008. A net loss of $20 million is projected for the five months Pierre was in bankruptcy (author's estimate), after $15 million professional fees, $10 million of interest on the Wachovia loan, and $14 million of depreciation/amortization. It is also believed that Pierre had a loss from March 1, 2008 to July 15, 2008, but Pierre did not file financial statements for the gap period.

Assuming the $4.3 million tax loss carry-forward as of March 2008 and the estimated $20 million loss during bankruptcy, the value of Pierre's tax losses is $9.7 million on a 40% tax rate. To realize the value of the tax loss carry-forward, it is critical for Pierre to avoid a change of control event, such that:

- Prepetition stockholders and creditors must continue to own at least 50% of the stock in the reorganized debtor;
- The stock received by creditors and counted in the ownership test must be for debt exchanged that was held by the creditors for at least 18 months prior to bankruptcy;
- A change of ownership control cannot take place within two years after the emergence from bankruptcy.

Employee Benefits

Pierre's retirement plan consisted of a 401(k) retirement plan. Pierre made matching contributions to the 401(k) retirement plan for up to 5% of an employee's voluntary contribution, limited to the lower of 5% of annual

Chapter 8: Analysis of Pierre's Operating Results & Balance Sheet

compensation or $15,500. Pierre's contribution was $0.7 million in FYE March 2008.

Pierre provides employee health insurance benefits to employees through self-insurance group medical plans. Pierre contributed $6.4 million to the group medical plans in FYE March 2008.

There is not any indication of any significant under-funding of retirement or health care obligations.

Chapter 9

- **Pierre's Credit Ratings**
- **Trading Value of Pierre's Debt**

"It ain't what you don't know that gets you into trouble. It's what you know for sure that just ain't so." Mark Twain

Credit Rating Agencies

Moody's and Standard and Poor's (S&P) were two of the first credit rating firms in the United States. They began grading railroad bonds in the late 1890's. After the 1929 stock market crash, the U.S. Treasury started using bond ratings in 1931 to measure the risk of investments held by banks. Regulators have increasingly relied on the ratings of credit rating agencies to measure the risk of the investments held by financial institutions.

In 1991, the U.S. Securities and Exchange Commission required money market mutual fund managers to place 95% of their investments into highly rated commercial paper. Financial institutions heavily rely on credit rating agency ratings to grade the credit risk of individual debt issues and overall portfolio risk. The credit agency rating agencies are used by banks, insurance companies, mutual funds, pension funds, government sponsored agencies, and other financial institutions. U.S financial institutions have $50.6 trillion of assets under management as of December 31, 2008 (*Flow of Funds of U.S.*, Federal Reserve Statistical Release, 2008).

Chapter 9: Pierre's Credit Ratings & Trading Value of Debt

Issuer Rating

An issuer or general corporate credit rating is an opinion on the general creditworthiness of an entity.

Issue Rating

An issue credit rating is the credit risk associated with a particular debt instrument or other financial obligation.

Long-Term Issuer Ratings

S&P's long-term credit ratings range from AAA (strongest) to D (lowest). Moody's comparable ratings range from Aaa and D.

Obligations rated below BBB- (S&P) and Baa3 (Moody's) are considered non-investment grade credits that have significant speculative characteristics.

Issuer or General Corporate Credit Rating

The issuer or general corporate credit rating is not specific to any particular debt instrument. The issuer credit rating does not take into account the recovery prospects, statutory/regulatory preferences, or the creditworthiness of guarantors, insurers, or other forms of credit enhancement that may pertain to the rating of a specific debt instrument.

Issue Credit Rating

An issue credit rating is the credit risk of specific debt issue, such as a rating on Pierre's Senior Notes or the Wachovia Credit Facility. The issue rating reflects the creditworthiness of guarantors, insurers, other forms of credit enhancement, subordination, and statutory and regulatory preferences.

If S&P can project recovery prospects exceeding 70% for an individual debt issue, the debt issue is typically rated higher than the corporate credit rating. Conversely, if S&P projects a recovery for a debt issue under 30%, the debt issue is typically rated lower than the corporate rating. A debt issue may be rated below the corporate credit rating when a debt issue is junior to other debt issues of a company or other obligations of a company.

Recovery Ratings for Issue Rating

For companies rated lower than BBB-, S&P assigns a recovery rating from 1 to 6 for the recovery prospects for a specific debt issue in event of issue default.

Part IV: Case Analysis of Pierre Foods

Analytical Framework for Determining Credit Ratings

A credit rating is based on business and financial analysis. The rating agencies believe that the ratings process cannot be reduced to a cookbook approach. The rating agencies believe their credit ratings include many subjective judgments. Credit ratings remain as much an art as a science—two companies with identical financial metrics can be rated very differently, to the extent that their business challenges and prospects differ.

Financial Ratios as Determinants of Credit Ratings

Cash flow analysis is usually the single most critical aspect of credit rating decisions.

Valuation: Measuring and Managing the Value of Companies (Koller, Gooedhart, Wessels, 2005) reported that a limited number of credit ratios explain credit ratings fairly well, with interest coverage as the single most significant indicator. For all U.S. and European firms in the authors' sample analysis, their research showed the interest coverage ratio as the key variable explaining S&P's credit ratings, with more than 45% of the rating differences explained by interest coverage.

For industrial companies rated by S&P, Table 9.0 shows the median EBITDA to interest ratio for companies rated AAA through CCC by S&P. Table 9.1 shows Pierre's EBITDA to interest ratio over time.

Table 9.0—S&P's Key U.S. Industrial Financial Ratios, Long-Term Debt Three-year (2004-2006 averages)

	AAA	AA	A	BBB	BB	B	CCC
Oper. income/revenue (%)	22.8	25.1	19.9	15.7	17.3	16.4	13.5
Disc. Cash flow/debt (%)	88.9	23.8	16.7	11.7	5.4	(0.1)	(3.7)
EBIT to interest coverage (x)	27.3	18.0	10.4	5.9	3.4	1.5	0.5
EBITDA to interest coverage (x)	31.0	21.4	12.8	7.6	4.6	2.3	1.2
FFO/ debt (%)	174.2	74.3	50.7	35.9	24.9	12.0	4.5
Free oper. cash flow debt (%)	133.1	43.0	26.0	15.4	7.2	2.2	(4.1)
Return on capital (%)	25.2	25.4	19.7	15.1	12.5	8.8	5.2
Debt/EBITDA (x)	0.5	1.0	1.6	2.2	3.2	5.4	7.7
Debt/debt plus equity (%)	12.6	6.1	38.4	43.7	51.9	74.9	100.6
No. of companies	6	15	118	213	297	345	32

Source: Reprinted with permission of S&P. S&P defines FFO as funds from operations.

Table 9.1—Pierre's EBITDA to Interest Coverage Ratio

FYE 3/6/04	FYE 3/5/05	FYE 3/4/06	FYE 3/3/07	Quarter 6/2/07	Quarter 9/1/07	Quarter 12/1/2007	FYE 3/1/08
1.51:1x	1.76x	2.52x	2.36x	1.42x	0.65x	1.08x	0.68x

Source: Calculated by author from Pierre's U.S SEC 10-Q and 10-K filings.

Chapter 9: Pierre's Credit Ratings & Trading Value of Debt

The S&P issuer credit rating for Pierre was B+/Negative on June 7, 2007. Pierre's EBITDA to interest ratio was 2.36:1 for FYE March 2007 which was comparable to the median EBITDA to interest ratio of 2.3:1 for a firm rated B by S&P.

S&P raised its credit rating on the Wachovia secured Credit Facility from B+ to BB+ on June 7, 2007 because S&P's introduced a new recovery rating methodology in 2007 for all secured debt issues. The new methodology provided for notching up the rating of a specific debt issue over the company's issuer credit rating. The notching was based on the assessment of the recovery rating for the specific debt issue in event of default.

Pierre's quarterly results for three months ending June 2, 2007 were released on July 18, 2007, approximately one year before Pierre's bankruptcy filing. Pierre reported a quarterly EBITDA to interest ratio of 1.42:1 for the June 2007 quarter, implying an S&P issuer credit rating of CCC as of July 18, 2007 based on the EBITDA to interest ratio.

It was not until September 25, 2007 that S&P downgraded Pierre's issuer credit rating from B+/Negative to B/Watch Negative. S&P evaluates many factors in the assignment of its credit ratings other than the EBITDA to interest ratio. One possible factor, among others, could have been the ownership of Pierre by Madison Dearborn. S&P may have believed that the strength and reputation of Madison Dearborn was an intangible factor for maintaining Pierre's credit rating above the S&P credit rating implied by the EBITDA to interest ratio.

Pierre's EBITDA to interest ratio continued to deteriorate in subsequent quarters, to 0.65:1 for the September quarter and 1.08:1 in the December quarter.

S&P downgraded Pierre's corporate credit rating from B/Negative to CCC+/watch/developing on June 3, 2008—with the S&P rating downgrade coming one day after Pierre gave notice that it would be late in filing its FYE March 2008 audited financial statements.

S&P must have continued to consider factors other than Pierre's EBTIDA to interest ratio in maintaining Pierre's credit rating higher than CCC prior to June 3, 2008.

Part IV: Case Analysis of Pierre Foods

Table 9.2 shows S&P's ratings history for Pierre's corporate credit rating and on Pierre's debt instruments.

Table 9.2—Standard & Poor's Credit and Recovery Ratings on Pierre Foods						
		Wachovia Secured Credit Facility			Unsecured Senior Notes	
Date	Issuer Credit Rating	Credit Rating	Recovery Rating	Recovery Percent	Credit Rating	Recovery Percent
06-11-04	B+/Negative	B+	3	50–70	B-	0–10
06-07-07	B+/Negative	BB+	2	70–90	B-	0–10
09-25-07	B/Watch Neg.	B+/Watch Neg.	2	70–90	CCC+/Watch Neg.	0–10
10-11-07	B/Negative	B+/Negative	2	70–90	CCC+/Negative	0–10
06-03-08	CCC+ Watch Developing	B- Watch Developing	2	70–90	CCC- Watch Developing	0–10
07-14-08	Default	Default	3	50–70	Default	0–10

Source: Pierre's SEC EDGAR filings, Bloomberg, Capital IQ, SEC filings by institutional debt holders

S&P Default Recovery Methodology

S&P believed that under a payment default scenario the Wachovia Credit Facility would achieve the greatest recovery through reorganization. Pierre's products were in demand. S&P used an Enterprise Value approach to determine the recovery prospects for Pierre's debt. S&P applied a multiple of five times to its estimate of Pierre's default level of EBITDA.

S&P assigned a 70%–90% recovery rating for the Wachovia loan in June 2007. The default EBITDA was based on S&P's simulated level of default EBITDA for the twelve month period June 2007 to June 2008.

On July 14, 2008, the date Pierre filed bankruptcy, S&P lowered the recovery rate from 70%–90% to 50%–70%.

S&P's recovery rating for the unsecured $125 million Senior Notes was 0%–10% throughout S&P's rating history for the Senior Notes.

Summary and Conclusion of Credit Agency Ratings

A company with a credit rating below BBB- remains a speculative credit. S&P rated Pierre as a speculative credit.

Although regulators and financial institutions have increasingly relied on the ratings of credit rating agencies for risk assessment, a credit agency rating is an opinion and not a guarantee of the current or future credit rating. Creditors have not been successful in suing credit rating agencies for harm caused by the reliance on credit rating opinions unless gross negligence or fraud on the part of the rating agency can be proven.

An investor has a fiduciary responsibility to perform its own independent credit analysis and evaluation of risk.

Chapter 9: Pierre's Credit Ratings & Trading Value of Debt

S&P Median Credit Ratios vs. U.S. Exchange Traded Non-Financial Companies

A cause for further study is whether the 1,077 U.S. industrial companies rated by S&P may have a higher average debt to equity ratio and lower average EBITDA to interest ratio as compared to all U.S. exchanged traded non-financial companies with annual revenue greater than $25 million (Table 4.2 companies in Chapter 4).

The Table 4.2 companies had a debt to EBITDA ratio of 1.80:1 (average) and 1.37:1 (median). The net debt to EBITDA ratio was 1.23:1 (average) and 0.25:1 (median). In contrast, the S&P data reports higher debt to EBITDA ratios for the companies rated by S&P. The S&P data shows that 86% of the industrial companies rated by S&P had a median debt to EBITDA ratio of 1.70:1 or greater.

The Table 4.2 companies had an EBITDA to interest ratio of 10.0:1 (average) and 10.4:1 (median). In contrast, the S&P data shows that 86% of industrial companies rated by S&P had a median EBITDA to interest ratio of less than 11.6:1.

S&P does not rate all U.S. industrial companies, for example, Apple Computer is not rated by S&P. Apple Computer had no debt and $24 billion of cash and investments as of June 30, 2008.

Market Trading Value of Pierre's Debt

Table 9.3 shows the market trading value for the $125 million unsecured Senior Notes and the $250 million Wachovia secured Credit Facility.

Trading Value of $125 million Senior Unsecured Notes

On March 31, 2008, Pierre's unsecured $125 million Senior Notes traded at 52% of par value. S&P assigned a 0%–10% recovery. On August 31, 2008, the Senior Notes traded at 8% of par.

Trading Value of $250 million Secured Wachovia Credit Facility

On March 31, 2008, the $250 million Wachovia secured Credit Facility traded at 67% of par value. S&P estimated a recovery of 70-90%. On June 11, 2008, S&P reduced the recovery estimate to 50%–70%. On June 30, 2008, the trading value for the Wachovia Credit Facility was 82.74% of par. Bloomberg does not report any trading activity for Wachovia Credit Facility after June 30, 2008.

Rabobank was a holder of $6.7 million of the Wachovia Credit Facility. Karen Boyer, Executive Director of Special Assets for Rabobank, testified in

Part IV: Case Analysis of Pierre Foods

Bankruptcy Court on December 10, 2008 (Bankr. D. Del, Ct. transcript) that trading for the Wachovia loan became active in May and June of 2009. Ms. Boyer reported that price quotes were anywhere from 70 cents to 80 cents on the dollar. She also reported that on November 18, 2008 Oaktree Capital offered 30 cents on the dollar for Rabobank's $6.7 million position in the Wachovia Credit Facility.

In a liquidation scenario for Pierre's business (Chapter 14), the estimated recovery for the Wachovia loan ranges between 33% (Debtor's Plan estimate) to 47.8% (independent analysis).

The Debtor's Reorganization Plan estimated a 73%–93% recovery for the Wachovia loan based on the estimate of Enterprise Value in the Debtor's Plan.

Table 9.3—Market Trading Value of Pierre's Debt

Date	Trading Value Percentage (Percentage of Par Value)		Dollar Trading Value (in millions of dollars)	
	Wachovia Facility [a]	Senior Note [a]	Wachovia Facility	Senior Note
09/30/07	100.00	92.00	$251	$115
10/17/08	unknown	84.75[b]	unknown	$106
12/31/07	96.55	73.00	$232	$ 91
03/31/08	67.00	52.00	$161	$ 65
06/03/08	(c)	25.87[b]	unknown	$ 32
06/06/08	(c)	29.37[b]	unknown	$ 37
06/10/08	(c)	29.25[b]	unknown	$ 37
06/30/08	82.74	11.50	$131	$ 65
08/31/08	unknown	8.00	unknown	$ 10
09/30/08	unknown	8.50	unknown	$11
10/31/08	unknown	8.00	unknown	$10
11/30/08	unknown (c)	8.00	unknown	$10

(a) Trading values from U.S. SEC EDGAR filings by Morgan Stanley Prime Income Trust, Federated High Yield Trust, Federated Insurance Series, Sun America Series Trust, Federated High Yield Trust, Federated High Income Bond Fund, and various subsidiaries of Fidelity Investments.
(b) Trades reported by Bloomberg Terminal.
(c) In the December 10, 2008 Bankruptcy Court transcript, Karen Boyer, Executive Director of Special Assets with Rabobank, testified trading became active in the Wachovia loan in late May and June 2008. Offers ranged from 70 to 80 cents on the dollar. Mr. Boyer reported that on November 18, 2008 Oaktree Capital offered Rabobank 30 cents on the dollar for Rabobank's $6.7 million position in the Wachovia loan.

Chapter 10

- **Events Leading to Chapter 11**
- **First-Day Orders**
- **DIP Loan**

"Capitalism without bankruptcy is like Christianity without hell."
Frank Borman, American Astronaut, Business Executive.

On September 1, 2007, nine months after the Wachovia Credit Facility financed 100% of the acquisition price of Zartic, Pierre was in default on the Wachovia financial covenant for the debt to EBITDA ratio ("the maximum leverage ratio").

On October 10, 2007, the leverage ratio and fixed charge ratio covenants were waived and reset (Table 10.0) in exchange for an increase in the interest rate. The rate increased by 1.75% on the Term Loan and 1.25% on the Revolver, resulting in a $4.1 million a year pro-forma increase in interest expense.

Table 10.00—Wachovia Credit Facility Covenants		
Rolling Four Quarters Ending	Maximum Leverage Ratio [a]	Minimum Fixed Charge Coverage Ratio [b]
Sep 2007	6.00:1	1.15:1
Dec 2007	6.90:1	1.10:1
Mar 2008	7.25:1	1.00:1
Jun 2008	7.25:1	1.00:1
Sep 2008	6.75:1	1.00:1
Dec 2008	6.50:1	1.00:1
Mar 2009	6.00:1	1.10:1
Jun 2009	6.00:1	1.10:1
Sep 2009 and after	5.50:1	1.10:1

Source: Pierre's SEC EDGAR 8-K filings filed with the SEC.

(a) The Wachovia Credit Agreement maximum leverage ratio was defined a funded debt less the lower of $5 million or actual cash balances, divided by four quarter rolling EBITDA.

(b) The Wachovia Credit Agreement fixed charge ratio was defined as four quarter rolling EBITDA less cash capital expenditures (excluding qualifying facility capital expenditures not to exceed $25 million) divided by (interest + CMLTD + cash taxes).

Part IV: Case Analysis of Pierre Foods

Black Swan Events

In late 2007 Pierre began to experience unprecedented levels of rapidly increasing prices for energy and food. Prices continued to escalate for food, raw material, fuel, packaging, and distribution cost. The Clovervale and Zartic acquisitions experienced increased costs associated with difficulties integrating the operations into Pierre's business. The combination of these factors contributed to a decline in Pierre's operating profits.

Subsequent to March 1, 2008, Pierre notified Wachovia Bank the Company would not comply with the financial covenants under the Wachovia Credit Agreement for fiscal year-end March 2008.

On June 2, 2008, Wachovia advised Pierre of a loan default for failing to deliver the FYE March 2008 audited financial statements by June 1, 2008. (The financial statements were filed with EDGAR on June 16, 2008).

Wachovia increased the loan interest rate to the default rate, an interest rate 2% higher than the non-default rate. The higher rate was applied retroactively to February 29, 2008, resulting in an additional $1.2 million of interest expense. Pierre was also prohibited from drawing on the Revolver, cutting-off $19 million of borrowing availability.

The default under the Wachovia Credit Facility caused a cross-default under the Swap Agreement. Pierre subsequently terminated the Swap, causing a $3.6 million settlement payment to be due on July 31, 2008.

Without availability under the Revolver, Pierre did not have cash available for the following cash payments:

- $6.2 million interest on the $125 million Senior Notes due on July 15, 2008;
- $3.6 million in payments on the Swap Agreement due on July 31, 2008;
- $5.1 million interest on the Wachovia loan due on August 19, 2008;
- $2.3 million of additional funds to secure U.S.D.A programs.

Oaktree Capital Begins Buying Claims and Proposes a Restructuring Plan

Pierre began working in May 2008 with equity sponsor Madison Dearborn to come up with a plan. Madison Dearborn decided they were not willing to invest more cash. The discussions then turned to bankruptcy.

Rabobank was a holder of $6.7 million of the Wachovia Credit Facility. Karen Boyer, Executive Director of Special Assets for Rabobank, testified in Bankruptcy Court there was a secondary market for trading in the Wachovia loan and the market became active for the Wachovia loan in May and June of 2009. The Wachovia Bank Agent had communicated to her that Oaktree Capital

Chapter 10: Events Leading to Chapter 11/First-Day Orders/DIP Loan

was starting to purchase claims. (Wachovia Bank, as Agent for the Credit Facility, was required to approve any purchase of the loan by a new holder).

In June 2008, Oaktree Capital began working on a restructuring plan with Pierre and the holders of the Wachovia Credit Facility. At that time, Oaktree Capital held $60 million (24%) of the Wachovia Credit Facility. (Oaktree Capital would eventually accumulate 92%).

The restructuring proposal included a DIP loan from Oaktree Capital. Oaktree Capital planned to exchange its $60 million of Wachovia debt for Pierre's stock and inject new cash in return for additional stock in Pierre. The remaining holders of the Wachovia Credit Facility would have their debt reinstated at par value.

In the December 10, 2008 Bankruptcy Court hearing, Ms. Boyer reported (Bankr. D. Del, Ct. transcript) that Rabobank believed Oaktree Capital also held a substantial portion (30% to 40%) of the $125 million Senior Notes based on reports from the Wachovia Agent.

In a June 19, 2008 conference call, according to the testimony of Ms. Boyer (Bankr. D. Del, Ct. transcript, Dec. 10, 2008), a few of the holders in the Wachovia Credit Facility were thinking the bankruptcy could be fast based on the Oaktree Capital proposal and support from the holders of the Wachovia debt. A fast bankruptcy could save $15–20 million in expenses. Some Wachovia debt holders were concerned a fight could occur in bankruptcy over Pierre's Enterprise Value, but the thought was that a bankruptcy could be fast because Oaktree Capital held a substantial portion (30% to 40%) of the $125 million Senior Notes. A 30% to 40% position would not be enough to deliver the votes of the unsecured class in bankruptcy, but it could block proposals by other members of the unsecured class.

The actual ownership of Senior Notes by Oaktree Capital has never been conclusively determined. Based on a review of the actual voting in the Chapter 11, Oaktree Capital's name did not appear as a voter for the Senior Notes. The Senior Notes were trading at 11% of par value. A buyer could have purchased $50 million (40%) of the Senior Notes for $5.5 million at a price of 11% of par. In the voting of the Senior Notes in the Debtor's Plan (Table 22.1 in Chapter 22), the only party holding a block close to $50 million was Bank of New York Mellon who had 11 votes counted for its reported $63.9 million par value position. The next largest voting block was 8 votes counted for the $15.6 million par value position reported by JP Morgan Chase.

The Wachovia holders negotiated in three different groups. Some of the holders of the Wachovia debt had concerns with linking the Oaktree Capital DIP loan to the Oaktree Capital restructuring plan and a concern that a

Part IV: Case Analysis of Pierre Foods

valuation fight could occur over Enterprise Value. The restructuring negotiations fell apart.

As news of Pierre's covenant defaults and worsening financial conditions spread in the weeks prior to Chapter 11, some of Pierre's vendors began restricting trade terms and asking for cash payments prior to shipping product.

Pierre's interest payment on the unsecured Senior Notes was due on July 15, 2008. With the Revolver borrowing availability cut-off, Pierre made the decision to file Chapter 11 on July 15, 2008 to complete a strategic restructuring.

First-Day Order for Wages, Salaries, Employee Benefits

The Bankruptcy Court authorized Pierre to pay up to $1.9 million of:

- Prepetition wages, salaries and other compensation;
- Reimbursable employee expenses;
- Other employee medical and similar benefits.

Pierre estimated $1.1 million of unpaid accruals for the forgoing items as of the date of the bankruptcy filing.

First-Day Order for Payments of Vendors

Pierre's July 15, 2008 Schedule of Assets & Liabilities reported $15.2 million of prepetition vendor payables, a decrease of $7.7 million from March 1, 2008. Pierre also reported an asset of $7.5 million for vendor prepayments that did not exist on March 1, 2008. In Chapter 13 of this book, the payments will be reviewed for disgorgement.

Pierre's July 15, 2008 motion in Bankruptcy Court for the payment of critical vendors estimated $15 million of total vendor payables, with $6.4 million of the $15 million owing to 130 critical vendors.

The Bankruptcy Court authorized the payment of up to $3.2 million for critical vendor claims, which was subsequently increased to $6.4 million in the final Court order without objection from any party of interest.

The median gross profit margin is 32.8% for U.S. exchange traded non-financial firms with revenue over $25 million (Table 4.2 in Chapter 4). A vendor's product turnover to a customer typically ranges 6–12 times a year. A vendor typically extends 30–60 days of credit to a customer. In bankruptcy, a vendor can quickly make up for any loss from 30–60 days of uncollectible sales based on the gross profit margin and sales turnover.

It is unlikely that any Senior Note holder had a gross margin in excess of 6%. Assuming a 6% gross margin, the principal on a lender's loan is recovered in 16 years.

Chapter 10: Events Leading to Chapter 11/First-Day Orders/DIP Loan

Pierre purchased $363 million of raw material a year from its vendors. Assuming an average 32.8% gross profit margin, the vendors earned gross profits of $119 million a year on sales to Pierre. Vendor payables were $15.2 million on the day of the bankruptcy filing. The Bankruptcy Court authorized Pierre to pay critical vendor prepetition claims up to $6.4 million. Pierre reported $7.2 million of prepayments to vendors on July 15, 2008. The Bankruptcy Trustee selected three vendors and four holders of the $125 million Senior Notes to serve on the unsecured Creditors Committee.

The Bankruptcy Court ordered Pierre to use reasonable business judgment in paying up to $6.4 million of the prepetition claims to critical vendors. Prior to payment, Pierre was required to enter into contracts with a vendor that provided the vendor would continue to extend credit to Pierre for an amount equal to the greater of the vendor credit extended at date of bankruptcy or the amount of credit extended 180 days prior to bankruptcy.

The extension of new credit during bankruptcy is an administrative claim rather than a prepetition claim. In effect, the critical vendors were permitted to swap their prepetition claims for administrative claims that had a higher expected recovery

The Bankruptcy Court also authorized the payment of claims for vendors who delivered goods classified as livestock under the Packers and Stockyards Act of 1921 or perishable agricultural commodities under the Perishable Agricultural Commodities Act of 1930 (collectively, the PSA/PACA Claimants). Pierre estimated $0.4 million in PSA/PACA claims. PSA/PACA claims imposed a statutory lien on Pierre's entire inventory, priming the lien of the Wachovia Credit Facility.

Pierre also had vendors with $2.6 million of potential warehouse and materialmens' lien claims, primarily relating to transportation and storage. The Bankruptcy Court authorized the payment up to $2.6 million for the warehouse and materialmens' claims.

First-Day Order for Debtor-In-Possession (DIP) Financing Facility

In May 2008, Pierre retained Perella Weinberg Partners (PWP) as its financial advisor to explore strategic restructuring and financing opportunities. The Wachovia Credit Lenders had split into three separate groups with three sets of advisors and three different views about how best to move the Company forward.

In June 2008, PWP requested and obtained proposals for DIP financing from each of the three Wachovia groups. None of the potential DIP lenders

Part IV: Case Analysis of Pierre Foods

were willing to provide DIP financing secured by liens junior to the first-lien held by the Wachovia Credit Facility.

Pierre negotiated with each of the Wachovia Credit Facility groups. Pierre selected a superpriority $35 million DIP Revolver proposal by OCM Principal Opportunities Fund IV (Oaktree Capital).

In the first-day Court motions, Pierre reported that Oaktree Capital, Pierre, and the Wachovia Credit Facility Lenders heavily negotiated the DIP facility prior to submitting it for approval to the Bankruptcy Court. The $35 million DIP Revolver had an interest rate of LIBOR plus 5.50% and included a 2% ($700,000) commitment fee and a $150,000 work fee. The DIP Revolver carried a maturity date of the earlier of nine months or the effective date of the confirmed reorganization plan. The DIP loan also had case milestone defaults for the following:

- Failure of Pierre to file a plan within 30 days after the final Bankruptcy Court approval of the DIP Revolver;
- Failure of Pierre to obtain entry of an Court Order approving Pierre's Disclosure Statement within 60 days of the filing of the plan;
- Failure of Pierre to obtain an Order confirming a plan acceptable to the DIP lenders within 90 days of approval of the Disclosure Statement;
- Failure of the effective date of the plan of reorganization to occur within 45 days of an Order confirming the plan;

The DIP Loan was granted superpriority status and the collateral was a first-lien on all of Pierre's assets, priming the lien of the Wachovia Credit Facility. The lien was subordinate to liens for unpaid taxes, purchase money security interests, capital leases, and other statutory vendor liens.

The lien of the DIP Lender and the Wachovia Credit Facility were subordinate to the following carve-outs:

- Fees of the Clerk of the Bankruptcy Court and the U.S. Trustee;
- Allowed fees and expenses of professionals retained by Pierre or any official committee approved by the Bankruptcy Court;
- Fees and expenses of professionals incurred subsequent to DIP Facility, in an aggregate amount not to exceed $2.5 million.

Chapter 10: Events Leading to Chapter 11/First-Day Orders/DIP Loan

The Court gave the DIP Facility superpriority status with a priming lien on the collateral securing the Wachovia Credit Facility because Pierre demonstrated it was unable to obtain credit otherwise and Pierre provided adequate protection to the Wachovia Credit Facility.

The DIP loan included other standard and customary covenants and events of default, as well as the following specific covenants and defaults:

- Default if Madison Dearborn ceased to own less than 51% of Pierre's stock or if a majority of the Pierre's Board of Directors were other than those Board Directors prior to bankruptcy;
- Customary covenants for limits on incurring debt, liens, dividends, changes in business, asset sales, investments, guarantees, leases, and prohibiting speculative transactions;
- Default if Pierre refinanced the Oaktree Capital DIP loan;
- Default if Lightning Management ceased to be Pierre's operational consultant debtor or John Schaeffer ceased to be the consultant on behalf of Lightning Management. Pierre paid Lightning Management a $500,000 fee immediately prior to the bankruptcy filing.

John Schaeffer's Background:
  - Employed by Lightning Consultants;
  - Consultant to Pierre beginning December 2007;
  - 1998–2007 President, CFO and COO. of Cornerstone Brands, a family of catalog companies for home, leisure and casual apparel;
  - 1992–1988 CFO and COO of Eastbay, a direct marketer of athletic footwear and apparel.

Part IV: Case Analysis of Pierre Foods

DIP Financial Covenants

Table 10.1 shows the DIP Revolver financial covenants. The DIP covenant required Pierre to have EBITDAR of $21 million for the eight months July 2008 to February 2009 (equivalent to $32 million of annualized EBITDAR).

Table 10.1—Debtor-In-Possession Loan Financial Covenants
($ millions)

Period	Minimum EBITDAR	Maximum CAPX
July 1, 2008 to August 2, 2008	(0.25)	1.8
July 1, 2008 to August 30, 2008	2.05	2.3
July 1, 2008 to September 27, 2008	4.55	2.8
July 1, 2008 to November 1, 2008	8.52	3.3
July 1, 2008 to November 29, 2008	11.42	3.8
July 1, 2008 to December 27, 2008	13.60	4.3
July 1 2008 tot January 31, 2009	17.02	4.9
July 1, 2008 tot February 28, 2009	20.90	5.3

Source: Pierre's July 16, 2008 Bankruptcy Court filing for interim Order for postpetition financing.

Adequate Protection Granted by the Prepetition Wachovia Credit Facility

In return for Pierre's use of cash collateral and DIP priming lien, the Bankruptcy Court provided the Wachovia Credit Facility with the following adequate protection:

- Cash payments of interest during bankruptcy at the non-default interest rate;
- Payment of letter of credit fees;
- Payment of reasonable fees and expenses, limited to one lead counsel, one local counsel, and one financial advisor;
- Reserved the right of the Wachovia Credit Facility to file secured claims against Pierre for prepetition and postpetition payment of interest at the default interest rate;
- Subject and subordinate to the carve-out and super priority claims provided to the DIP Lender, the Court provided the Wachovia Credit Facility a superpriority claim in an amount equal to the aggregate diminution in value of the prepetition collateral, including the diminution resulting from the priming lien.

Chapter 10: Events Leading to Chapter 11/First-Day Orders/DIP Loan

Preliminary DIP Loan Court Hearing and Order on July 16, 2008

In Pierre's July 16, 2008 Bankruptcy Court hearing, Jon Henes, attorney with Kirkland & Ellis representing Pierre, argued for the DIP loan and adequate protection (Bankr. D. Del, Ct. transcript):

> "it is to adequately protect the lenders from a diminution in the value of their interest in the collateral...the best way to adequately protect the lenders and everyone in this case is to continue to operate the business. ...we have beef...If we shut this Company down because we do not have access to cash collateral, we would have spoiled smelly beef. You would not be able to go sell that for a lot of money, so I think we all are clear that we need to used the cash collateral and continue to operate.... I think we have adequately protected them by paying the non-default rate of interest, by paying Wachovia's professionals, and by giving replacement liens, by continuing to operate the business."

GE Capital, Morgan Stanley Investment, Kampen Assets, and Z Capital (the GE Group) held a portion of the Wachovia Credit Facility. The GE Group objected because they wanted to receive the default rate of interest as adequate protection.

Mr. Henes argued that Pierre was protecting the lenders by just operating the business and the issue of a default rate should be determined at the date of the claims period. He believed that if it turned out the Wachovia Facility was oversecured, a final determination could be at the end of the case under Section 506(b) of the Bankruptcy Code for the payment of interest at the default rate.

The GE Group also objected because they wanted representation by separate counsel and for the Debtor to pay for the legal expense. In addition, the GE Group requested access rights to information from Pierre; rather than relying on their rights under the Wachovia Credit Facility because the Wachovia Agent might decline to request information that the GE Group believed might be necessary. The GE Group believed the Wachovia Agent was not aggressively protecting the rights of the Wachovia Credit Facility Lender Group.

Counsel for the GE Group expressed concern that Oaktree Capital held both secured and unsecured debt. Moreover, there was concern with the Oaktree Capital DIP loan having case milestone defaults for the reorganization plan. The GE Group was concerned the Pierre would file a plan "the DIP lender loves, because it is Oaktree Capital" (Bankr. D. Del, August 16, 2008 Ct. transcript).

Part IV: Case Analysis of Pierre Foods

An Ad Hoc group of the unsecured Senior Notes, holding 48% of the Senior Notes, also expressed concern that the Oaktree Capital loan had default provisions for dates relating a schedule of approvals for the Debtor's reorganization plan.

Counsel for Oaktree Capital argued the DIP approval of $35 million was only 14% of the amount of the Wachovia Credit Facility and was not a lot of money in the context of the Wachovia's loan, but a lot of money for the Debtor as it worked towards its reorganization plan.

The Bankruptcy Judge gave preliminary approval for the Oaktree Capital DIP loan, subject to a future hearing for final approval.

Final Hearing and Court Order for DIP Loan Approval & Other Matters

On August 13, 2008, the Bankruptcy Court approved a request to increase the critical vendor payments from the $3.2 million in the initial Court Order to $6.4 million (no objection was filed to the Debtor's motion).

There were a number of changes to the final DIP Court Order based on discussions between the Creditors Committee and the DIP lender. The DIP Lender would permit Pierre to refinance the DIP loan whereas previously this was an event of default.

With respect to the milestone days, the DIP Lender gave the Creditors Committee the right to extend any deadline by 15 days. The DIP Lender also agreed that it would not be a default under the DIP loan if a change of control occurred due to the resignation of the Debtor's Board of Director Members, unless the result left fewer than three Board Members.

The GE Group objected to the Perella Weinberg fees for its work as Pierre's financial advisor. The fees consisted of a $300,000 initial fee, a $150,000 monthly fee, and $2,000,000 transaction fee for restructuring due at the end of the case. Steve Yoder, with law firm Potter, Anderson & Corroon, representing the GE Group, summarized the belief of the GE Group in the August 13, 2008 Court hearing (Bankr. D. Del, Ct. transcript):

> "PWP would do nothing other than perhaps convert the Wachovia secured Credit Facility to equity under some plan that everybody else deemed to be a plan that made sense, and approve that plan, perhaps over the objection of the GE Group, and the plan would deny the GE Group a full recovery and then charge $2 million for doing so. The GE Group believed this $2 million payment was not adding any value to do anything other than to convert debt to equity."

The Bankruptcy Judge approved the final DIP order and the PWP success fee.

Chapter 11

Prepetition Claims

"This Chapter 11 is the preferable form of a Chapter 11" Joe Gensor

Summary of Prepetition Claims

Based on Pierre's July 15, 2008 Schedules of Assets/Liabilities, information in Pierre's first-day Court motions, and claims tracked by Kurtzman Carson, Pierre had the following prepetition claims:

- $252.7 million for the Wachovia secured Credit Facility;
- $131.2 million unsecured Senior Notes (including $6 million interest);
- $1.8 million estimated balance on capital leases;
- $1.0 million to Butler County Water for an unsecured priority claim;
- $6.4 million for critical vendor claims. The Court authorized payment of up to $6.4 million of the claims;
- $2.6 million for vendor claims for potential warehouse & materialmens' claims. The Court authorized payment of up to $2.6 million of the claims;
- $0.4 million for vendor claims for PSA/PACA potential liens. The Court authorized payment of up to $0.4 million of the claims;
- $5.8 million of other general unsecured vendor claims based on the Debtor's $23 million of unsecured claims itemized in the Debtor's Schedule of Assets/Liabilities. The $5.8 million of vendor claims is net of the other specific vendor claims itemized above and excludes $2.4 million deferred compensation (below) and the $6.4 million for letters of credits that have been classified in the Wachovia Credit Facility claim;
- $2.4 million claims for deferred compensation to Pierre's President Norbert Woodhams and former Sales Manager Robert Naylor;
- $1.1 million for prepetition wages, salaries, reimbursable employee expenses, and other employee medical and similar benefits. The Court authorized the payment of up to $1.1 million for these claims;
- Rejected executory contracts. $4.6 million property lease claim by Interstate Warehouse. $1.1 million NASCAR claim for an advertising contract running through the year 2013.

Part IV: Case Analysis of Pierre Foods

On the date of Pierre's bankruptcy filing, Pierre had $1.5 million of cash, a $7.5 million asset for prepayments to vendors, and a $7 million tax refund receivable pending collection. Moreover, in the 136 days prior to bankruptcy, Pierre reduced its vendor payables by $7.7 million and its obligation under the Wachovia Credit Facility by $12.0 million. Pierre had potential liquidity of $35.7 million as follows:

($millions)
1.5	Cash
7.5	Prepayments to trade vendors
7.0	Tax refund receivable
7.7*	Potential preference payments to trade vendors
5.6*	Potential preference payments to Wachovia Credit Facility
6.4*	Potential preference for replacement letters of credits Wachovia Credit Facility
35.7	

* Preference payments reviewed in Chapter 13 of this book

Prepetition $125 million Senior Notes (Unsecured)

Pierre's $125 million of Senior Notes had a 9.875% interest rate. Interest payments were due on January 15 and July 15 of each year. The Senior Notes were issued on June 30, 2004 and matured in July 2012. The Senior Notes were unsecured obligations of Pierre Foods, Inc.

The Senior Notes were subordinate in right of payment to the Wachovia Credit Facility. The Senior Notes were not subordinate to vendor payables. The Senior Notes were guaranteed by each of the direct and indirect subsidiaries of Pierre but the guarantees were subordinate to the guarantees for the Wachovia Credit Facility.

Institutional Holders of Senior Notes

U.S. National Bank & Trust was the Trustee for the Senior Note. SEC filings revealed that holders of the Senior Notes included:

Fidelity Investments	Federated Investments
Great American Life Insurance	Annuity Investors
Nationwide Fund Advisors	Allstate Life Insurance
Liberty Life Assurance	American Heritage Life

Chapter 11: Prepetition Claims

Largest Unsecured Creditors

Pierre's largest unsecured creditors at the date of the bankruptcy are listed in Table 11.0 below:

Table 11.0—Pierre's Top Unsecured Creditors ($ millions)	
Unsecured Creditor	Amount
U.S. National Bank as Trustee for Senior Notes (including interest)	131.2
Interstate Warehouse Distributors	4.6
Archer Daniels Midland	2.5
Norbert Woodhams deferred compensation	1.3
Robert Naylor severance & deferred comp.	1.1
NASCAR	1.1
Butler County & Water	1.0
Duke Energy	0.4
Genesis Baking	0.3
Flowers Baking	0.3
Kraft Food	0.3
Americraft Carton	0.2
Echo Lake Farm Produce	0.2
Genpak	0.2
Swift	0.2
All other	2.5 [a]
Total estimated unsecured claims	147.4 [a]

Source: Debtor's July 15, 2008 Schedule of Assets/Liabilities and claims register reported by Kurtzman Carson. All other claims and total claims have been estimated by the author based on case information

List of Debtor's Unexpired Leases to be Rejected

The leases rejected by the Pierre in bankruptcy are in Table 11.1.

A $4.6 million claim was filed by Interstate Warehouse but a lease rejection was not filed by Pierre for Interstate Warehouse based on a review of Court filings.

Pierre had $2.7 million of capital leases on March 1, 2008, with payments of $1.7 million due in 12 months. Based on scheduled lease payments, the balance on capital leases has been estimated at $2.8 million on the date of bankruptcy. Pierre's claims for rejected equipment leases were $991,370 (Table 11.1), therefore it roughly estimated that Pierre accepted capital leases of $1 million (author estimate). The annual payment savings from car, truck, and trailer leases were $379,992 a year based on the Debtor's August 15, 2008 Court Order for the rejection of certain leases.

Pierre also assumed or renegotiated other contracts. The annuals savings is unknown because the Court permitted the re-priced contracts to remain confidential.

Part IV: Case Analysis of Pierre Foods

Pierre's cash flow saving from the rejection of the capital and leases is unknown. The savings are estimated to be between $400,000 and $800,000 a year, or more (author estimate).

Pierre also had $7.3 million of future operating lease payments due as of March 1, 2008, with $5.4 million payable between March 1, 2008 and February 28, 2009. The operating lease payments were scheduled to decrease to $1.7 million a year for FYE March 2010 and $0.1 million for FYE March 2011. Therefore, based on the scheduled decreases in operating lease payments, EBITDA should increase $3.6 million a year beginning March 1, 2009 and an additional $1.6 million a year beginning March 1, 2010 (author estimate).

Table 11.1—Leases to be Rejected by Debtor

Lessor	Category	Items	Claim Filed
Interstate Warehouse	Real estate	Warehouse space	$4,600,000 [a]
NMHG	Machinery	(22) forklifts	$ 158,082
GE Capital	Office equip.	Copier	
Ikon	Office equip.	(3) copiers	
Citi Capital	Office equip.	Copier	
Millennium Business	Office equip.	(12) copiers	
Transport Services	Auto	(5) 1999 utility vehicles	
Baltimore	Auto	6 automobiles	
Mike Albert Leasing	Auto	2005 Chevy cargo van & 2006 Ford	
Camargo Cadillac	Auto	2006 Chevy Hummer	
Kings Toyota	Auto	(2) 2006 & (1) 2007 Toyota Sequoia	$ 54,078
Kerry Ford	Auto	(2) 2007 Ford F-150 trucks & 2007 Ford	
Fairfield Lincoln	Auto	2007 Lincoln Mark IV	
Idealease of Atlanta	Auto	(4) International 9400 vehicles	
Infiniti of Dayton	Auto	2007 Infiniti M35 auto	
Jake Sweeney Chev	Auto	2006 BMW	
Kings Cove Auto	Auto	2007 Lexus	
Lexus River Center	Auto	2008 Lexus	
Penske	Equipment	Rolling stock	$147,379 [b]
Crown Credit	Equipment		$631,831 [b]
		Total	$5,591,370

Source: Pierre's Schedule of Leases Rejected filed with the Bankruptcy Court on August 15, 2008.

(a) The $4.6 million claim by Interstate Warehouse was not listed as a rejected lease in Debtor's schedule of rejected leases filed with the Bankruptcy Court. Interstate Warehouse filed a $4.6 million claim based on a review of the Kurtzman Carson claims register.

(b) Penske and Crown Credit were not listed as rejected leases on the Debtor's schedule of rejected leases but, from a review of the Kurtzman Carson Claims register, they both filed the claims against Pierre.

Rejection of Other Contracts

Pierre rejected a long-term advertising contract with NASCAR who filed an unsecured claim for $1.1 million. The annual savings from the cancelled contract was $200,000 a year.

Chapter 11: Prepetition Claims

Pierre also rejected over 400 individual marketing and rebate agreements and the existing Employee Stock Option Plan.

The annual savings from the other contracts rejections could result in an expense savings for the Debtor. An estimate of the savings was not disclosed in the Debtor's Plan or court filings.

$252.7 million Wachovia Credit Facility (Secured by Lien on All Assets)

The $252.7 million Wachovia secured Credit Facility consisted of the following:

- $224 million Term Loan;
- $14 million balance on the $40 million Revolver;
- $6.4 million letters of credit. The obligation was released in August 2008 as the DIP lender issued replacement letters of credit;
- $4.2 million of unpaid interest;
- $3.6 million swap termination fee;
- $0.4 million of legal & professional fees.

The Revolver had a maturity date of June 30, 2009.
The Term Loan had a maturity date of June 30, 2010.

Wachovia Bank was the administrative agent under the Wachovia Credit Facility. The Wachovia Credit Facility was originally opened with Wachovia (Wachovia merged into Wells Fargo Bank in December 2008). The borrower was Pierre Foods, Inc., with loan guarantees by all other companies in the Pierre Food Group, including PF Management, PF Holding and all subsidiaries of Pierre Foods, Inc.

The loan was secured by a first-lien on all present and after-acquired assets in the Pierre Food Group of companies, including personal property, real property, intangible assets, and the stock of each subsidiary, including all of the stock interest owned by PF Management and PF Holding.

The Wachovia Facility Term Loan required quarterly payments of $375,000 with a balloon of $141.4 million due June 2010. Pierre was required to make additional annual principal payments on the Wachovia Credit Facility based on Pierre's annual debt to EBITDA ratio, as follows:

Debt to EBITDA Ratio	Annual Required Principal Payments
< 4.50:1	50% of annual net cash flow
4.50:1 or greater	75% of annual net cash flow

Part IV: Case Analysis of Pierre Foods

Pierre actual principal payments on the Wachovia Term Note were as follows:

Fiscal Year	Principal Payments
March 2005	$16.5 million
March 2006	$17.8 million
March 2007	$14.7 million
March 2008	$ 3.5 million

In connection with an Amendment No. 3 to increase in the loan to finance the acquisition of Zartic in December 2006, the scheduled quarterly repayments on the Wachovia Term Loan were reduced from $375,000 a quarter to $250,000 per quarter. During the quarter ending June 2, 2008, Pierre made a $2 million prepayment on the Wachovia Term Loan and was not required to resume scheduled quarterly payments until February 28, 2009. Chapter 13 in this book will review the $2 million payment for disgorgement as a preference payment.

On October 10, 2007, Wachovia waived covenant compliance for the Leverage Ratio on the June 2007 financial statement and the interest rate was increased to the Wachovia Prime Rate plus 3.00% should the debt to EBITDA ratio exceed 5.0:1. Any future default would cause the interest rate to increase by an additional 2.00%.

The Wachovia loan financial covenants were previously set forth in Table 7.7 (Chapter 7) and the amended covenants in Table 10.0 (Chapter 10). Other affirmative and negative covenants in the Wachovia Credit Facility included:

- Default of change in control, defined as Madison Dearborn ceasing to own/control less than 51% of Pierre's stock;
- Fundamental changes in the business to merge, dissolve, liquidate consolidate into other entities;
- Limitations on asset sales;
- The Wachovia Credit Facility maintaining its first-lien priority;
- Limitations on debt;
- Default for failure to pay amounts due under the loan;
- Filing for bankruptcy.

Chapter 11: Prepetition Claims

Each Lender in the Wachovia Credit Facility had the ability to sell their loan to other parties, subject to:
- for the Term and Revolver, to any existing Lender in the Wachovia Credit Facility;
- for the Term Loan, to any other person/entity subject to approval by the Administrative Agent;
- for the Revolver, any other person/entity subject to approval by the Administrative Agent and the Borrower, but Borrower approval was not required if the Wachovia Credit Facility was in default.

Because Oaktree Capital was not a party to the original Wachovia Credit Facility, Wachovia Bank, as Agent for the Facility, was required to approve the sale of any portion of the Term Note to Oaktree Capital. The $224 million Wachovia Term Note accounted for 90% of the Wachovia Credit Facility.

The lack of constraints on the future holders of the Wachovia Credit Facility had important implications for Pierre and holders of the Wachovia debt.

Amendments or waivers to the Wachovia Credit Facility required the consent of over 50% of the holders, except 100% consent was required of all holders for changes in loan amounts, interest, postponing payments due, or to release all or substantially all of the collateral.

Institutional Holders for the Wachovia Credit Facility

As of October 10, 2007, the Wachovia Credit Facility Lenders consisted of 44 institutional investors (or affiliates) as listed in Table 11.2.

Table 11.2—Initial Holders of the Wachovia Secured Credit Facility

Wachovia	Eagle Loan Trust	Navigator
Antares	Fidelity Funds	Pangaea
Ares	Flagship CLO Funds	Prospero
Atlas Funding	Foothill Group	Pyramis
Ballantyne Funding	Grand Central Asset Trust	Qualcomm Global Trading
Ballrock	General Electric Capital	Rabobank
CIT Lending Services	General Motors Trust Bank	Schooner
Confulent	Harch	Stanfield Capital
CUNA	Harford	Stanfield Group
Callidus	Landmark Funds	Sumitomo
Beecher	LaSalle Bank	WB Loan Funding 1
Bushnee	MAPS Funds	Venture III
CBNA	Morgan Stanley Prime Income	Van Kampen Loan Fund
Denali Capital	Mutual Life Insurance	

Source: Pierre's U.S. SEC EDGAR filing.

Part IV: Case Analysis of Pierre Foods

With 44 Lenders in the Wachovia Credit Facility, the loan per lender would have averaged $5.6 million, assuming equal dispersion of the loan among the Lenders. The make-up of the Wachovia Lenders consisted primarily of constituents of the syndicated senior-secured lending market.

In the most recent decade, the syndicated loan market has become an increasingly important part of the U.S. capital markets. Banks, who typically arrange and agent these leveraged loans, often act primarily as investment bankers/arrangers whose primary function is to raise capital for the borrower, rather than acting solely as an investor holding the loan.

The institutional investors in the syndicated loan market consist primarily of structured investment funds, mutual funds, hedge funds, pension funds, and insurance companies. Commercial banks and finance companies tend to place more emphasis on borrower relationships, tend to hold their loans to maturity, and are more likely to work with a borrower in the event of financial distress. Other institutional investors are more likely to sell their loans in the market in the event of distress and are more likely to trade the loans based on loan pricing and changes in credit agency ratings.

In commercial lending, it is important to underwrite who will initially hold the debt, how much they will hold, and who is permitted to own the debt in the future.

Chapter 12

Validity of Guarantees Securing Wachovia Credit Facility

"It's not much fun to be a banker these days. One leading European banker says a poll showed that the only groups now held in lower regard are prostitutes and convicted felons. There are plenty of people who would be quite happy to see a few bankers join the latter group." Floyd Norris, "Failing Upward at the Fed", New York Times, February 26, 2009.

Pierre Foods, Inc. was the borrower in the Wachovia Credit Facility. All of the companies in the Pierre group of companies guaranteed the Wachovia Credit Facility.

Pierre Foods, Inc. and its subsidiaries were the only entities with tangible assets. The only asset held by the parent of Pierre Foods, Inc. was the stock of Pierre Foods, Inc. The parent did not have any direct liabilities, however it guaranteed the Wachovia loan.

The issue for review is the validity of the guarantees of the subsidiaries of Pierre Foods, Inc. as well as the pledge of collateral in those subsidiaries securing the guarantees.

Subject to certain conditions, Section 548 of the Bankruptcy Code provides that a transfer of property may be voided that was made within two years before bankruptcy.

Part IV: Case Analysis of Pierre Foods

The key issue for guarantees of Pierre's subsidiaries was:
- whether the subsidiaries received reasonably equivalent value in consideration of their guarantees; and
- whether the subsidiaries became insolvent because of the guarantees, leaving them with unreasonably small capital and debt beyond their ability to pay.

The most recent extension of credit on the Wachovia loan in connection with the subsidiary guarantees was in 2006 for the acquisitions of Clovervale (August 2006) and Zartic (December 2006). The assets held directly by the Clovervale and Zartic corporations accounted for approximately 20% of all of the assets in the consolidated Pierre group of entities. The assets of the corporation Pierre Foods, Inc. (excluding stock in subsidiaries) accounted for 78% of all of the assets in the consolidated group of Pierre entities.

Form the data presented below, it is concluded that the subsidiary guarantees are valid based on the following factors;
- The majority of the Wachovia loan proceeds in 2006 were used to complete the acquisition price of Clovervale and Zartic;
- Clovervale and Zartic had $134 million of assets, $21 million of liabilities, a $113 million net worth, and a $52 million tangible net worth;
- Clovervale and Zartic were solvent after the acquisition;
- The time between the date of the debt/acquisitions and the date of the bankruptcy filing was 23 months for Clovervale and 19 months for Zartic.

Table 12.0 shows the March 31, 2008 balance sheet for Pierre Foods, Inc. and the guarantor subsidiaries.

As of March 1, 2008, the combined guarantor entities had $85 million of assets, $7 million of liabilities, and a $78 million net worth. Pierre Foods, Inc. carried the investment in subsidiaries at $78.5 million (compared to $112.5 million at the time of the initial formation of the subsidiaries).

In summary, due diligence was performed on the validity of the guarantees in a test for fraudulent conveyance. A court challenge as to the validity of the collateral guarantees is likely to be unsuccessful, time consuming, and costly.

Chapter 12: Validity of Guarantees Securing Wachovia Credit Facility

Table 12.0—Breakout of Pierre Foods, Inc. and Subsidiary Guarantors

(in $ millions)	Fiscal Year End March 1, 2008			
	Pierre Foods, Inc.	Guarantors	Eliminating Entries	Total
Cash	5.5	0	0	5.5
Receivables	45.5	0.9	0	46.4
Inventory	56.2	8.5	0	64.7
Refundable taxes	(6.2)	13.0	0	6.8
Deferred taxes	9.8	4.2	0	14.1
Prepaid items	3.9	1.0	0	4.9
PP&E	52.4	32.0	0	84.4
Intangibles	50.3	17.8	0	68.1
Goodwill	43.9	0	0	43.9
Deferred loan fees	7.1	0	0	7.1
Investment in subsidiaries	78.5	0	(78.5)	0
Intercompany accounts	0	7.4	(7.4)	0
Other	3.0	.4	0	3.4
Total Assets	350.0	85.4	(85.9)	349.4
Wachovia Secured debt	241.0	0	0	241.0
Unsecured Notes	125.0	0	0	125.0
Other debt	0.5	2.1	0	2.6
Interest rate swap liability	6.9	0	0	6.9
Trade payables	14.9	8.0	0	22.9
Other accruals	17.2	5.7	0	22.9
Accrued promotions [a]	6.0 [a]	0	0	6.0 [a]
Deferred taxes	22.9	(8.8)	0	14.1
Intercompany accounts	7.4	0	(7.4)	0
Total Liabilities	441.8	6.9	(7.4)	448.7
Common Stock	150.2	112.8	(112.8)	150.2
Accumulated deficit	(242.0)	(34.3)	34.3	(242.0)
Shareholder's equity	(91.8)	78.5	(78.5)	(91.8)

Source: Pierre's U.S. SEC EDGAR filing.

(a) Accrued promotions are for the liability for promotions to customers. If Pierre's customers take advantage of the promotions, the resulting liability becomes a contra to the customer's account receivable balance.

Chapter 13

Disgorgement of Preference Payments

"If stupidity got us into this mess, why can't it get us out?"—Will Rogers

Wachovia Credit Facility Preference Payments

The Bankruptcy Court granted adequate protection for the prepetition Wachovia Credit Facility in return for the priming lien granted to the $35 million DIP loan and the use of cash collateral. The adequate protection consisted of a lien on all of Pierre's postpetition assets, payment of interest, and a superpriority lien to the extent the priming lien caused any loss of collateral value to the Wachovia claim. The superpriority lien was subordinate to the DIP Loan and carve-outs.

The adequate protection Court Order was subject to disallowance and disgorgement. The Bankruptcy Court gave parties of interest up to 75 days, and the Creditors Committee up to 60 days (after formation), to file a motion to challenge an avoidance action or any other objection as it pertained to the Wachovia loan obligation, documents, or collateral. If not timely challenged, then the prepetition Wachovia obligations would be deemed allowed claims, not

Chapter 13: Disgorgement of Preference Payments

subject to re-characterization or avoidance. There was never a challenge by a party of interest.

Table 13.0 shows a $5.2 million reduction in the prepetition Wachovia Credit Facility obligation from March 1, 2008 to July 15, 2008 (136 days prior to bankruptcy).

Table 13.0—Change in Wachovia Loan Balance 136 days prior to Bankruptcy
(in $ millions)

	March 1, 2008	July 15, 2008	Variance
Loan balance	241.0	238.0	3.0
Interest	6.2	4.2	2.0
Swap Liability	4.0	3.6	0.4
Undrawn letters of credits	6.4	6.3	0.1
Totals	257.6	252.2	5.5

Source: Pierre's first-day Bankruptcy Court motion on July 15, 2008 and U.S. SEC EDGAR filings.

Table 13.1 Pierre shows $12.1 million of potential disgorgement from the Wachovia Credit Facility for: (1) $5.7 million of preference payments made 90 days prior to bankruptcy and (2) $6.4 million for the reduction in the letters of credit obligation when the DIP Lender issued replacement letters of credits.

Table 13.1—Analysis of Wachovia Loan Balance for Disgorgement
(in dollars)

Amount	Date	Purpose
312,837	4/30/2008	Unknown
4,918,516	5/01/2008	Unknown
993,623	5/13/2008	Sale of building—per SEC filing
2,000,000	6/12/2008	Proceeds insurance casualty—per SEC filing
422,193	6/30/2008	Unknown
8,647,169		Total payments received 90 days to bankruptcy
(2,000,000)		Exclude proceeds insurance casualty (Wachovia collateral)
(993,623)		Exclude proceeds sale of office building (Wachovia collateral)
5,653,546		Reduction in Wachovia loan balance 90 days prior to bankruptcy
6,400,000		DIP Lender replacement of letters of credits issued by Wachovia
12,053,546		Amount to be Disgorged from the Wachovia Credit Facility

Source: Pierre's July 15, 2008 Statement of Financial Affairs filed with the Bankruptcy Court on September 3, 2008 and U.S. SEC EDGAR filings.

The Bankruptcy Court had avoiding powers to undo a transfer of money made 90 days before the petition date under Section 547 of the Bankruptcy Code. The cash payments received are preference payments if they were received within 90 days prior to bankruptcy and if Pierre was insolvent. For purposes of Section 547 of the Bankruptcy Code, Pierre is presumed to be insolvent for any payment made 90 days prior bankruptcy. To disgorge the payments from a lender, the cash payments must have allowed the lender to

Part IV: Case Analysis of Pierre Foods

receive more than it would have received in a Chapter 7 liquidation of the business, unless the payments to the lender were made according to ordinary business terms.

It is argued that the $5.6 million reduction in exposure was not made according to ordinary business terms and the payments were not regularly scheduled Wachovia loan payments. $5.2 million of the payments were made on April 30, 2008 and May 1, 2008. Pierre was under financial distress at that time. Subsequent to March 1, 2008, Pierre advised Wachovia that it would not be able to deliver its FYE March 2008 financial statements by the required June 2, 2008 due date. Pierre received a notice of loan default from Wachovia on June 2, 2008.

It is argued that the payments effectively allowed Wachovia to receive more than it would have in a liquidation of Pierre. The liquidation analysis in the Debtor's Plan (Chapter 14) projects a 33% recovery for the Wachovia Credit Facility in a liquidation of the business. The independent liquidation analysis (Chapter 14) projects a recovery of 39% in a 3 month liquidation period and a 48% recovery in a 9 month liquidation period. If the $5.6 million of assets had not been converted to payments on the Wachovia loan, then Wachovia would have recovered no more than $2.7 million (48% high recovery estimate times $5.6 million of assets converted).

In conclusion, the potential recovery of preference payments from Wachovia is $2.9 million (52% of the $5.6 million). A party of interest should have filed a motion to disgorge $2.9 million from the Wachovia Credit Facility.

In addition, the DIP Loan issued letters of credit that replaced $6.4 million of letters of credits issued under the prepetition Wachovia Credit Facility. A party of interest should have filed a motion to authorize a bankruptcy emergence loan to prime the collateral on the Wachovia Facility for up to $6.4 million, without impairment to the Wachovia claim.

Trade Vendor Preference Payments

Pierre made $7.5 million in prepayments to trade vendors 90 days prior to the bankruptcy filing. Pierre did not have any significant prepaid amounts for vendors on the Company's March 1, 2008 balance sheet. Pierre also reduced vendor payables by $7.7 million from March 1, 2008 and the date of bankruptcy.

There was never a challenge by a party of interest for the disgorgement of the amounts paid to trade vendors.

The payments were not in the payment of debt and the payments allowed vendors to receive more than they would have received in a liquidation of Pierre. The liquidation analysis in the Debtor Plan projected a 0% recovery for

Chapter 13: Disgorgement of Preference Payments

unsecured claims. Therefore, a party of interest should have filed a motion to disgorge trade vendors of $15.2 million of preference payments. The case analysis assumes that $9 million (60%) of the $15.2 million in preference payments would be recovered from the vendors.

Chapter 14

- **Wachovia Under or Over Secured**
- **Initial Estimate of Recoveries Based on Assets & Enterprise Value**

"Experience seems to most of us to lead to conclusions, but empiricism has sworn never to draw them." George Santayana

Chapter 14 will evaluate the Wachovia Credit Facility collateral position and provide an independent estimate of the expected recoveries for the classes of claims.

The independent analysis uses four valuation cases: (1) three month liquidation, (2) nine month orderly liquidation, (3) fair market value basis without goodwill, and (4) fair market value with goodwill (the full Enterprise Value).

The independent valuation and recovery analysis is as of the July 15, 2008 bankruptcy date, prior to the $35 million DIP loan. The inclusion of the $35 million DIP loan does not affect the estimate of recovery because the assumed net liquidation proceeds are net of liquidation expenses, including a 3% Trustee Fee and other required costs to operate the Debtor during the liquidation period. The purpose of the DIP loan was to keep the business operating until the earlier of the liquidation of the business or the emergence from bankruptcy.

Chapter 14: Wachovia Under or Over Secured & Estimate of Recoveries

Matrix for Values and Recoveries for Classes of Claims

Table 14.0 is a summary of recoveries for the classes of claims based on: (1) the independent analysis and (2) the Debtor's Plan.

Table 14.0
Recovery by Class of Claim for Various Valuation Assumptions for Independent Analysis as Compared to Debtor's Plan

(in $ millions) Classes of Claim	Claim	Recovery - Independent Analysis (see Table 14.1 for supporting details)				Recovery Debtor's Plan	
		Liquidation		Operate the Business		Liquidate	Operate Business
		Quick (3 mo.)	OLV (9 mo.)	FMV	Enterprise Value	12 months to liquidate	Enterprise Value
Professional fees	$15.9	$3.2 / 0%	$3.2 / 0%	$15.9 / 0%	$15.9 / 100%	$6.8 / 0%	100%
Class 1: Priority tax claims	$0.9	0%	0%	0%	100%	0%	100%
Class 1. Butler County Water	$1.0	0%	0%	0%	100%	0%	100%
Class 1. PACA/PSA payables	$0.4	0%	0%	0%	100%	0%	100%
Class 1. Vendor claims warehouse	$2.6	0%	0%	0%	100%	0%	100%
Class 1. Vendor claims 503(b)(9)	$6.4	0%	0%	0%	100%	0%	100%
Class 2. Capital lease	$1.8	100%— estimated balance. Assumes Pierre accepts $1.1 million of capital leases					
Class 3. Wachovia Credit Facility	$252.7	39.1%	47.8%	76.7%	100%	33% (a)	73% - 92% (a)
Class 4. Unsecured Senior Notes	$131.2	0%	0%	0%	100%	0%	12%
Class 4. Unsecured vendors	$6.2	0%	0%	0%	100%	0%	12%
Class 4. Contract reject claims	$5.7	0%	0%	0%	100%	0%	12%
Class 4. Unsecured employee	$2.4	0%	0%	0%	100%	0%	12%
Class 4. Unsecured WARN Costs	$14.0	0%	0%	N/A	N/A	N/A	N/A
Class 5. Equity	-	0%	0%	0%	(b)	0%	0%

Source: Table 14.1 provides the supporting detail for Table 14.0.
(a) The Perella Weinberg (PWP) liquidation analysis in the Debtor's Plan (Appendix E to the Debtor's Plan) showed a 33% recovery for the Wachovia Credit Facility in the event of a 12 month liquidation. The Debtor's Plan projected a 73%–92% range of recovery for the Wachovia Credit Facility based on range of PWP's estimated Enterprise Value. The PWP estimate of Enterprise Value (Exhibit D to Debtor's Plan) was $232 million, with the low and high value from $205–$255 million.
(b) The prepetition stockholders will receive stock in the reorganized Pierre. The percentage of stock distributed to the classes is set forth in Chapter 25.

Part IV: Case Analysis of Pierre Foods

Under or Over Secured—Wachovia Credit Facility

If a loan is undersecured, then a case can be made against the payment of interest on the loan during bankruptcy. Moreover, the loan can be bifurcated into a secured and unsecured claim. Instead, Pierre requested the payment of interest on the Wachovia loan in return for a DIP loan that primed the Wachovia lien. The Creditors Committee did not contest the adequate protection or file a motion to treat the Wachovia claim as undersecured.

Excluding the $1.8 million of capital leases, the Wachovia loan represented 100% of Pierre's secured debt. The Wachovia Credit Facility had a first-lien on all of Pierre's assets, including intangibles. In addition, Wachovia had a lien on the full value of the business because it had a lien on all of the common stock of Pierre.

The independent analysis assumes the Debtor will continue to use all of the assets securing the Wachovia claim after emergence from Chapter 11. The value for the Wachovia collateral is the fair market value if the Debtor plans to continue to use the assets in the business.

The independent analysis assumes two different cases for fair market value: (1) fair market value of all tangible assets, excluding the goodwill earning power of the business and (2) fair market value of tangible and intangible assets, including goodwill. The fair market value of the business is based on the estimate of the Alternative Enterprise Value in Chapter 24.

The independent analysis shows a recovery for the Wachovia Credit Facility of : (1) 76.7% based on the fair market value of assets excluding goodwill and (2) 100% based on the fair market value including goodwill. If the estimate of Alternative Enterprise Value is accepted, then the Wachovia claim is fully secured.

The Perella Weinberg estimate of Enterprise Value resulted in a recovery for the Wachovia Credit Facility of between 73% and 92% (as presented in the Debtor's Plan).

If the Enterprise Valuation in the Debtor's Plan is accepted, the Wachovia Credit Facility is undersecured. Using the $232 million mid-point PWP estimate of Enterprise Value, then $58.9 million of the Wachovia Credit Facility claim should be classified as an unsecured claim and $173.1 million as a secured claim.

In conclusion, it is argued that Wachovia Credit Facility claim is conclusively a fully secured claim because the estimate of Alternative Enterprise Value is accepted as the correct valuation.

Chapter 14: Wachovia Under or Over Secured & Estimate of Recoveries

Table 14.1— Independent Analysis of Asset Value Recovery, Liquidation Costs, & Claim Recovery

(in $ millions)	Book Value 7/15/08	Quick %	Quick $	OLV %	OLV $	FMV %	FMV $	Enterprise Value %	Enterprise Value $
Cash	$1.6	100%	1.6	100%	1.6	100%	1.6	100%	1.6
Tax refund receivable	7.0	100%	7.0	100%	7.0	100%	7.0	100%	7.0
Accounts receivables	33.3	90%	30.0	95%	31.6	100%	33.3	100%	33.3
Less: reserve bad debt	(0.7)	100%	(0.7)	100%	(0.7)	100%	(0.7)	100%	(0.7)
Less: rebate/promotions	(5.4)	100%	(5.4)	100%	(5.4)	100%	(5.4)	100%	(5.4)
Inventory:									
Packaging	4.2	10%	0.4	50%	2.1	100%	4.2	100%	4.2
Meat, cheese, & material	11.2	70%	7.8	85%	9.5	100%	11.2	100%	11.2
Finished goods	50.1	70%	35.0	85%	42.6	100%	50.1	100%	50.1
Other inventory	.4	10%	.0	50%	0.2	100%	.4	100%	.4
Reserve for obsolescence	(2.2)	100%	(2.1)	100%	(2.1)	100%	(2.2)	100%	(2.2)
Gross value machinery/equip.	74.2								
Less: depreciation	(28.9)								
Net book value M & E	45.3	25%	11.3	40%	18.1	1.2x	54.4	1.2x	54.4
Construction in progress	1.3	25%	0.3	40%	0.5	100%	1.3	100%	1.3
Spare parts	3.1	10%	0.3	35%	1.1	100%	3.1	100%	3.1
Buildings	28.4	50%	14.2	70%	19.9	100%	28.4	100%	28.4
Real property	4.0	50%	2.0	70%	2.8	100%	4.0	100%	4.0
Deposits–Utility & other	0.7	0%	0	0%	0	100%	0.7	100%	0.7
Professional retainers	2.6	0%	0	0%	0	0%	0	0%	0
Prepaid insurance	0.9	0.75%	0.7	0.50%	0.4	100%	0.9	100%	0.9
Prepayments to vendors	7.5	100%	7.5	100%	7.5	100%	7.5	100%	7.5
Goodwill (a)	0.0	0%	0	0%	0	0%	0		335.9 (a)
Gross liquidation proceeds	193.3		109.9		136.7		199.8		535.7
Trustee fee	-		(3.2)		(4.1)		N/A		N/A
Wind-down costs	-		(2.0)		(5.7)		N/A		N/A
Capital Lease balance	(1.8)		(1.8)		(1.8)		(1.8)		(1.8)
Vendor PACA/PSA claims	(0.4)		(0.4)		(0.4)		(0.4)		(0.4)
Vendor potential lien claims	(2.6)		(2.6)		(2.6)		(2.6)		(2.6)
Vendor Butler Water utility	(1.0)		(1.0)		(1.0)		(1.0)		(1.0)
Net available	187.5		98.9		121.1		194.0		529.9
Less: Wachovia obligation	(252.7)		(252.7)		(252.7)		(252.7)		(252.7)
Wachovia Recovery %	74.1%		39.1%		47.8%		76.7%		100%
Excess (shortfall)	(65.2)		(153.8)		(131.6)		(58.7)		277.2
Administrative claims:									
Priority tax claims	(0.9)		(0.9)		(0.9)		(0.9)		(0.9)
Professional fees	-		(3.2)		(3.2)		(15.9)		(15.9)
503(b)(9) vendor claims	(6.4)		(6.4)		(6.4)		(6.4)		(6.4)
Recovery Admin. claims	0%		0%		0%		0%		100%
Excess (shortfall)	(72.5)		(164.3)		(142.1)		(81.9)		254.0
Unsecured Claims:									
WARN cost	-		(6.6)		(6.6)		N/A		N/A
Senior Notes	(131.2)		(131.2)		(131.2)		(131.2)		(131.2)
Vendor claims	(6.2)		(6.2)		(6.2)		(6.2)		(6.2)
NASCAR contract rejection	(1.1)		(1.1)		(1.1)		(1.1)		(1.1)
Interstate Warehouse contract	(4.6)		(4.6)		(4.6)		(4.6)		(4.6)
Deferred compensation	(2.4)		(2.4)		(2.4)		(2.4)		(2.4)
Employee Wage & Benefits	(1.1)		(1.1)		(1.1)		(1.1)		(1.1)
Excess funds	(219.1)		(317.5)		(295.3)		(228.5)		107.4
Recovery Unsecured	0%		0%		0%		0%		100%

Source: Pierre's July 15, 2008 Schedules of Assets/Liabilities filed with the Bankruptcy Court, Pierre's October 29, 2008 Plan, and assumptions as set forth in this Chapter.

(a) $335.9 million of goodwill based on the $514 million estimate of Alternative Enterprise Value in Chapter 24.

Part IV: Case Analysis of Pierre Foods

Assumptions Used in Collateral Valuation & Liquidation

Liquidation Period

Perella Weinberg's (PWP) liquidation analysis assumed a 12 month liquidation period. The independent analysis assumes 3 and 9 month liquidation periods.

The majority of Pierre's inventory consists of meat, cheese, bread, and other commodities that can be readily sold. The time to assemble a sandwich is short. There is no significant risk of loss in the cycle between raw material, finished goods, receivables, and cash collections. Inventory and receivable turns are relatively quick at 60 days and 30 days, respectively. Receivables and inventories account for 51% of tangible assets. In summary, a receivable and inventory liquidation period of 90 days is reasonable.

Equipment and land/building are 25% and 17% of tangible assets, respectively. It is assumed there will be minimal requirements to retain personnel to liquidate the remaining equipment and real property. Based on the type of equipment in the business, the equipment can remain idled without any significant damage to its value.

Receivables

The analysis of the receivable liquidation percentage is after Pierre's allowance for bad debts and net of promotions/rebates. For receivables, the analysis assumes quick and orderly liquidation percentages of 87.9% and 93.8%, respectively. PWP's recovery estimate for receivables was 91.8% on the same basis of comparison.

Inventory

For inventory, the analysis assumes quick and orderly liquidation percentages of 64.5% and 82.1%, respectively. This compares to the 65% liquidation percentage estimated by PWP in a 12 month liquidation period.

Equipment

Based on consultation with a leading equipment specialist in the asset-based lending industry, PWP's estimated recovery of 70% of the net book value of equipment is high. The Debtor has many specialized types of stainless steel food processing lines of equipment. The estimated liquidation value is 15% to 25% of gross equipment value (25% to 40% of the net book value).

Chapter 14: Wachovia Under or Over Secured & Estimate of Recoveries

In the case of fair market value and Enterprise Value, the independent analysis assumes the fair market value of the equipment is 1.2 times the net book value. It is assumed Pierre has depreciated the equipment more rapidly than the actual physical deterioration. The 1.2 times mark-up increases the value of the equipment by $9.1 million.

Land and Building

The analysis assumes quick and orderly liquidation percentages for real property of 50% and 70%, respectively. PWP has estimated 52% in its 12-month liquidation.

Trustee Liquidation Fee

The analysis deducts the 3% standard and customary Trustee liquidation fee for the quick and orderly liquidation.

The Trustee liquidation fee and wind-down costs are paid prior to the secured Wachovia claim, or any other claims, because the expenses are assumed to be necessary to liquidate the assets and are a benefit to the Wachovia claim and other claims.

Administrative Claim—Wind-Down Costs During Liquidation Period

In PWP's liquidation analysis, PWP estimated $28.4 million of costs to liquidate the business in 12 months, which includes $14 million for the WARN Act, $6.8 million for professional fees, and $7.6 million for other costs.

The WARN Act requires a company with over 100 employees to give employees 60 days advance notice of plant closings and mass layoffs. In Pierre's first-day Court motion for the payment of wages, Pierre estimated monthly payroll costs and payroll taxes of $3.3 million a month. Therefore, 60 days for the WARN Act notice results in $6.6 million of payroll costs to layoff the employees. The independent analysis assumes $6.6 million for WARN costs that are paid in the 3 and 9 month liquidation periods. The WARN costs are assumed to be junior in claim status to the secured Wachovia claim.

Although PWP estimates $6.8 million of professional fees, the independent analysis assumes a $5 million cap on professional fee expense during the liquidation period ($1.8 was paid for prior to bankruptcy in the form of retainer fees). Therefore, the independent analysis assumes only $3.2 million for future professional fees for both the 3 and 9 month liquidation periods. The $5 million cap on professional fees is consistent with the court approved $5 million professional fee cap in the August 13, 2008 Bankruptcy Court Order. The professional fees are projected to increase to $15.9 million in the independent

Part IV: Case Analysis of Pierre Foods

analysis for the case of valuations based on fair market value and Enterprise Value. Pierre incurred $15.9 million of professional fee expense, as disclosed in the Debtor's Operating Report for the period ending December 27, 2008.

PWP included $7.6 million for other wind-down costs, including labor ($2.8 million), utilities ($4.3 million), and other costs ($0.6). The PWP wind-down costs included a compensation program to retain key employees during the liquidation period. The independent analysis assumes that $7.6 million of wind-down costs are pro-rated over 3 months ($2 million) and 9 months ($5.6 million). The wind-down costs are paid prior to the Wachovia loan because the expenses are necessary to operate the business and liquidate the assets for the benefit of the Wachovia claim.

Warehouse/Mechanics Liens

$2.6 million of warehouse/mechanic vendor potential liens based on the Pierre's first-day Court motions to pay vendors. The claims have statutory priority over the lien of the Wachovia Credit Facility. The warehouse/mechanic lien claims are paid prior to the Wachovia Credit Facility claim.

Other Priority Liens

Claims under the Packers and Stockyards Act of 1921 or Perishable Agricultural Commodities Act of 1930 (PSA/PACA). Pierre estimated $0.4 million of PSA/PACA claims in the first-day Court motion for payment of vendor claims. The PSA/PACA imposes a statutory lien on Pierre's inventory of livestock and perishable agricultural commodities. The PACA/PSA is paid prior to the Wachovia Credit Facility Claim because it is a statutory lien priming the Wachovia lien.

Unsecured Claims

Unsecured vendor and employee claims are based on Pierre's July 15, 2008 Schedules of Assets/Liabilities, first-day Court motions, and the schedule of official claims tracked by Kurtzman Carson.

Pierre and its subsidiaries reported $22.4 million of general unsecured claims in the July 15, 2008 Schedules of Assets and Liabilities. Included in the $22.4 million is a $6.4 million claim for the letters of credit that have been reclassified to the Wachovia Credit Facility claim.

The $22.4 million of unsecured claims also includes $2.4 million of deferred compensation claims for Pierre's executive officers Norbert Woodhams and Robert Naylor—their claims are shown as a separate line item in the liquidation analysis.

Chapter 14: Wachovia Under or Over Secured & Estimate of Recoveries

Excluding the reclassification of the letters of credits and employee claims, the remaining unsecured claims are $13.6 million as follows:

- $1.0 million to Butler County Water & Sewer for an unsecured priority claim (a separate line item in the liquidation analysis);
- $6.4 million of 503(b)(9) vendor claims (a separate line item in the liquidation analysis). The $6.4 million of 503(b)9 vendor claims are for goods delivered 20 days to the date of the bankruptcy;
- $6.2 million for other general unsecured vendor claims and contract rejection (excludes the Interstate Warehouse and NASCAR contract rejection that is shown on a separate line item in the liquidation analysis).

Executory Contract Rejections

The largest contract rejection claims is a $4.6 million claim for a property lease filed by Interstate Warehouse and a $1.1 million claim on a long-term advertising contract filed by NASCAR.

$1.8 million of capital lease balances are estimated as of the date of bankruptcy. Based on the Debtor's schedule of lease rejections, it is estimated $1.1 million of capital leases are accepted. The claims for rejected capital leases are included in the $6.2 million claims for unsecured vendor claims.

In the event of a liquidation of Pierre's business, many more contracts would be rejected, resulting in a substantial increase in claims. These claims have not been estimated in the liquidation analysis in the Debtor's Plan or in the independent analysis.

Other Employee Claims

Based on the first-day Bankruptcy Court motions, Pierre estimated $1.1 million of claims for prepetition wages, salaries, reimbursable employee expenses, and other employee medical and similar benefits. The Bankruptcy Court approved $1.1 million for the foregoing expenses in the first-day Court Order.

Chapter 15

Wachovia Credit Facility Claim: Unimpaired or Impaired Treatment

"Few things are harder to put up with than the annoyance of a good example"
Mark Twain

If the Wachovia Credit Facility can be treated as an unimpaired claim, then the Wachovia Credit Facility class cannot vote or participate in a plan of reorganization. If the Wachovia Credit Facility claim is unimpaired, it will be possible for greater value to be allocated to the junior classes, assuming sufficient Enterprise Value and a feasible plan.

Section 1124 of the Bankruptcy Code defines a claim as unimpaired if it leaves unaltered the legal, equitable, and contractual rights of the creditor.

Section 1124 also provides that a claim can be classified as unimpaired if the plan does not otherwise alter the legal, equitable or contractual rights of the creditor even if there is a provision in a prepetition agreement that allows the creditor to accelerate the claim because of an the event of default. In this case, the reorganization plan must:

- Cure other defaults;
- Reinstate the maturity date of the claim prior to the default;
- Compensate the creditor for damages from any reasonable reliance on the covenants that caused the default;
- With respect to any other non-monetary default, the debtor is required to compensate the creditor for any actual money loss incurred by the creditor.

Chapter 15: Wachovia Credit Facility: Unimpaired or Impaired

The Senate footnotes to Section 1124 of Chapter 11 of U.S.C Title 11 comment as follows:

> "a claim or interest is unimpaired by curing the effect of a default and reinstating the original terms of an obligation when maturity was brought on or accelerated by the default. The intervention of bankruptcy and the defaults represent a temporary crisis which the plan of reorganization is intended to clear away. The holder of a claim or interest who under the plan is restored to his original position, when others receive less or get nothing at all, is fortunate indeed and has no cause to complain. Curing of the default and the assumption of the debt in accordance with its terms is an important reorganization technique for dealing with a particular class of claims, especially secured claims."

The Wachovia Revolver had a maturity of June 30, 2009. A bankruptcy judge could determine that a plan is not feasible if the maturity date of a bank revolving line of credit has a maturity date only six months after the emergence from Chapter 11.

The Wachovia Term had a balloon of $141.4 million due June 30, 2010. If the maturity date of the Term Loan is reinstated, the loan comes due within 18 months after Pierre exits bankruptcy. Refinance risk exists in June 2010.

The Wachovia Credit Facility's lien position is an issue with respect to the treatment of the Wachovia claim as an unimpaired claim. The Wachovia loan was secured by a first-lien on all of Pierre's assets. The Bankruptcy Court approved a $35 million DIP loan that gave the DIP Lender (Oaktree Capital) a priming lien over the Wachovia lien. The Wachovia debt is therefore impaired by the priming lien for the balance on the DIP Revolver and the exposure for the letters of credits issued under the DIP Revolver.

If commercial banks controlled 75% of the dollar amount of the secured Wachovia claims, a reorganization plan reinstating the Wachovia claim as 100% debt would be more likely to receive approval from the Wachovia class. In fact, if banks controlled, it would be more likely that 75% of the Wachovia holders would be agreeable to an extension of the loan maturity and in renegotiating the affirmative and negative covenants in the loan agreement. By charter, commercial banks are generally required to invest in interest bearing securities and prefer interest paying first-lien debt.

On the other hand, if a distressed opportunistic investor controlled 92% of the Wachovia class and was angling for greater value and stock ownership, the

Part IV: Case Analysis of Pierre Foods

distress investor would be expected argue for the treatment of the Wachovia claim as an impaired claim.

Oaktree Capital controlled 92% of the Wachovia class. Oaktree Capital could deliver the votes to approve any feasible plan that offered a recovery greater than the amount a holder was entitled to receive in a liquidation of the business.

Oaktree Capital could also benefit from a lower estimate of Enterprise Value for Pierre because greater debt and equity could be allocated to an impaired Wachovia class of claims.

During the presentation of the Debtor's Reorganization Plan in the next Chapter, the reader should keep in mind that immediately prior to Pierre's emergence from bankruptcy:

- The DIP loan balance was zero and the obligation for letters of credits issued under the DIP Facility was $9.1 million. $2.5 million of the letters of credits were related to professional fees that would be paid off in cash at emergence from bankruptcy;
- Pierre had $14.2 million of cash balances (Pierre collected a $7 million tax refund during bankruptcy);
- A motion should have been filed by the Debtor or Creditors Committee to disgorge preference payments of $15.7 million from vendors and $9.3 million from the Wachovia Credit Facility ($2.9 million for payments and $6.4 million for exposure reduction in letters of credit).

This leads to the next Chapter on the Debtor's Plan as sponsored by Oaktree Capital.

Chapter 16

- **Rush to Exit Chapter 11**
- **Debtor's Plan of Reorganization**

"If a man is offered a fact which goes against his instincts, he will scrutinize it closely, and unless the evidence is overwhelming, he will refuse to believe it. If, on the other hand, he is offered something which affords a reason for acting in accordance to his instincts, he will accept it even on the slightest evidence."
Bertrand Russell

Pierre, Oaktree Capital, and the Wachovia debt holders worked on a restructuring plan for bankruptcy through June 2008. Certain Wachovia holders were against linking Oaktree Capital's DIP loan to Oaktree Capital's restructuring plan. There was also some concern over an Enterprise Value fight by the Senior Note holders (Bankr. D. Del, Ct transcript 12/10/08). The negotiations fell apart and Pierre filed bankruptcy on July 15, 2008.

In the December 10, 2008 Bankruptcy Court confirmation hearing for the Debtor's Plan, John Henes, the attorney with Kirkland & Ellis who represented Pierre, commented (Bankr. D. Del, Ct. transcript):

> Pierre's management felt very fortunate to have a company such as Oaktree Capital buy Pierre's debt, make a DIP financing commitment, and negotiate with the Creditors Committee for a plan to de-lever the balance sheet, allowing Pierre to emerge from Chapter 11 in a stronger position and able to thrive in the future.

Part IV: Case Analysis of Pierre Foods

A Rush to Exit Bankruptcy

The Creditors Committee formed on July 28, 2008 and hired Imperial Capital as its financial advisor two days later. In the December 10, 2008 confirmation hearing for the Debtor's Plan, Eric Carson, managing Director of Imperial Capital, testified (Bankr. D. Del, Ct. transcript), that Oaktree Capital had provided a term sheet proposal to the Creditors Committee in late August 2008. The proposal offered a small recovery to the unsecured creditors in the form of Pierre's stock. Oaktree Capital gave the Creditors Committee one week to respond to the offer. Abid Qureshi, an attorney with Akin Gump who represented the Creditors Committee, characterized the Oaktree Capital offer in Court (Bankr. D. Del, Ct. transcript, 12/10/08) on behalf of Mr. Carson, as: "a take-it-or-leave-it offer, the alternative to which was a cramdown."

Creditors Committee Reaches Plan Agreement in One Month

The Creditors Committee met with Oaktree Capital in the middle of September to discuss the Oaktree Capital term sheet offer (Bankr. D. Del, Ct. transcript, Dec. 10, 2008). The parties negotiated for the evening and part of the following day. Phone negotiations continued between the parties throughout September 2008. The Creditors Committee, with four members holding Senior Notes and three members holding vendor claims, desired more than a nominal recovery in Pierre's stock. In addition, the Creditors Committee was concerned with the subordination provision in the Senior Notes. Under the Senior Note Indenture, the Wachovia debt had to receive payment in full prior to any distribution to the Senior Notes.

Oaktree Capital and the Creditors Committee reached an agreement for a plan that paid 12 cents on the dollar in cash to all of the unsecured creditors. The plan would require any secured Wachovia holder, who accepted a settlement under the plan, to release their right to require the Senior Note holders to pay their distribution to the Wachovia class.

On September 29, 2008, Pierre filed its first plan of reorganization in Bankruptcy Court. The Debtor and the Creditors Committee had agreed on a plan for the unsecured creditors, approximately one month after the formation of Creditors Committee.

Compensation Structure for Financial Consultants Gives Incentive for Quick Plan

The financial advisors' compensation was structured for faster case resolution. Imperial Capital received a payment of $1 million. The fee arrangement was $100,000 a month and a $500,000 success fee. Pierre's

Chapter 16: Rush to Exit Chapter 11 and Debtor's Plan

Investment Banker, Perella Weinberg Partners, received a $300,000 initial fee, a $150,000 monthly fee, and $2,000,000 restructuring fee due at the end of the case. The fees to Imperial Capital and Perella Weinberg were approximately 20% of the estimated $18 million (12%) cash payout to the unsecured creditors.

Make-up of the Creditors Committee Favors Vendors Over Senior Note Holders

The unsecured Creditors Committee was represented by three vendors and four Senior Note holders. The Senior Notes held 86% of unsecured claims.

The vendors significantly improved their position prior to bankruptcy and during bankruptcy. Vendor payables were $22.9 million on March 1, 2008 and $15 million when Pierre filed bankruptcy. Prepaid amounts to vendors were zero on March 1, 2008 and $7.5 million when Pierre filed bankruptcy. In first-day Bankruptcy Court Order, $9 million was approved for payment to critical vendor prepetition claims.

The median gross profit margin for an exchange traded U.S. firm is 31%. Pierre's inventory turnover was 5.4 times a year. A vendor can quickly recover a prepetition loss from future sales to a reorganized debtor.

The vendors benefited from an improvement in their position prior to bankruptcy, during bankruptcy, and could benefit from future sales to a financially sound Pierre.

Under a vendor's paradigm, it would be rational for a vendor to support a plan by Pierre to emerge quickly from bankruptcy with a conservative capital structure.

The Creditors Committee formed at the end of August 2008 and agreed to recovery in the Debtor's first plan filed on September 29, 2008. Although the debtor's final Plan was filed on October 29, 2008, there was no change in recovery to the unsecured creditors between the September and October final Plan.

The unsecured Senior Notes who were subordinated to the Wachovia claim, were permitted to retain a 12% cash recovery under the Plan without paying the amounts over to the Wachovia claim as required by the subordination.

It is assumed that in one month the Creditors Committee: (1) evaluated Pierre's Enterprise Value, (2) compared the Debtor's Plan to other possible feasible plans for the benefit of the unsecured class, and (3) negotiated a plan with Oaktree Capital and Pierre.

Part IV: Case Analysis of Pierre Foods

Concern over Enterprise Value Fight

Josh Scherer, Investment Banker for Perella Weinberg, testified in the December 10, 2008 confirmation hearing for the Debtor's Plan (Bankr. D. Del, Ct. Transcript). Mr. Scherer was involved in the estimate of Pierre's Enterprise Value. Mr. Scherer testified that Pierre Foods never pushed Perella Weinberg to come up with a lower or higher Enterprise Valuation. He also acknowledged that Oaktree Capital was involved in the valuation process, nevertheless, in his opinion, Oaktree Capital did not control the valuation process.

Mr. Scherer testified the Senior Note holders were of the opinion that Pierre's Enterprise Value should be significantly higher than Perella Weinberg's estimate. According to Mr. Scherer, Pierre's management had assured its customers and vendors the bankruptcy would be quick and Pierre's management was worried that a protracted public fight over Enterprise Value might result in the loss of some significant customers and vendor support.

Risk of Loss of Customer and Vendor Support

Pierre's liquidity may have been an issue at the date of bankruptcy, but by the end of November 2008 Pierre had $14 million of cash and a zero balance on the DIP Revolver. The Bankruptcy Court had previously approved cash payments to the prepetition claims for critical vendors to keep shipping product. Moreover, vendor sales to Pierre during bankruptcy were protected as administrative claims.

Pierre's cash flow was not an issue in bankruptcy. In the five months of bankruptcy, Pierre had $18.2 million of EBITDA. Pierre's only cash interest expense during the five-month bankruptcy was $9 million for the Wachovia loan. Pierre's operations were building cash in bankruptcy, during the worst economic recession since the Great Depression.

Pierre's customer warranty and products claims were not an issue in bankruptcy. A consumer was not likely to delay buying a sandwich for immediate consumption because of Pierre's financial condition.

To mitigate vendor and customer concerns, Pierre's management could have provided reports to customers and vendors during bankruptcy on the Company's cash liquidity, positive cash flow, and growing cash balances. The risk of customers not receiving product from Pierre was prior to the bankruptcy filing.

Chapter 16: Rush to Exit Chapter 11 and Debtor's Plan

DIP Trigger for Plan Submittal

Was Pierre's management in a rush to file a plan because Oaktree Capital had a default trigger in the DIP loan if a reorganization plan was not filed by the end of September 2008?

Pierre reported the following DIP Credit Facility exposure and cash balances during bankruptcy:

Monthly Report ($ millions)	Cash	DIP Loan	Reserve Letters Credits
September 27, 2008	$ 4.4	$10.4	$8.7
November 1, 2008	$ 8.3	$ 6.5	$9.1
November 29, 2008	$14.2	$ 0.0	$9.1

If Oaktree Capital called the DIP loan at the end of September for the failure of Pierre to submit a Plan, then according to the liquidation analysis in the Debtor's Plan, Oaktree Capital would have recovered 35% of its 92% investment in the Wachovia loan. Based on the trading prices of Pierre's debt prior to bankruptcy, it is estimated that Oaktree Capital paid 67% to 83% of the par for the Wachovia debt. Given Pierre's liquidity and financial performance in bankruptcy, it was unlikely that Oaktree Capital would call the DIP loan and take a loss.

Pierre had until November 15, 2008 to submit a Plan under the Bankruptcy Code. Moreover, Bankruptcy Courts will typically grant a debtor reasonable extensions of time for plan submittal.

By November 29, 2008, Pierre had $14.2 million in cash and a $9.1 million obligation under the DIP loan for letters of credits. Pierre's $193 million of tangible assets would have adequately covered a $9.1 million DIP loan with super-priority status and a priming lien.

Did Oaktree Capital's Proposed Cash Investment Rush a Plan?

Oaktree Capital was not proposing or committing to any additional cash injection into Pierre's capital structure in the Debtor's Plan.

Incentives for Pierre's Management and the Debtor Plan

Although Pierre's management had a fiduciary responsibility to its shareholders, management did not own a significant amount of prepetition stock in Pierre. The following hypothesis is offered for Pierre's speedy Plan: in addition to the DIP default deadline for submitting a Plan, Pierre's management was operating on the belief, assumption, or hope that Oaktree Capital would be the new ownership group because of Oaktree Capital's significant debt ownership and reputation as a large, successful distressed investor who had

Part IV: Case Analysis of Pierre Foods

access to capital and the public markets. Under the circumstances, Pierre's management most likely believed the prepetition shareholders would receive a zero recovery; Oaktree Capital would be the new boss. The best Plan for management and employees would be a remerged Pierre with as little debt in the capital structure as possible.

Are the Financial Advisors Responsible for the Debtor's Plan?

In the December 10, 2008 confirmation hearing for the Debtor's Plan, Cynthia Hughes, Pierre's Chief Financial Officer, testified (Bankr. D. Del, Ct. transcript) that she had relied on the financial experts and advisors hired by Pierre. Ms. Hughes was asked if Pierre's financial advisors had communicated to her that Oaktree Capital's goal was to make an equity play for Pierre to take over ownership. Mr. Henes, the attorney representing Pierre, objected to the question to the extent the asked her to disclose any legal advice she may have received from her advisors (Bankr. D. Del, Ct. Transcript 12/10/08).

In a Chapter 11 bankruptcy, the Bankruptcy Code gives Pierre's management the exclusive right to submit and recommend a plan of reorganization in the first 120 days and the courts typically grant reasonable extensions beyond 120 days. Pierre's financial advisors were not the parties with the exclusive right to submit and recommend a plan.

Oaktree Capital: Hope for a Bigger and Brighter Future for Pierre

A Registration Rights Agreement and Management Services Agreement between Oaktree Capital and Pierre offered the hope of bigger plans for the future of the Pierre.

The Registration Rights Agreement gave Oaktree Capital the right to require Pierre's management to file for an initial public offering of stock. Moreover, Pierre agreed to pay Oaktree Capital a $1.5 million annual management fee in connection with a Management Services Agreement. Under the Management Services Agreement, Pierre was also required to pay a $4.5 million fee to Oaktree Capital should Pierre consummate an initial public stock offering or sell one or more of the Pierre companies (through merger or otherwise), or sell all or substantially all of Pierre's assets.

The payment of the management fees to Oaktree Capital under a Management Services Agreement was disclosed in the October 29, 2008 Plan Disclosure Statement as follows: "the Shareholders Agreement between the Debtor and Oaktree Capital provides for the payment to Oaktree Capital of customary management fees for sponsored deals."

Chapter 16: Rush to Exit Chapter 11 and Debtor's Plan

In the December 10, 2008 confirmation hearing on the Plan, Cynthia Hughes, Chief Financial Officer of Pierre, testified (Bankr. D. Del, Ct. transcript) that she was not aware of the Management Services Agreement. The Chief Financial Officer of Pierre was not aware of an agreement that would pay Oaktree Capital an annual management services fee of $1.5 million and an initial public offering success fee of $4.5 million.

The Management Services Agreement was filed with the Bankruptcy Court on December 8, 2008 in the Second Amended Plan for Technical Modifications—three days after the final date for voting on the Debtor's Plan.

The hope that Oaktree Capital might support a future public offering for Pierre may have been an incentive for Pierre's management to move fast on a plan sponsored by Oaktree Capital. Oaktree Capital was bringing human capital to the table, its reputation and experience as a possible future equity sponsor for a public offering.

There may have been more incentive for Pierre's management to agree to a speedy Plan. The Debtor's Plan disclosed a Management and Director Incentive and Severance Program. A copy of the compensation program was not included in the Debtor's Plan or Plan Supplements. Rabobank received a copy of the compensation plan several days prior to the December 10, 2008 confirmation hearing. The compensation plan was not filed as a document with the Bankruptcy Court. If the management compensation program included a provision to compensate management with stock, then a future public offering of Pierre's stock could provide management with an opportunity to monetize the stock award.

The Debtor's Plan

The Debtor filed its first Plan in Bankruptcy Court on September 29, 2008. The Debtor's Plan paid unsecured creditors, including the $125 million Senior Notes, 12 cents on the dollar in cash. The plan proposed the following recovery for the prepetition secured Wachovia claim:

- A $96 million Note, maturing in 6 years. No principal amortization. LIBOR plus 2.50% floating interest rate. Secured by a second-lien on all assets behind a $35 million first-lien exit credit facility;
- A $50 million Note, maturing in eight years. 14% interest rate. Interest payable in cash or payment-in-kind (PIK Note). Secured by a third-lien on all assets;
- 100% of the stock in the reorganized Pierre.

Part IV: Case Analysis of Pierre Foods

Subsequent to the September 29 Plan, the Debtor submitted its First Amended Plan on October 28, 2008 and its Second Amended Plan on October 29, 2008 (the final Debtor's Plan).

The Debtor did not provide specific dollar estimates for all of the claims against Pierre. The claims have been estimated based on Pierre's July 15, 2008 Schedules of Assets/Liabilities, first-day Court motions, and the schedule of official claims register tracked by Kurtzman Carson. Recoveries for the estimated claims based on the Debtor's final Plan are in Table 16.0 and are summarized below:

- DIP Facility to be paid in full (the balance was zero at November 29, 2008). Although $9.1 million of letters of credits were outstanding under the DIP Facility, $2.5 million secured professional fees that would be paid in cash at emergence; therefore only $6.6 million of letters of credits were required to be replaced;
- $15.9 million of professional fees to be paid in full;
- $0.4 million PACA/PSA priority vendor claims to be paid in full. The payment was authorized in the first-day Court orders;
- $2.6 million to be paid in full for vendor claims that could create warehouse/materialmens' priming liens. The payment was authorized in the first-day Court orders;
- $1.0 million to be paid in full for Butler County water as an unsecured priority claim;
- $6.4 million for 503(b)(9) vendor claims. The Court authorized the payment of up to $6.4 million for critical vendor claims in first-day Orders;
- 12% cash payment for the remaining $6.2 million of unsecured vendor claims and other miscellaneous claims for contract rejection;
- 12% cash payment for the $4.6 million real property contract unsecured claim by Interstate Warehouse;
- 12% cash payment for the $1.1 million advertising contract rejection unsecured claim by NASCAR;
- $1.0 million of estimated accepted capital leases treated as unimpaired;
- $1.9 million for prepetition employee wages and other related employee claims. Pierre was authorized to pay up to $1.9 million of these claims in a fist day Bankruptcy Court Order;

Chapter 16: Rush to Exit Chapter 11 and Debtor's Plan

- 12% cash payment assumed for $2.4 million unsecured deferred compensation claim for Pierre's President and former Vice-President Sales;
- 12% cash payment for the $131.6 million unsecured Senior Note claim (claim includes $6.6 million prepetition interest);
- 0% recovery for prepetition stockholders;
- The Debtor's Plan estimated a 73%–92% recovery for the Wachovia claim. The author estimates a 70%–82% recovery for the Wachovia claim as follows:
  - Cash payment from zero to 12% ($30 million). Josh Scherer, investment banker with PWP, testified in Bankruptcy Court on December 12, 2008 (Bankr. D. Del, Ct. transcript) that the cash payment would be $15–$25 million. Karen Boyer, Executive Director of Special Assets at Rabobank, testified in Bankruptcy Court on December 10, 2008 (Bankr. D. Del, Ct. transcript) that she had a phone conversation on December 2, 2008 with PWP. PWP advised her the cash payment would be $23 million (9.3% of the claim), but he cautioned the final payout could differ;
  - 35% recovery in an $85 million second-lien, subordinated Note, with an eight-year maturity. Interest rate 14%. Interest payable in cash or PIK, at the option of the Pierre;
  - 35% recovery in stock with an estimated value of $85 million. The Wachovia claim receives 100% of Pierre's stock in the form of 8% cumulative Preferred Stock with a par value of $0.01 (the $85 million value for stock is the difference between Perella Weinberg's mid-point Enterprise Value of $232 million and the projected exit debt of $147 million).

The Debtor's Plan was very vague on the cash payout for the Wachovia claim, with the cash payout between $0–$30 million (12%). It is difficult to reconcile the Debtor's Plan estimated recovery of 73% to 92% for the Wachovia claim. The Debtor's Plan did not provide a detailed reconciliation of the recovery. It is not clear if any discount was provided for the type of securities received in exchange for the first-lien interest paying Wachovia Credit Facility.

The prepetition Wachovia debt had mandatory cash interest payments and also had a first-lien on all assets. The replacement securites included Preferred Stock and a second-lien PIK Note that was subordinated to a $95 million Exit Credit Facility.

Part IV: Case Analysis of Pierre Foods

An insitution that has a charter to hold first-lien, interest-paying debt typically prefers to receive cash and/or debt securiites with terms similar to the prepetition debt.

A subordinated second-lien loan does not have the same value as the first lien-loan. The Debtor's Plan did not discuss if the value allocated to the Preferred Stock provided for any discount for selling the stock or for the other constraints as discussed in sections below.

Dilution of Preferred Stock Under Debtor Plan

The issuance of 100% of the Preferred Stock to the prepetition Wachovia Credit Facility claim was subject to dilution by any equity to be issued in connection the new Management and Director Incentive and Severance program. A copy of the agreement was provided to Rabobank several days before the Plan confirmation hearing but the agreement was not filed as a document with the Bankruptcy Court.

Constraints on Selling Preferred Stock Under Debtor Plan

All of the claims receiving Preferred Stock, except for Oaktree Capital, had to wait 18 months to sell their stock, unless they sold their stock to Oaktree Capital.

If Oaktree Capital received an offer for the purchase of Pierre's stock and agreed to sell, Oaktree Capital was obligated to give Pierre's other Preferred Stockholders the right to sell their shares to the offering party at the same price. If the purchaser offered fewer shares than the sellers were offering to buy, Oaktree Capital and the other Preferred Stockholders were to pro-rate the number of shares based on their respective ownership percentages. The forgoing provision did not apply for any sales of shares by Oaktree Capital up 10% of the Preferred Stock held by Oaktree Capital.

Prior to any Pierre Preferred Stockholder accepting an offer to sell their shares, Oaktree Capital had the right of first refusal—the right to buy the shares first from the selling Preferred Stockholder at the same selling price.

Requirement to Sell Preferred Stock Under the Debtor Plan

If Oaktree Capital proposed a sale of the majority of Pierre's Preferred Stock, then Oaktree Capital had the option to require Pierre's other Preferred Stockholders to sell at the same price.

Chapter 16: Rush to Exit Chapter 11 and Debtor's Plan

Table Summarizing Debtor's Plan

Table 16.0 summarizes the final Debtor's Plan.

Table 16.0—Summary of Debtor's Reorganization Plan [a]					
Class	Description	Amount ($ millions)	Treatment	Projected Recovery	Vote
	Administrative	$ 6.8 Professional fees $ 5.4 Vendors post petition $12.2 Total estimated Admin. fees	Pay 100% in cash	100%	No
	DIP Loan	$0 at 11/29/08 $9.1 letters of credit ($2.5 of letter credit for professional fees)	Pay in full ($0 bal. on 11/28/08) Replace $6.6 letters of credits	100%	No
	IRS claim	$0.9 (estimate)	Pay over 5 yrs. (unimpaired)	100%	No
1	Other priority	$0.4 vendor PACA/PSA $2.6 vendor warehouse/materialmen $6.4 vendor 503(b)(9) claims $1.0 vendor Butler County water $10.4 Total priority	Pay 100% in cash Note: the first-day orders authorized the immediate payout of these priority claims	100%	No
2	Other secured	$1.8 capital leases. Assume $1.1 accepted	Pay in cash, accept, or or return equip. (unimpaired)	100%	No
3	Wachovia	$224.0 - Term Loan $ 14.0 - Revolver $ 6.4 - Letters of Credit $ 3.6 - Swap termination fee $ 4.3 - Interest $ 0.6 - Legal & fees $252.9 Subtotal	- $0 to $30 in cash; - 100% of Pierre's stock; - $85 PIK Note (8 yrs.); 14% interest rate; 2nd lien on assets, No required amortization; 50% excess cash flow to loan subordinate to $95 Exit Loan	73 – 92% Debtor Plan Estimate	Yes
4	Unsecured Sr. Note Unsecured-Other (a)	$131.2 (includes $6.2 interest) $ 6.2 other vendor claims $ 1.3 Woodhams deferred comp. $ 1.1 Naylor severance & comp. $ 1.9 Employee wages & other $ 4.6 Interstate Whse contract claim $ 1.1 NASCAR contract claim $ 147.4 Total Estimated Unsecured	$17.5 cash payout =12% of $145.5 (excludes $1.9 employee wages as the first-day order authorized the payment of $1.9 wages)	12%	Yes
5	Equity	$0	(Impaired). Deemed to reject		No
6	Inter-company	No money paid out	(Impaired). Deemed to accept		No

Source: Amounts have been estimated by the author based on the Debtor's Plan, Kurtzman Carson claims register, and other case information.

Chapter 17

Exit Financing for Debtor's Plan

"A bank is a place that will lend you money if you can prove you don't need it."
Bob Hope

$95 million First-Lien Exit Credit Facility

The Exit Credit Facility proposed in the Debtor's Plan replaced the DIP Financing Facility and consisted of a $95 million first-lien Exit Credit Facility with a term of four years. The Debtor's Plan projected that Pierre would draw $55–$60 million at emergence from Chapter 11. The Exit Credit Facility was provided by Wells Fargo Foothill and Bank of America. The $95 million Exit Credit Facility consisted of a Revolver and Term Loan as follows:

- **Revolver**: $75 million Exit Revolver, with an advance rate equal to 85% of the eligible receivables plus the lower of: (a) $42.5 million, (b) 65% of the book value of eligible inventory, or (c) 85% of the orderly liquidation value of eligible inventory;
- **Term Loan**: The maximum Term Loan could not exceed the lower of: (1) $20 million and (2) 85% of the orderly liquidation value of equipment plus 60% of the fair market value of real property.
  The Term Loan repayment began in February 2009. The Term Loan matured in four years and required quarterly principal payments that effectively amortized the loan over seven years.

Chapter 17: Exit Financing for Debtor's Plan

The interest rate on the Exit Credit Facility was between LIBOR plus 3.5% and 4.0% for the Revolver and LIBOR plus 4.5% to 5.0% for the Term Loan. The rate depended on Pierre's senior debt to EBITDA ratio. The Exit Facility term sheet filed with the Debtor's Plan did not reference an interest rate floor. The Debtor's Plan projections assumed a LIBOR rate floor of 3.5%.

The Exit Credit Facility had customary financial covenants. The Exit Credit Facility required Pierre to make the following payments on the Exit Loan:
- 50% of Pierre's annual excess cash flow;
- 50% of cash proceeds from stock sales.

$85 million, 14% Exit PIK Note (Second-Lien and Subordinate)

Part of the settlement for the Wachovia Credit Facility claim included an $85 million Note. The Note was secured by a second-lien on all assets, subordinate in collateral and payments to the first-lien Exit Facility. The Note matured in December 2016 and was non-amortizing. The interest rate was fixed at 14%. Pierre had the option to pay the interest in cash or to add the interest to the principal balance (PIK Note). The Note could be prepaid without a penalty. Oaktree Capital was the administrative agent under the Note.

The $85 million Note required the following additional payments:
- If Pierre sold additional stock for cash consideration, Pierre was required to apply 50% of the net proceeds to the PIK Note. The right to receive the payment was subordinate to the first-lien Exit Credit Facility.
- Beginning with fiscal year-end February 2010, Pierre was required to pay 50% of annual excess cash flow the Note balance. The right to receive the payment was subordinate to the first-lien Exit Credit Facility.

The $85 million PIK Note had the following restrictive covenants:
- New debt to be issued by Pierre was limited to Permitted Debt, which included: (1) debt for the purchase assets, not to exceed $30 million during the eight-year term of the Note, (2) first-lien debt not to exceed $105 million, including the first-lien $95 million Exit Facility, (3) debt balances that were refinanced, and (4) other debt not to exceed $7.5 million;
- Limitations on Pierre granting liens on its assets to other parties. Permitted Liens included liens for leases and for liens on Permitted Debt (defined above);
- Prohibited Pierre from merging without the consent of the required holders of the $85 million PIK Note;

Part IV: Case Analysis of Pierre Foods

- Limitations on asset disposals;
- Change of control—a default if Permitted Holders of Pierre's stock failed to own and control more than 50% of the stock. The Permitted Holders were Oaktree Capital and other parties receiving stock in the Debtor's Plan;
- Restrictions on distributions and dividends to holders of Pierre's stock.

Amendments or waivers to the $85 million Note Credit Agreement required the consent of more than 50% of the holders, except that 100% consent was required for:

- Changes in loan amounts;
- Changes in the interest rate;
- Postponement of payments;
- For a release of substantially all of the collateral

Oaktree Capital or Pierre had the option to replace any lender who declined to agree to an amendment or waiver for the $85 million Note.

Chapter 18

Sources & Uses of Cash in Debtor's Plan

"There is nothing wrong with a woman welcoming all men's advances as long as they are in cash." Zsa Zsa Gabor

The Debtor's Plan did not include a sources and uses of funds for Pierre's emergence from Chapter 11. Based on the information in the case, an estimate of the sources and uses of funds has been developed in Table 18 for purposes of analysis.

Karen Boyer, Executive Director of Special Assets for Rabobank, testified in the December 10, 2008 Plan confirmation hearing (Bankr. D. Del, Ct. transcript) that the Debtor's Plan was vague on the payout for the secured Wachovia Credit Facility.

The Debtor's Plan estimated a $0–$30 million cash payout to the Wachovia Credit Facility claim. Ms. Boyer contacted Perella Weinberg (PWP) in early December to request a sources and uses of funds. PWP advised Ms. Boyer that PWP would prefer to discuss the sources and uses of funds in a phone conversation (Bankr. D. Del, Ct, 12/10/08). In the phone conversation, PWP advised Rabobank that estimated cash distribution to the Wachovia claim was $25 million (9.3% of the claim), although the final amount was subject to change.

Although the final Plan payout percentage was never disclosed by the Debtor in Court filings, it is conjectured that the cash payout to the Wachovia claim was 12% in order to bring the cash payout on par with the 12% cash payout for the unsecured claims.

Table 18.0 estimates the sources and uses of funds. The analysis assumes that Pierre's uses its $14.4 million cash as of November 29, 2008 to fund claim payouts. Table 18.0 projects a post closing first-lien Revolver balance of $22.7 million.

Pierre filed a December 27 post emergence balance sheet, reporting cash of $4.4 million and a Revolver balance of $11.7 million—the Revolver balance was $7.3 million net of cash.

Part IV: Case Analysis of Pierre Foods

The $15.4 million variance between the Revolver balance of $7.3 million (net of cash) on the December 27 balance sheet and the $22.7 million Revolver balance estimated in the sources and uses of funds is centered on:

- A $4.0 million decrease in inventories & receivables from November 29 to December 27, and
- $11.4 million of claims not paid out as of the December 27.

The $11.4 million of remaining unpaid claims are estimated to consist of:

- $8 million of professional fees ($7.9 million of the $15.9 million professional fees were paid out prior to December 27), and
- $3.4 million of cash payments on other remaining claims.

Table 18.0—Estimated Sources & Uses of Funds at Bankruptcy Exit Based on Debtor Plan ($ millions)

	Uses of Cash (estimate)
	Secured claims with administrative priority:
$0	DIP Revolver ($0 balance immediately prior to exit from bankruptcy)
	Prepetition secured claims:
$29.8	Wachovia Credit Facility (payout estimated = 12% of $248 claim)
	Administrative claims:
$11.1	Professional fees ($15.9 less $3.0 paid prior to 11/27/08 less $1.8 retainer)
$ 3.3	Interest expense accrued on DIP & Wachovia Credit Facility
$ 5.4	Accounts payable balance incurred post petition (100% payout)
	Other prepetition unsecured:
$15.7	9.75% Senior Note (payout 12% of $131.1 million)
$ 1.7 [a]	Other unsecured claims of $14.6 million (12% of $14.6 million)
$67.0	Uses of cash
	Source of Cash (estimate)
$14.2	Reduction in cash (assume Debtor uses all of its $14.2 million cash as of 11/29/08)
$ 7.2	Post 11 payable vendor credit granted ($7.2 per post exit balance sheet dated 12/27/08)
$ 2.9	Accruals (change from 11/27/08 to 12/27/08, excluding professional fees)
$20.0	First-lien Exit Term Loan draw
$22.7	First-lien Exit Revolver draw (force figure to balance the sources & uses of cash)
$67.0	Sources of funds

Source: Estimate developed by author based on case information. The Debtor did not file a sources and uses of funds statement in connection with the case.

(a) $ 6.2 unsecured vendor claims (excludes vendor claims payments authorized in first-day orders).
    $ 2.4 unsecured Norbert Woodhams and Robert Naylor deferred compensation claim.
    <u>$ 5.7</u> assumed contract claims for NASCAR and Interstate Warehouse.
    $14.3 times 12% = $1.7 million cash payout

Liquidity Assuming Disgorgement of Preference Payments, Increase in Payables, Equipment Sale, and Zero Claim Payout

Assume the following:

Chapter 18: Sources & Uses of Cash in Debtor's Plan

- Operations are cash flow breakeven in the next 12 months;
- Pierre maintains its December 27, 2008 inventory and receivable level;
- Reserve for letters of credit decreases to $6.6 million because the letters of credit for professional fees are released after the payment of professional fees;
- Pierre completes a sale of equipment for $1.1 million—on November 10, 2008 Pierre accepted an offer for $1.2 million for the sale of 426 items of equipment in the Cedartown plant that Pierre closed in February 2008. Based on a review of the offer from the Gordon Group, it appeared the transaction could close in the first quarter of 2009.
- In accordance with Debtor's Plan projections, vendor payables increase to $17 million, providing an additional $10 million of cash working capital;
- The estate recovers $9.0 million (60%) of the $15.2 million preference payments to vendors (as estimated in Chapter 13 of this book);
- The estate recovers $2.9 million for preference payments to the Wachovia Credit Facility (as estimated in Chapter 13 of this book).

Given the above assumptions, Table 18.1 shows the balance is $19.7 million on the Exit Facility (Revolver & Term Loan combined)

Table 18.1—Balance on Debtor's Plan Exit Facility after Disgorgement & Increase in Vendor Float
(in $ millions)

	Uses of Cash (estimate)
42.7	Previously projected Exit Term Loan and Revolver
-1.1	Proceeds from pending sale of equipment
-10.0	Increase in vendor trade payables
-9.0	Disgorgement of prepaid vendor amounts
-2.9	Disgorgement of amounts to Wachovia Credit Facility
19.7	Balance on Exit Facility

Source: projections and estimates by author.

Suppose further that the Debtor Plan does not pay out a 12% cash distribution to the Wachovia claim and to unsecured claims. Without the 12% cash payouts, Table 18.2 shows Pierre would have a zero balance on the Exit Credit Facility and $20.9 million of cash balances. The $20.9 million cash balance is after the Debtor's cash payout of $15.9 million for professional fees and after $6.6 million of cash is reserved for letters of credits.

Part IV: Case Analysis of Pierre Foods

Table 18.2—Balance on Debtor's Plan Exit Facility Without 12% Cash Payouts and after Disgorgement and Increase in Vendor Float

($ millions)	Uses of Cash (estimate)
19.7	Balance on Exit Facility
-29.8	Claw-back of cash payout to Wachovia Credit Facility
-17.4	Claw-back of the 12% cash payout to unsecured claims
27.5	Cash Balance
-6.6	Cash reserve to establish required letters of credits
20.9	Net cash balance

Source: projections and estimates by author.

The Wachovia claim also benefited from the DIP Lender replacing the $6.4 million of letters of credits issued under the Wachovia Credit Facility. Therefore, an Exit Credit Facility with a priming lien of up to $6.4 million would not cause impairment to the Wachovia Credit Facility relative to the position of the Wachovia claim at the date of bankruptcy.

The next two Chapters will evaluate the feasibility of the Debtor's Plan in terms of liquidity, capital structure, and cash flows.

Chapter 19

Feasibility of Debtor's Plan: Debtor's Projected Balance Sheet

"We're reeling, everything is up on the table and we are going to be under this cloud for a while. For a long time, people have been so focused on earnings that corporate America realized that they can get away with playing games with the balance sheet, and it's catching up with them." Ram Kolluri

Debtor's Post Chapter 11 Balance Sheet: Key Metrics

The purpose of this Chapter is to determine the feasibility of the Debtor's Plan in terms of adequate liquidity and capital structure.

Table 19.0 presents Pierre's balance sheets for March 1, 2008, November 29, 2008, and post exit as projected in the Debtor's Plan.

Part IV: Case Analysis of Pierre Foods

Table 19.0—Post Chapter 11 Balance Sheet Key Metrics in Debtor's Plan

(in $ millions)	FYE 3/1/08	Interim 11/29/08	FYE 2/28/09	FYE 2/28/10	FYE 2/28/11
Cash	6	14	0	0	0
Receivables	46	38	50	52	53
Inventory	65	61	67	67	69
Plant, property, equipment	80	76	76	78	79
Goodwill & intangibles	112	107	87	87	87
Total assets	349	323	289	293	298
Payables	23	5.3	6	17	19
Accruals	37	23.6	31	22	22
Accrued interest Wachovia		3.3			
CMLTD 1st Lien Term Note			2.8	2.8	2.8
CMLTD other	(a)		0.8	0.2	0
CMLTD 2nd Lien Note			0 (c)	0 (c)	0 (c)
DIP Revolver balance		0			
Revolver Exit Facility			36	39	38
Long-term debt for 1st Lien Note			19	16	14
Prepetition Wachovia Facility	241 (b)	246	0 (c)	0	0
Exit 2nd Lien Note to Wachovia			85 (d)	92	99
Prepetition unsecured Claim	125 (b)	131	0	0	0
Prepetition capital lease/other debt	2	0	0	0	0
Prepetition unsecured claims		29	0	0	0
Total debt	368	371	142	147	150
Tax liability			$20 (e)	$14 (e)	$9 (e)
Total liabilities	441	453	199	201	200
Stockholders equity	(92)	(129)	90	92	97
Total liabilities. & equity	349	323	289	293	298

(a) The auditor classified 100% of debt on 3/1/08 as CMLTD because of debt defaults, including the $241 million balance on the Wachovia loan and the $125 million Senior Notes.

(b) On 3/1/08, the auditor classified the debt as CMLTD because of debt defaults. The debt is listed in this cell as long-term debt to allow the reader to compare debt amounts with other prior year periods.

(c) The Debtor's Plan converts a portion of the Wachovia claim to an $85 second-lien, PIK Term Note, subordinate to the $75 million Exit Facility Revolver and the $20 million Exit Facility Term Loan.

(d) At Plan exit, the $245 million prepetition Wachovia Credit Facility receives $29.8 million cash, a second-lien PIK Note of $85 million, and 100% of the 8% cumulative Preferred Stock in Pierre.

(e) The Debtor's tax advisor estimated emergence tax liability of $25 million for FYE 2010 to FYE 2012. The Debtor estimated the tax would be paid every 2–4 months over a 3-year period beginning June 15, 2009. The Debtor's Plan does not detail the reason for the tax. It is possible the tax is because of a gain on the cancellation of debt.

Debtor Plan—Debtor's Ability to Retain Sufficient Liquidity and Capital

A key test under the Bankruptcy Code is for the Debtor to retain sufficient liquidity and capital resources under a plan. The Debtor's budget projects minimal working capital needs for FYE February 2010 and February 2011 ($0.06 million in FYE February 2010 and $0.8 million in FYE February 2011).

Chapter 19: Feasibility of Debtor's Plan—Debtor's Projected Balance Sheet

Pierre's projects a $56 million balance on the Exit Credit Facility on February 28, 2009. From Table 18.0 (Chapter 18), it was estimated that $47.2 million of cash was paid out for the 12% distributions in the Debtor's Plan. The Debtor's projected statement of cash flows does not show the cash payouts in the Debtor's Plan because the Debtor's statement of cash flows is dated subsequent to the cash payouts.

Pierre projects $6 million of vendor payables at February 28, 2009—a payable turn of only 6 days based on $363 million of annual raw material purchases. Pierre's Plan projects payables will increase to $17.2 million on February 28, 2010 because of an increase trade vendor terms (16.7 day payable turnover). The increase in trade payables will provide $11.2 million of working capital.

Based on Pierre's financial projections, Pierre would not require a $95 million Exit Credit Facility and cash balances would be $31.1 million, assuming the following:

- No cash payout of $47.2 million (12% of prepetition claims);
- $11.9 of preference payments are recovered from vendors and the Wachovia Credit Facility;
- Vendor payable terms return to normal, for a $11.2 million increase in working capital;
- Pierre holds receivables/inventories to levels at December 27, 2008. It is not clear why Pierre projects a $22 million increase in receivables/inventories from December 27, 2008 to February 28, 2009. The Debtor's Plan does not forecast any significant increase in sales.

Debtor Plan—Balance Sheet Capital Structure

On February 28, 2009, Pierre's Plan projects total assets of $289 million, including $90 million of goodwill/intangibles. Perella Weinberg estimated an Enterprise Value of $232 million. Table 19.1 estimates the value of Preferred Stock in the Debtor's Plan at $90.8 million.

Table 19.1—Estimated Value of Preferred Stock per Debtor's Plan
(in $ millions)

232.0	Enterprise Value estimated by Perella Weinberg in Debtor's Plan
(36.2)	Revolver balance projected in Debtor's Plan on February 28, 2009
(20.0)	Term Loan opening balance per Debtor's Plan
(85.0)	PIK Note
90.8 (a)	Estimated value of Preferred Stock per Debtor's Plan

(a) The Debtor's Plan balance sheet dated February 28, 2009 projected a net worth of $90 million.

Part IV: Case Analysis of Pierre Foods

Feasibility of Debtor's Plan Debt Structure and Debt Service

On February 28, 2009, the Debtor's Plan projects a $36.2 million balance on the Revolver and $38.8 million of borrowing availability on the Exit Revolver.

The principal payments due in one year on the first-lien Exit Term Loan are $2.8 million a year. The Exit Facility matures in four years. At the maturity date of the Term Loan, Pierre should in position to renew the Exit Term Loan based on the collateral coverage, subject to satisfactory operating performance.

The $85 million PIK Note does not have required debt service. The PIK Note matures in eight years.

In conclusion, based on the Debtor's projections, liquidity is adequate and the debt service is minimal. The Debtor's Plan passes the test of feasibility based on the analysis of capital structure. The Debtor's Plan will be tested in Chapter 20 for the feasibility of cash flow coverage.

Chapter 20

Feasibility of Debtor's Plan: Debtor's Projected Income Statement & Cash Flows

"The only function of economic forecasting is to make astrology look respectable" John Kenneth Galbraith

The purpose of this Chapter is to determine the feasibility of the Debtor's Plan in terms of the ability of the Pierre's operations to provide sufficient cash flow to cover debt service obligations.

Table 20.0 summarizes Pierre's operating results prior to bankruptcy, during bankruptcy, and for three fiscal years after bankruptcy as projected by in the Debtor's Plan.

Part IV: Case Analysis of Pierre Foods

Table 20.0—Post Chapter 11 Income Statement & Cash Flows in Debtor's Plan

(in $ millions)	FYE 3/5/05	FYE 3/4/06	FYE 3/3/07	FYE 3/1/08	164 days 7/15/08 to 12/27/08	FYE 2/28/09	FYE 2/28/10	FYE 2/28/11
Sales	410	432	488	643	293	645	665	713
Gross margin percentage	25.8%	28.3%	29.5%	23%	24%	24%	23%	23%
SG&A	66	68	85	126	51	145	118	125
Depreciation/amortization	26	32	32	39	13	28	12	11
Operating income	15	24	28	(17)	5.2	(20)	20	25
Charge-off goodwill/impairment				229				
Interest expense	26	22	25	42		26 [d]	16 [d]	17 [d]
Chapter 11 professional fees					15			
Pre-tax income	(11)	2	3	(288)		(45)	4	8
Cash Flow Metrics:								
Adjusted EBITDA	45	56	60	29	18 [c]	34	32	36
Interest expense	26	22	25	42		26	16	17
CMLTD 1st lien Debt & lease	0.4	0.3	1.6	1.6 [a]		3.6	3.0	2.9
CMTLD Wachovia 2nd lien loan [b]	0	0	0	0		0	0	0
Cash Flow before CAPX	19	34	33	(15)		4	13	16
CAPX (excluding acquisitions)	6	7	9	8		7	13	12
CAPX financing [e]								
Tax liability						6 [f]	6 [f]	6 [f]
Net Cash Flow	13	27	24	(23)		(9)	(6)	(2)
Ratios:								
EBITDA to total interest	1.73x	2.55x	2.40x	0.69x		1.3x	2.0x	2.1x
EBITDA to interest on 1st lien Debt						9.4x	10.7x	12.4x
EBITDA to debt service	1.70x	2.51x	2.26x	.07x		1.14x	1.6x	1.8x
Debt / EBITDA	5.87x	4.38x	5.98x	12.7:1		4.2x	4.6x	4.1x
Debt	$264	$245	$359	$368		$142	$147	$150
Business Valuation Metrics:								
PWP Enterprise Value estimate	$232	$232	$232	$232	$232	$232	$232	$232
PWP Enterprise Value to EBITDA	5.16x	4.14x	3.87x	8.0:1		6.8x	7.2x	6.4x
PWP Enterprise Value to sales	0.57x	0.54x	0.48x	0.36:1		0.36x	0.35x	0.33x

Source: Table 20.0 has been prepared by the author from Pierre's: (1) U.S. SEC EDGAR filings, (2) Operating Reports filed with the Bankruptcy Court, and (3) the October 29, 2008 Plan.
Note: Pierre did not release Financials between March 2, 2008 and the July 15, 2008 bankruptcy filing.
(a) At FYE 3/1/08, the auditor classified 100% of Pierre's debt in CMLTD due to debt defaults. For purposes of comparison to prior year and the budget, Table 20.0 does not classify the debt in CMTLD.
(b) In the Debtor's Plan, the prepetition Wachovia secured claim has been converted to a second lien, $85 million PIK Note. The Note does not have any required principal repayments, except for 50% of net excess cash flow should cash flow be sufficient, but the payment is subordinate to the first-lien Exit Facility.
(c) Prior to professional fee expenses of $15.9 million during bankruptcy and other reorganization expense.
(d) For projected interest expense, the Debtor assumed a LIBOR floor of 3.5% on the first-lien Exit Credit Facility. The rate was LIBOR plus 3.5% on the Revolver and LIBOR plus 4.5% on the first-lien Term Loan. The interest on the $85 million Note can be payment in cash interest or by adding the interest to the Note balance.
(e) The Debtor Plan assumed no financing of CAPX.
(f) The Debtor's tax advisor estimated an emergence tax liability of $25 million for FYE 2010–2012. The tax is paid every 2–4 months over 3 yrs. beginning 6/15/09. The Debtor's Plan does not detail the reason for the tax. It is possible that the tax may be in part due to a gain on the extinguishment of debt in the Debtor's Plan.

Chapter 20: Feasibility of Debtor's Plan: Income Statement & Cash Flows

Reasonableness of Sales Forecast in Pierre's Plan

Pierre's Plan projects sales of $645 million in FYE March 2010, with sales increasing to $713 million in FYE March 2011. For the 164 days in bankruptcy, Pierre had sales of $292.6 million, or $651 million on an annualized basis. Pierre's sales forecast is conservative based on the level of sales in bankruptcy.

Reasonableness of the EBITDA Forecast in Pierre's Plan

Pierre projected EBITDA in the Plan as follows:

FYE Year-End	Amount
March 2009	$34 million
March 2010	$32 million
March 2011	$36 million

For the 164 days in bankruptcy, Pierre's EBITDA was $18.2 million, or $40.5 million on an annualized basis.

Pierre's projected EBITDA is conservative compared to the annualized EBITDA during bankruptcy. Bankruptcy is a period of distress and reorganization. Future results should benefit from the rejection of executory contracts and rationalization of operations.

Debtor's Plan Projected EBITDA to Debt Service Coverage

The Debtor's Plan projected an EBITDA to interest ratio of 2.0:1 for FYE March 2010. Pierre can elect to add the interest on the $85 million PIK Note to the loan balance. The ratio of EBITDA to cash interest expense (excluding PIK interest) is 10.7:1 for FYE March 2010.

Debtor's Plan Projected Working Capital and CAPX

Pierre projects minimum working capital needs based on a steady state of operations. Pierre projects $13 million of annual CAPX. Pierre's historical CAPX averaged $6–$8 million a year in the most recent four years. Based on Pierre's small projected increase in sales in the Debtor's Plan, it is not clear why Pierre projected an increase in CAPX.

Debtor's Plan Projected CMLTD and Net Cash Flow

The Plan has minimal current maturities of long-term debt—$2.8 million a year on the $20 million first-lien Exit Term Loan (balloon balance due in 2012). The second-lien $85 million PIK Note matures in 2016.

Part IV: Case Analysis of Pierre Foods

Pierre projected net cash flow (EBITDA net of debt service, CAPX, and tax) as follows:

FYE Year-End	Net Cash Flow
March 2009	Deficit $9 million
March 2010	Deficit $6 million
March 2011	Deficit $2 million

The Debtor Plan does not explain the source of funds to repay the $85 million PIK Note when it matures in 2016.

Reasonableness of Projected EBITDA in Debtor's Plan

Pierre projects EBITDA of $32 million in FYE March 2010. In contrast, Pierre's average annual Adjusted EBITDA was $43.0 million for the five years prior to bankruptcy. Moreover, FYE March 2004 and 2008 results should be excluded to normalize EBITDA because of the following factors:

- FYE March 2004 had expenses that were eliminated after Madison Dearborn acquired Pierre;

- The 2006 acquisitions of Zartic/Clovervale increased sales by 20%;

- Pierre intends to discontinue the Zar Tran business and exit commodity chicken sales. It is assumed the discontinuance of these operations will have a favorable impact on EBITDA;

- FYE 2008 experienced rapidly rising commodity prices that adversely affected profits. Pierre's financial projections were provided to Perella Weinberg on September 2, 2008. Therefore, it is assumed that the financial projections and assumptions were developed in August 2008, a time when raw material inflation was high. Raw material prices decreased significantly after bankruptcy and into 2009;

- In 2008, Pierre had $2.7 million of professional fees, including fees for the integration of Clovervale and Zartic and costs/fees related to the Wachovia Credit Facility;

- In 2008, Pierre had a $2.1 million of expense primarily due to bad debt associated with the bankruptcy of a customer and for increases in insurance, wages, and travel;

- In 2008, Pierre had an $1.6 million increase in marketing expense from the implementation of an inventory reduction initiative;

Chapter 20: Feasibility of Debtor's Plan: Income Statement & Cash Flows

- In 2008, Pierre had an $1.3 million increase in freight, primarily from increased fuel surcharges;
- In 2008, Pierre had an $1.4 million increase in costs in connection with the Zartic plant fire;
- Operating lease payments are scheduled to decrease $1.1 million a year beginning March 1, 2009. Pierre also rejected lease and executory contracts that are expected to reduce lease expense between $0.4 million and $0.8 million a year, or possibly more (author estimate).

Comparison of Historical EBITDA to Debtor's Plan EBITDA

Pierre had historical average annual Adjusted EBITDA of $53.6 million for the three years FYE March 2005–2007. In contrast, Pierre's Plan projects $32.6 million of EBITDA for FYE March 2010.

Pierre's Historical EBITDA Margins Compared to Industry Peers and Exchange Traded U.S. Firms

Pierre's EBITDA margins are 8.3% based on $53.6 million of annual normalized EBITDA for FYE March 2005–2007 as compared to 11% EBITDA margins for industry peers and 12.1% EBITDA margins for U.S. based exchange traded non-financial stocks.

Feasibility of the Debtor's Plan: Cash Flow

The Debtor's Plan under estimates EBITDA and over estimates CAPX as compared to historical normalized EBITDA and CAPX.

Pierre's projected cash flow is not sufficient to repay principal on the $85 million PIK Note. The Debtor Plan has not explained how the PIK Note will be repaid. Assuming Pierre's historical normalized EBITDA, Pierre's cash flow is adequate to service the PIK Note.

Although the Debtor's projected cash flow is not sufficient to repay the PIK Note, the Debtor's Plan remains feasible because the PIK Note maturity is in the distant future.

Chapter 21

Objections to the Debtor's Plan

"If ignorant both of your enemy and yourself, you are certain to be in peril."—Sun Tzu

Objections to the Plan of Reorganization

The Debtor received eight objections to the confirmation to Plan. Six of the objections were resolved prior to the Plan confirmation hearing, leaving objections from the U.S. Bankruptcy Trustee and Rabobank. Rabobank held $6.3 million of the Wachovia Credit Facility.

U.S. Trustee Objection

The U.S. Bankruptcy Trustee objected that the Plan provided for the exculpation of Oaktree Capital, the Plan Sponsor. The exculpation prohibited a party from suing Oaktree Capital in connection with the Plan, unless the cause was the result of Oaktree Capital's gross negligence or fraud. The Bankruptcy Judge ruled in favor of the exculpation for Oaktree Capital.

The U.S. Trustee also objected to the Debtor's Plan paying the expenses of Trustee for the $125 million Senior Notes on the basis the Trustee for the Senior Notes should seek an administrative award or have the expenses paid as an official member of the Creditors Committee. If the Trustee for the Senior

Chapter 21: Objections to the Debtor's Plan

Notes did not receive full payment for its expenses, then the Trustee would have a lien against the amounts received by the holders of the Senior Notes, reducing the recovery for the Senior Notes. The Bankruptcy Judge ruled in favor of the payment of expenses to the Trustee.

Rabobank Objections

Rabobank sought to exclude the votes of Oaktree Capital on the basis Oaktree Capital was an insider whose votes should not count toward Plan acceptance. Rabobank asserted that Oaktree Capital decided to make a play to acquire Pierre by purchasing both prepetition and postpetition claims. Oaktree Capital had acquired 92% of the Wachovia Credit Facility claims. Rabobank had reason to believe that Oaktree Capital was also purchasing the unsecured Senior Notes that made up the majority of impaired Class 4. As discussed in Chapter 10, Oaktree Capital's ownership of Senior Notes has never been conclusively established, although the Agent for the Wachovia Credit Facility reported to Rabobank that Oaktree Capital had purchased 30%–40% of the Senior Notes (Bankr. D. Del, Ct. transcript, 12/10/08)

According to Rabobank (Bankr. D. Del, Ct. objection by Rabobank, 12/5/08), a month before Pierre's bankruptcy filing, Oaktree Capital asked Rabobank to consent to a pre-packaged bankruptcy plan proposed by Oaktree Capital. Oaktree Capital had purchased $60 million (24%) of the secured Wachovia Credit Facility. The Oaktree Capital proposal was as follows:

- Oaktree Capital to provide a $30 million DIP loan;
- Oaktree Capital to convert its $60 million position in the Wachovia loan into new common stock in exchange for 60% of the Pierre's common stock;
- Wachovia loan to be reinstated at par (net of Oaktree Capital's $60 million position converted to stock);
- Oaktree Capital to provide a $25 million capital infusion for 25% of Pierre's stock (this offer implies a value of $100 million for 100% of the stock in Pierre);
- $125 million unsecured Senior Notes to be converted into new common stock equal to 15% of Pierre's stock (this conversion implies a value of $125 million for 100% of the stock in Pierre).

Under Oaktree Capital's pre-package plan, pro-forma debt would consist of a new $30 million DIP loan and the $185 million Wachovia Credit Facility (the

Part IV: Case Analysis of Pierre Foods

original $245 million Wachovia Credit Facility less the $60 million debt owned by Oaktree Capital and converted to stock).

The transactions would provide Pierre with $55 million of new working capital ($30 million DIP loan and $25 million from stock sale to Oaktree Capital).

Rabobank argued that it consented to the proposed Oaktree Capital DIP loan and believed the Rabobank loan would be reinstated at par. Rabobank believed that Oaktree Capital baited Rabobank's consent for a DIP loan by showing Rabobank a plan that reinstated the Rabobank's claim at par. Oaktree Capital then continued to purchase the claims of the competing lenders. The Debtor filed bankruptcy and Oaktree Capital, according to Rabobank, performed a "switch" in treatment of the Wachovia Credit Facility.

Rabobank's first knowledge that Oaktree Capital had radically altered the prepackage bankruptcy plan was in October 2008 when it reviewed the first plan filed by the Pierre. Rabobank was shocked to discover Oaktree Capital was no longer infusing $25 million or any new capital; that the secured Wachovia Credit Facility claim would no longer be reinstated at par. Rabobank was shocked to discover that, aside from a fractional cash payment of 12 cents on the dollar, the Wachovia Credit Facility claim would be relegated to stock in the Debtor and a deeply subordinate position on an $85 million PIK Note due in 8 years.

Rabobank argued that the Class 4 unsecured claims (most of which Rabobank believed were owned by Oaktree Capital) were receiving far better treatment than the stock for debt proposed in Oaktree Capital's term sheet prior to bankruptcy. Class 4 claims were receiving 12 cents on the dollar, despite the fact they would receive zero in a liquidation of the Debtor based on the Debtor's liquidation analysis in the Plan.

Rabobank argued that when Oaktree Capital performed the "bait and switch", it was not a third party free to look out solely for its own interests. By virtue of its purchase of some of the Wachovia Credit Facility, it became a member of the Wachovia Lending Syndicate bound by the implied covenant of good faith and fair dealing in the Wachovia Credit Facility. Rabobank asserted that it was a breach of the terms of the Wachovia Credit Agreement to use the mechanism of bankruptcy to: (1) convert the Wachovia loan from first-lien status on the collateral to second-lien status and (2) exchange the Wachovia debt for stock in Pierre. Rabobank believed this Plan treatment evaded the unanimous consent required by the Wachovia Credit Agreement for such conversion.

Moreover, according to Rabobank, through its suspected purchase of unsecured Senior Notes, Oaktree Capital became bound by the subordination

Chapter 21: Objections to the Debtor's Plan

provisions and should not be allowed to use the Plan to evade those provisions. The Debtor's Plan required any Wachovia holder receiving a settlement to waive their rights to enforce the subordination provision.

Rabobank also objected because the new stockholders under the Debtor's Plan were not being treated fairly. The Shareholders Agreement in the Plan gave Oaktree Capital rights to sell its stock but restricted all other stockholders to a 36-month holding period. In addition, the Debtor Plan gave Oaktree Capital "bring along rights" that allowed Oaktree Capital to require all holders of Pierre's stock to sell their stock to a buyer of Pierre's stock for the same price that Oaktree Capital sold its shares to the same buyer.

Rabobank objected because the Shareholder's Agreement in the Debtor's Plan entitled Oaktree Capital the right to compensation for services it performed for Pierre under a Management Services Agreement, the terms of which had not been disclosed. Rabobank was unclear as to why the reorganized Pierre needed to pay a "hedge fund" like Oaktree Capital to manage its business.

Oaktree Capital subsequently provided Rabobank with a copy of the proposed Management Services Agreement (the Management Services Agreement was not filed with the Bankruptcy Court until after the vote on the Plan). Rabobank then objected because the Management Services Agreement proposed to pay Oaktree Capital a fee of $1.5 million a year and locked in Oaktree Capital as Pierre's investment banker. Pierre was committed to a $4.5 million fees to Oaktree should Pierre consummate an initial public offering or sell one or more of its companies (through merger or otherwise), or sell all or substantially all of their assets.

Prior to the confirmation hearing, the Debtor Plan was amended as follows:

- Reduction in the selling time restriction of the stock held by other Pierre stockholders from 36 months to 18 months;
- Other Pierre stockholders were permitted to tender stock to any party offering to buy Pierre's stock.

Rabobank agreed to withdraw all of its objections (Bankr. D. Del, Ct. transcript, 12/10/08) to the Debtor's Plan in return for Oaktree Capital amending the Stock Registration Rights Agreement to provide "piggyback rights" for only Rabobank. Under the piggyback registration, if Pierre's management proposed to register Pierre's stock for a public offering, Oaktree Capital's shares were also permitted to participate in the registration.

Chapter 22

Voting Results for Debtor's Plan

"Democracy is the worst system devised by man, except for all the others."
Winston Churchill

Voting Results for Classes 1, 2, and 6

Claims in Classes 1, 2, and 6 were not impaired in the Debtor's Plan and the holders of such claims were deemed to have voted to accept the Plan.

The prepetition stockholders in Class 5 were not voting on the Plan because they were not receiving a distribution. As such, they were deemed to have voted to reject the Plan.

Claims in classes 3 (Wachovia) and 4 (Senior Notes and other unsecured claims) were entitled to vote on the Plan.

Oaktree Capital owned 92% of the claims in Class 3. As Sponsor of Pierre's Plan, Oaktree would vote to approve the Pierre's Plan.

If the unsecured creditors in Class 4 did not approve the Plan, the Debtor planned to seek Bankruptcy Court approval to cramdown Class 4.

Vote Results for Class 3 Claims

Oaktree Capital held 92.33% of Class 3 claims, controlled through 21 entities (First Street Holdings 1 to 21). Table 22.0 shows the Class 3 holders and the voting results. In summary, 97.3% of the dollar amount and 96.3% of the number of votes in Class three voted to accept the Plan. Rabobank was the only dissenter in Class 3.

Chapter 22: Voting Results for Debtor's Plan

Table 22.0—Class 3 Voting Results

Class 3 Holder	Claim (millions$)	Number of Votes	% of Class in Dollars	Vote
Rabobank	$6.7	1	2.73%	Rejected
First Street Holdings 1 through 21 LP, all affiliates of Oaktree Capital	$227.2	21	92.23%	Accepted
Wachovia NA	$5.4	1	2.22%	Accepted
Harch CLO II & III	$4.8	2	1.95%	Accepted
Denali Capital CLO	$0.9	1	0.36%	Accepted
Spcp Group	$1.0	1	0.42%	Accepted
WBNA	$0.2	1	0.09%	Accepted
Total Wachovia Credit Facility Claims	$246.3	28	100.0%	

Source: Filing with Bankruptcy Court

Vote Results For Class 4 Claims

94% of the dollar amount and 89% of the number of votes in Class 4 accepted the Plan. Table 22.1 summarizes the Class 4 votes.

Table 22.1—Class 4 Voting Results

Class 4 Holder	Claim	No. Votes	Vote
Broadbridge on behalf of Brown Brothers Harriman, Citibank, Bank New York Mellon	$13.2	6	Accept
Bank of New York Mellon	$63.9	11	Accept
JP Morgan Chase	$15.6	8	Accept
State Street Bank & Trust	$12.9	9	Accept
Mellon Trust of New England	$3.9	4	Accept
US Bank	$0.4	4	Accept
Broadbridge on behalf of Citi Group	$2.1	Not counted	Voted late
Goldman Sachs Asset Management (GSAM)	$2.0	Not counted	Abstained
Wells Fargo Bank NA	$3.1	Not counted	Abstained
Subtotal of $125 million Sr. Notes Ballots Returned	$117.1		
Class 4 Votes Counted over $200,000:			
- NASCAR	$1.0	1	Accept
- Roy Nichols	$0.5	1	Accept
- David Clark (former Vice-Chairman of Pierre)	$2.0	Not counted	Abstained
Class 4 Votes Under 200,000:			
- Class 4 Votes Counted & Accepting	$3.3	226	
- Class 4 Counted & Rejecting	$0.4	33	Rejected
Total of all Class 4 Votes Counted and Accepting Plan	$114.7 (99.6%)	270 (89%)	
Total of all Class 4 Votes Counted and Rejecting Plan	$ 0.4 (0.4%)	33 (11%)	
Total of all Class 4 Votes Counted	$115.1 (100%)	303 (100%)	

Source: Filing with Bankruptcy Court

Exit From Bankruptcy

On December 10, 2008, the Bankruptcy Court confirmed Pierre's Plan of Reorganization. On December 12, 2008 Pierre emerged from Chapter 11.

Part IV: Case Analysis of Pierre Foods

New Chief Executive Officer Appointed

At the emergence from bankruptcy, William Toler was appointed as the new Chief Executive of Pierre. Mr. Toler had 25 years of industry experience. He had previously served as a special advisor to Oaktree Capital. His experience included the following positions:

- President of Pinnacle Foods—July 2005 to November 2008;
- Provided consulting services to Aurora Foods;
- President North American ICG Commerce, a procurement company;
- President of Campbell Sales Company—1995 to 2000. Responsible for $4 billion in sales, including Campbell Soup Company's flagship soup brands Condensed, Chucky and Select, V-8 beverages, and Prego and Pace sauces ;
- V.P. of Sales and Integrated Logistics at Nabisco—1992 to 1995;
- V.P. National Sales Manger for Reckitt & Colman—1989 to 1992;
- He began is career at Procter & Gamble—1981 to 1989.

New Board Members of Reorganized Pierre

In accordance with the Debtor's Plan, at the emergence from bankruptcy, five individuals were appointed to serve on Pierre's Board of Directors. The members were the new Chief Executive Officer, William Toler, and the following four individuals:

Steven Kaplan - Chairman of Board

- Mr. Kaplan co-founded Oaktree Capital in 1995;
- Positions at Oaktree Capital: Head of Principle Group, Portfolio Manager, Director of Oaktree Capital Management, LLC

His prior experience included

- Managing Director of Trust Company of the West (TCW) and portfolio manager of TCW Special Credits Fund V;
- Partner with the law firm Gibson, Dunn & Crutcher and responsible for the firm's East Coast bankruptcy and workout practice;
- His experience includes specializing in transactions for the purchase and sale of companies undergoing financial restructurings;
- B.S. degree in Political Science summa cum laude from the State University of New York;
- J.D. from the New York University School of Law.

Chapter 22: Voting Results for Debtor's Plan

Matthew Wilson - Director
- Prior to joining Oaktree Capital, he was an officer at H.I.G. Capital, leading leveraged buyouts, recapitalizations, and distressed debt transactions;
- Previously, he was at J.H. Whitney & Co., as an associate of the firm's middle market buyout group;
- Began his career in Investment Banking Division at Merrill Lynch;
- B.A. degrees with Distinction in Economics and History from the University of Virginia;
- M.B.A. from the Harvard Business School.

Dean Hollis - Director
- Served as President ConAgra Foods Consumer Foods and International division;
- Oversaw the largest segment of the ConAgra Foods portfolio, including leading consumer brands and customer branded businesses, consisting of over 40 global brands in 110 countries;
- From 1987, he served in a variety of senior level positions at the ConAgra Foods Consumer Foods.

Margaret Cannella - Director
- 30 year career with JP Morgan Chase as a research analyst and the global head of credit research and U.S. corporate strategy;
- Previously, responsible for high-yield and high-grade credit research at Citigroup for ten years;
- Specialized in covering retailing, supermarket, food and beverage sectors;
- Graduate of Princeton University with a degree in East Asian Studies;
- MBA from Columbia University Graduate School of Business.

Chapter 23

Perella Weinberg's Estimate of Enterprise Value

"Try not to become a man of success, but rather try to become a man of value."
Albert Einstein

Perlla Weinberg Partners (PWP), Pierre's Investment Banker, estimated the Enterprise Value of Pierre in Exhibit D to the Debtor's October 29, 2009 Plan. The PWP analysis reflects work performed by PWP based on information for Pierre's business and assets that were provided to PWP as of September 2, 2008. The PWP Enterprise Value estimate was based on the financial projections prepared by Pierre, Alvarez & Marsal, and other professionals. PWP assumed the financial projections were prepared in good faith and reflected the best available estimates as to future operating and financial performance of Pierre.

The PWP estimate of Pierre's Enterprise Value ranged between $208 million and $255 million. PWP assigned a final Enterprise Value of $232 million to Pierre Foods.

Chapter 23: Enterprise Value Determined by Perella Weinberg

The $232 million PWP Enterprise Value equals:

- 6.8x the FYE March 2009 EBITDA of $34 million in Pierre's budget;
- 7.2x FYE March 2010 EBITDA of $36 million in Pierre's budget;
- 4.3x annual average EBITDA of $53.6 million for the three years FYE March 2005–2007.

PWP used the following valuation methodologies to estimate Pierre's Enterprise Value:

- Comparable firm analysis based on the current trading values for comparable companies. PWP analyzed the Enterprise Value for comparable companies as a multiple of projected calendar year-end EBITDA for 2008 and 2009. These multiples were then applied to Pierre's calendar year-end. The detail of this analysis was not disclosed in the Debtor's Plan;
- Discounted cash flow based on the present value of the projected unlevered after-tax cash flows for a determined period plus the present value of the terminal value of cash flows. PWP's discounted cash flow valuation was based on a three year calendar year projection for 2009–2011. PWP discounted the projected cash flows using Pierre's estimated risk-adjusted cost of capital, the weighted average cost of capital, and calculated the terminal value of the business. The detail of the analysis was not disclosed in the Debtor's Plan;
- Precedent transactions analysis. An analysis of the purchase price as a multiple of various operating statistics for companies in similar lines of business to Pierre. The transaction multiples were calculated based on the purchase price, including any debt assumed, to acquire companies that were comparable to Pierre. Unlike PWP's comparable public company analysis, the valuation in the precedent transactions included a "control" premium. The detail of this PWP valuation analysis was not disclosed in the Debtor's Plan.

Analysis cannot be performed to determine the reasonableness of the PWP estimate of Enterprise Value because the Debtor's Plan does not fully disclose the details and assumptions used in the PWP Enterprise Valuation.

Part V
Presentation of an Alternative Enterprise Value for Pierre

Chapter 24

Alternative Enterprise Value

"The absence of alternatives clears the mind marvelously." Henry Kissinger

Chapter 24 develops an alternative estimate for Pierre's Enterprise Value.

Enterprise Value Estimated by Grant Thornton in June 2001
In June 2001, Pierre engaged Grant Thornton to evaluate the fairness of the 2001 buyout offer from Pierre's management. Grant Thornton's opinion was filed by Pierre in a June 25, 2002 U.S. SEC EDGAR filing.

Grant Thornton used three methods to estimate Enterprise Value:

- Comparable company analysis, using Bridgford, Hormel, and Rymer;
- Comparable sale transaction analysis based on 15 recent business combinations;
- The discounted cash flow method.

Comparable Companies Used by Grant Thornton in 2001
Table 24.0 shows the sales and EBITDA multiples for the comparable company analysis.

Table 24.0—Comparable Firm EBITDA & Sales Multiples for the Year 2001		
Company	EBITDA Multiple	Sales Multiple
Bridgford Foods	7.9x	0.8x
Hormel Foods	11.3x	1.0x
Rymer Foods	(5.7x)	0.1x
Industry Median	7.9x	0.8x

Source: Pierre's U.S. S.E.C. EDGAR DEF 14A filing on June 25, 2002.

Grant Thornton reported that the three firms were comparable but not identical to Pierre (Rymer was unprofitable in 2001 and sold its assets in 2002 to Colorado Boxed Beef).

Based on differences in size, growth, and geographic diversity, Grant Thornton adjusted the sales and EBITDA multiples for the three firms down by

Part V: Presentation of Alternative Enterprise Value for Pierre

20% for Pierre. Grant Thornton assigned multiples for sales and EBITDA of 0.6x and 6.3x, respectively.

Comparable Transactions Used by Grant Thornton in 2001

Grant Thornton reviewed 15 business combination transactions in the food processing industry. A median Enterprise Value to sales multiple of 0.88x was considered appropriate. The multiple was adjusted downward by 20% for differences in size, growth, and geographic diversity. On the basis of the comparable transactions, Grant Thornton assigned a final sales multiple to Pierre of 0.7x. The Grant Thornton analysis did not report on comparable transaction Enterprise Value to EBITDA multiples.

Discounted Cash Flow Analysis Used by Grant Thornton in 2001

In June, Grant Thornton performed discounted cash flow analyses to estimate the Enterprise Value for Pierre under four different scenarios. Pierre's management provided projected income statements for the Grant Thornton analysis. All four scenarios focused on projected income statements and debt-free net cash flows for fiscal years 2002–2007 (Sales were $242 million in 2002 vs. $643 million in 2008).

The four different scenarios were as follows:

- Case one: sales growth of 11.6% in 2002 and 3.0% a year from 2003–2007. Gross profit margin was assumed to decrease from 33.7% in 2002 to 32.3% in 2007. After 2007, free cash flow was assumed to grow 4.0% a year;
- Case two, three, and four: sales growth of 11.6% in 2002 and 10.0% per year from 2003–2007. Gross profit margin was assumed to increase from 33.7% in 2002 to 34.5% in 2007. An acquisition was projected in 2003 and a plant expansion in 2006. After 2007, free cash flow was assumed to grow 4% a year. The only difference between the case two and three was an assumption in case three that 25% of Senior Notes were purchased for 50% of face value. In case four, 50% of the Senior Notes were purchased for 50% of face value.

Grant Thornton calculated Enterprise Value by applying a discount rate of 18% to the annual debt-free net cash flows in the projected income statements and to the estimated value terminal at the end of 2007. After 2007, the terminal cash flows were assumed to grown 4% into perpetuity.

Grant Thornton arrived at the 18% discount rate by calculating an estimated cost of capital using the capital asset pricing model for the cost of equity capital

Chapter 24: Alternative Enterprise Value

based on data from recognized industry sources, including Ibbotson Associates *2001 Stock Bonds Bills and Inflation Yearbook* and the Federal Reserve's Statistical Release on Interest Rates. The cost of debt was based on the interest rate on Pierre's existing debt and an estimated premium Grant Thornton believed would be required for additional debt. The Grant Thornton valuation (in Pierre's SEC filing) did not provide the specific amounts used for: (1) the risk-free rate, (2) the equity risk premium, (3) the Beta value, or (4) any other risk premiums.

Grant Thornton's weighted average cost of capital was based on the capital structures of companies in the food industry as determined by reviewing the data for SIC codes in the *Ibbotson's Cost of Capital 2001* Yearbook—the specific details were not disclosed.

Table 24.1 shows the Grant Thornton valuation based on the discounted cash flow method. The Enterprise Value assigned by Grant Thornton for Pierre was $57.5 million (case 1), $74.9 million (case 2), $64.6 million (case 3), and $65.0 million (case 4).

After Grant Thornton subtracted the $121 million of debt, the value of the equity was negative and Grant Thornton assigned a zero value to Pierre's stock.

It is difficult to understand the Grant Thornton valuation based on discounted cash flow method because the implied Enterprise Value to EBITDA multiple ranges between 1.8x to 3.8x (Table 24.1). The multiple seem extraordinarily low.

Table 24.1—EBITDA Multiples Implied by the Grant Thornton Discounted Cash Flow

($millions)	Year	2002	2003	2004	2005	2006	2007
Case 1	Sales	235	247	254	262	270	278
	Operating Profit	12.8	11.8	11.1	11.0	10.9	10.6
	Depreciation (estimated)	6.9	6.9	6.9	6.9	6.9	6.9
	EBITDA	19.7	18.7	18.0	17.9	17.8	17.5
	Enterprise Value	57.5	57.5	57.5	57.5	57.5	57.5
	Implied EBITDA Multiple	2.9x	3.0x	3.2x	3.2x	3.2x	3.3x
(Case 2, 3, 4)	Sales	235	264	294	326	360	397
	Operating Profit	12.8	15.0	17.9	22.3	27.1	31.4
	Depreciation (estimated)	6.9	6.9	6.9	6.9	6.9	6.9
	EBITDA	19.7	21.9	24.8	29.2	34.0	38.3
	Enterprise Value	74.9	74.9	74.9	74.9	74.9	74.9
	Implied EBITDA Multiple	3.8x	3.4x	3.0x	2.6x	2.2x	1.9x
Case 3 & 4)	Operating Profit	12.8	10.0	15.1	19.5	24.3	28.5
	Depreciation (estimated)	6.9	6.9	6.9	6.9	6.9	6.9
	EBITDA	19.7	16.9	22.0	26.4	31.2	35.4
	Enterprise Value	65.0	65.0	65.0	65.0	65.0	65.0
	Implied EBITDA Multiple	3.3x	3.8x	2.9x	2.5x	2.0x	1.8x

Source: Pierre's U.S. S.E.C. EDGAR DEF 14A filing on June 25, 2002.

Part V: Presentation of Alternative Enterprise Value for Pierre

Final Enterprise Value Estimated by Grant Thornton in 2001

A significant consideration in the Grant Thornton opinion was the existence of a change of control agreement between Pierre and James Richardson and David Clark. Richardson and Clark would be entitled to receive an aggregate payment in excess of $11 million for a change of control. The significance of the payment for change of control was to increase the cost of the purchase to a buyer and thus diminish the return to the buying shareholders.

To set the floor on the range of Pierre's Enterprise Value, Grant Thornton weighted the discounted cash flow method 50%, the comparable company method 25%, and the comparable transaction method 25%.

Grant Thornton's final valuation for Pierre was an EBITDA multiple between 6.4x and 7.0x and a sales multiple between 0.54x and 0.59x.

Pierre's October 2008 Enterprise Value Based on the 2001 Grant Thornton Multiples

The final EBITDA multiple from the 2001 Grant Thornton analysis will be used to estimate Pierre's Enterprise Value as of October 2008 based on Pierre's $53.6 million of average annual EBITDA for the years FYE March 2005–2007 (Pierre's "normalized EBITDA").

Pierre's FYE March 2004 EBITDA is excluded because it was before the Madison Dearborn acquistion that eliminated certain expenses and before the acquistions of Zartic/Clovervalue.

FYE 2008 EBITDA is excluded because of $27.9 million of unusual expenses were incurred in 2008. Without these expenses, FYE March 2008 pro forma Adjusted EBITDA would have been $47.9 million. The unusual expenses of $27.9 million are as follows:

- $18.9 million of higher raw materials from rapidly rising commodity prices;
- $2.7 million of one-time costs related the Wachovia loan;
- $2.1 million of expense from the bankruptcy of a customer and increases in insurance, wages, and travel;
- $1.3 million higher fuel costs. Oil prices hit a high of $140 a barrel in 2008;
- $1.4 million from a plant fire that increased production costs;
- $1.5 million of costs for the closure of Pierre's Cedartown, Georgia plant;
- Operating lease payments are scheduled to decrease $1.1 million a year beginning March 1, 2009. Pierre also rejected lease and executory contracts that are expected to reduce lease expense between $0.4 million and $0.8 million a year, or possibly more.

Chapter 24: Alternative Enterprise Value

Assuming the average 2001 Grant Thornton EBITDA multiple, Pierre's Enterprise Value is $358 million based on Pierre's $53.6 million of normalized EBITDA.

Assuming the 2001 Grant Thornton lower range sales multiple, Pierre's Enterprise Value is $348 million based on Pierre's $643 million of sales in 2008.

Enterprise Value Based on October 2008 Analysis of Bridgford & Hormel

Bridgford Foods

Bridgford Foods manufactures and sells frozen, refrigerated foods, and snack foods. Table 24.2 shows Bridgford's Enterprise Value to EBITDA and Sales for the most recent four years. Bridgford Foods had a market capitalization of $58.5 million at October 1, 2008.

Bridgford Food's Enterprise Value to EBITDA multiple is 23x based on its average annual EBITDA for the most recent three years. The EBITDA multiple is 6.7x based on Bridgford's 1Q09 EBITDA (on an annualized basis). Pierre's Enterprise Value is $359 million based on the Bridgford Food's 6.7x EBITDA multiple and Pierre's $53.6 million of normalized EBITDA.

Bridgford Food's sales multiple is 0.46x based on 1Q09 annualized sales. Pierre's Enterprise Value is $295 million based on the Bridgford sales multiple and Pierre's $643 million of sales in 2008.

Table 24.2—Bridgford Foods Enterprise Value to EBITDA and Enterprise Value to Sales

(in millions)	3 months annualized 1Q09	FYE Oct 2008	FYE Oct 2007	FYE Oct 2006	FYE Oct 2005
Sales	126.0	121.0	125.1	134.2	130.8
EBITDA	8.7	(2.6)	2.7	5.2	2.0
Debt	0.0	0.0	0.0	0.0	0.0
Equity Value 10/1/08	58.5	58.5	58.5	58.5	58.5
Enterprise Value 10/1/08	58.5	58.5	58.5	58.5	58.5
	Ratio	Ratio	Ratio	Ratio	Ratio
Enterprise Value to EBITDA	6.7x	n/a	21.7x	11.2x	29x
Enterprise Value to Sales	0.46x	0.48x	0.47x	0.44x	0.45x

Source: U.S. SEC EDGAR filings by Bridgford

Hormel

Hormel manufactures and sells meat and food products in the U.S. and internationally. Pork and turkey are the major raw materials for its products. Hormel also sells branded and value-added products in addition to commodity fresh meat products. Hormel had a market capitalization of $4.9 billion as of October 1, 2008.

Part V: Presentation of Alternative Enterprise Value for Pierre

Hormel's Enterprise Value to EBITDA multiple is 9.3x based on its average annual EBITDA for the most recent three years. Pierre's Enterprise Value is $493 million based on Hormel's 9.3x EBITDA multiple and Pierre's $53.6 million of normalized EBITDA.

Hormel's sales multiple is 0.79x. Pierre's Enterprise Value is $507 million based on the Hormel sales multiple and Pierre's $643 million of sales in 2008.

Table 24.3
Hormel Foods Enterprise Value to EBITDA and Enterprise Value to Sales

(in $ millions)	FYE Oct 2008	FYE Oct 2007	FYE Oct 2006	FYE Oct 2005
Sales	6,755	6,193	5,745	5,412
EBITDA	639	609	572	541
Debt 10/1/08	352	352	352	352
Equity Value 10/1/08	4,992	4,992	4,922	4,922
Enterprise Value 10/1/08	5,344	5,344	5,344	5,344
	Ratio	Ratio	Ratio	Ratio
Enterprise Value to EBITDA	8.36x	8.78x	9.34x	9.88x
Enterprise Value to Sales	.79x	.86x	.93x	.99x

Source: U.S. SEC filings by Hormel

Enterprise Value Based on Madison Dearborn's Acquisition Multiple for Pierre in June 2004

Madison Dearborn purchased Pierre in June 2004 for $422 million. The purchase price was equal to:

- 16.9 times Pierre's FYE March 2004 Adjusted EBITDA;
- 7.4 times Pierre's FYE March 2004 pro-forma Adjusted EBTIDA (pro-forma assumes the elimination of certain expenses post Madsion Dearborn acquiston);
- 9.4 times Pierre's FYE March 2005 EBITDA;
- 1.17 times Pierre's FYE March 2004 sales and 1.02x FYE March 2005 sales.

Pierre's Enterprise Value is $399 million based on the 7.4x pro-forma Adjusted EBITDA multiple implied by the Madison Dearborn acquisition price and Pierre's $53.6 million of normalized EBITDA.

Pierre's Enterprise Value is $655 million based on the 1.02x sales multiple implied in the Madison Dearborn acquisition price.

October 2008 Enterprise Value to EBITDA for Industry Peers

Table 24.4 shows EBITDA multiples for 16 publicly traded U.S. firms in the packaged foods and meats industry who have market capitalizations under $2

Chapter 24: Alternative Enterprise Value

billion ("Industry Peer"). As of October 2008, the Industry Peer EBITDA multiple was 9x (median) and 9.6x (average).

Table 24.4—Enterprise Value to EBITDA Multiples for Packaged Foods & Meat Industry for Firms with Market Capitalizations less than $2 billion

	EBITDA FYE 2008	Market Cap. 10/1/2008	Debt 10/1/2008	Enterprise Value 10/1/2008	Enterprise Value To FYE 2008 EBITDA
(in $ millions)					(ratio)
Median of firms below					9.0x
Average of firms below					9.6x
Sanderson Farms	(19.8)	798	177	975	(49.2x)
Smithfield Foods, Inc.	613.2	2,524	3,477	6,001	9.79x
Diamond Foods, Inc.	30.3	474	206	680	22.4x
Seneca Foods	55.8	146	279	425	7.62x
Treehouse Foods	141.9	955	552	1,507	10.6x
Del Monte	481.9	1,420	1,832	3,252	6.75x
The Hain Celestial Group	107.5	1,189	321	1,511	14.0x
American Italian Pasta	89.5	326	242	568	6.3x
Green Mountain Coffee	60.7	1,041	96	1,137	18.7x
Lance Inc.	53.4	713	82	795	14.9x
Lancaster Colony Corp	100.7	1,070	80	1,150	11.4x
Cal-Maine Foods	249	640	130	770	3.1x
Tootsie Roll Industries	80.4	1,583	7.5	1,591	19.8x
J&J Smack Foods Corp.	70	632	0.5	632	9.0x
B&G Foods	93.7	168	0.5	169	1.8x
Bridgford	(2.7)	58	no debt	58	(82.x)

Source: Custom data screen developed through Capital IQ screening by the author. Capital IQ is not responsible for the actual data results returned in the screening or in the table.
Market capitalizations as of October 1, 2008

Pierrre's October 2008 Enterprise Value Based on Industry Peer Enterprise Value to EBITDA

Pierre's Enterprise Value is $482 million based on the 9x Industry Peer median EBITDA multiple and Pierrie's $53.6 million of normlized EBITDA.

Pierre's October 2008 Enterprise Value Based on Peer Enterprise Value to Sales

Pierre's Enterprise Value is $417 million based on the Industry Peer sales muliple of 0.65x and Pierre's $643 million of sales in 2008.

Part V: Presentation of Alternative Enterprise Value for Pierre

Pierre's Enterprise Value Based on Recent Comparable Sale Transactions from July 2007 to May 2009

Nine business combinatons between July 2007 and May 2009 as reported by Capital IQ are reviewed below for the comparable transaction basis.

July 2007—Acquisition of U.S. Food Service

Clayton, Dubilier & Rice and Kohlberg Kravis Roberts purchased U.S. Foodservice from Koninklijke Ahold in July 2007 for $7.1 billion. In 2006, U.S. Foodservice had sales of $19.2 billion and an operating profit of $81 million. The acquisition price to sales multiple was 0.4x. An EBITDA multiple is not available.

U.S. Foodservice sells food products to restaurants, healthcare facilities, lodging, gaming, and governmental customers. The Company also sells flatware, glass items, dining supplies, and cookware.

January 2008—Acquisition of Performance Foods

VISTAR Corporation acquired Performance Foods in January 2008. The acquisition price to sales and EBITDA multiples were 0.2x and 10.4x, respectively.

Performance Food sells a wide variety of brand food and non-food products to independent restaurants, hotels, cafeterias, schools, healthcare facilities, and other institutional customers.

February 2008—Acquisition of Watts Brothers Frozen Foods

Lamb Weston, a subsidiary of ConAgra, acquired Watts Brothers Frozen Foods in February 2008 for $233 million. In 2007 Watts Brothers had annual sales of $100 million. The acquisition price to sales multiple was 2.3x. An EBITDA multiple is not available.

Watts Brothers Frozen Foods engages in farming, food processing, packaging, and cold storage operations. The Company sells frozen vegetables, such as corn, peas, blends, beans, and carrots.

April 2008—Acquisition of Nonni's Food

Vivartia acquired Nonni's Food for $320 million in April 2008. In 2007 Nonni had sales of $187 million and EBITDA of $32 million. The acquisition price to sales and EBITDA multiples were 1.7x and 10x, respectively.

Nonni's Food manufactures and sells biscotti, bagel chips, pita chips, flatbreads, toasts, crackers, croutons, and bread crumbs. It sells to grocery

Chapter 24: Alternative Enterprise Value

stores, club outlets, restaurants, convenience stores, and military and vending channels.

August 2008—Acquisition of Post Cereal

Ralcorp acquired Post Cereal from Kraft Foods for $2.6 billion in August 2008. In 2006 Post Cereal had annual sales of $1.1 billion and EBITDA of $234.2 million. The acquisition price to sales and EBITDA multiples were 2.4x and 11.2x, respectively.

Post Cereals manufactures cereals under the brands Honey Bunches of Oats, Pebbles, Post Selects, Spoon Size Shredded Wheat, Grape Nuts and Post Raisin Bran.

August 2008—Acquisition of Holsum Bakery

Flowers Foods acquired Holsum Bakery for $140 million in August 2008. Holsum Bakery had annual sales of $146 million. The acquisition price to sales multiple was 0.96x. An EBITDA multiple is not available.

Holsum Bakery manufactures and sells breads, buns, and rolls to retail grocers, convenience stores, restaurants, and other various institutions.

September 2008— Acquisition of Pop Secret Popcorn

Diamond Foods acquired the Pop Secret Popcorn business from General Mills for $188 million in September 2008. The Pop Secret Popcorn business had annual sales of $103 million. The sales and EBITDA multiples were 1.8x and 8.6x, respectively.

Pop Secret Popcorn offers microwave popcorn products under the brand name Pop Secret. The business was started in 1985.

October 2008—Acquisition of Star-Kist Foods

Dongwon Enterprise acquired Star-Kist Foods from Del Monte Corporation for $363 million in October 2008. Star-Kist Foods had annual sales of $560 million. The sales multiple was 0.64x. An EBITDA multiple is not available. Star-Kist Foods sells tuna products.

January 2009—Acquisition of Weston Foods, Inc.

Grupo Bimbo acquired Weston Foods from Dunedin Holdings for $2.5 billion in January 2009. The acquired business had annual sales of $2.2 billion and EBITDA of $255 million. The sales and EBITDA multiples were 1.1x and 9.8x, respectively.

Part V: Presentation of Alternative Enterprise Value for Pierre

Weston Foods produces and sells fresh, frozen, and specialty bakery products.

Pierre's Enterprise Value Based on Recent Comparable Transactions

Table 24.5 summarizes the EBITDA and sales multiples for the nine recent comparable transactions. The average Enterprise Value to EBITDA multiple was 10.0x for the comparable companies reviewed. Assuming Pierre's normalized EBITDA of $53.6 million, Pierre's Enterprise Value is $531 million based on the average EBITDA multiple of 10x for nine recent comparable transactions.

Table 24.5—Summary of Comparable Sale Transactions July 2007 to January 2009

Date	Company Acquired	Annual Sales	EBITDA	Acquisition Price to Sales	Acquisition Price To EBITDA
Jul 2007	U.S. Food Service	$7.1 billion	Unknown	0.4x	Unknown
Jan 2008	Performance Foods	$6.3 billion	$116.9 million	0.2x	10.4x
Feb 2008	Watts Brothers	$100 million	Unknown	2.3x	Unknown
Apr 2008	Nonni's Food	$187 million	$32 million	1.7x	10x
Aug 2008	Post Cereal	$1.1 billion	$234.2 million	2.4x	11.2x
Aug 2008	Holsum Bakery	$146 million	Unknown	0.96x	Unknown
Sep 2008	Pop Secret Popcorn	$103 million	$21.9 million	1.8x	8.6x
Oct 2008	Star-kist	$560 million	Unknown	0.64x	Unknown
Jan 2009	Weston Foods	$2.2 billion	$255 million	1.1x	9.8x
				Median of above:	10.0x
				Average of above:	10.0x
	Pierre Foods	$643 million	$53.6 million	Pierre's Enterprise Value is $531 million (assuming Pierre's normalized 2005–2007 EBITDA and the above median comparable acquisition multiples)	

Source: Source: Custom data screen developed through Capital IQ screening by the author. Capital IQ is not responsible for the actual data results returned in the screening or in the table.

Discounted Cash Flow Method of Valuation

Pierre's Enterpise Value is estimated by discounting Pierre's free cash flow at an appropriate discount rate. The discount rate will be based on Pierre's estimated cost of capital less and an assumed growth rate for Pierre's cash flow.

Two methods will be used to estimate the cost of capital: (1) the build-up method and (2) the Captial Asset Pricing Model (CAPM).

Chapter 24: Alternative Enterprise Value

The cash flows discounted to determine the Enterprise Value are the cash flows available to equity and debt.

Free cash flow in the model is defined as follows:

      earnings before interest and taxes x (1 − tax rate)
      +   depreciation and other non-cash charges
      -   capital expenditures
      +/- changes in working capital

Many courts have cited the U.S. Supreme Court's opinion in the 1941 case of Consolidated Rock when determining the value of a debtor at the date of the plan of reorganization. Consolidated Rock established the key criteria in valuing a company is its earning capacity rather than its market value during the bankruptcy because market value will be harmed by the bankruptcy. According to the Supreme Court, this estimate of earning capacity should be based on an informed judgment which embraces all facts relevant to future earning capacity, including, the nature and condition of the properties, the past earning records record, and all circumstances which indicate whether or not that record is a reliable criterion of future performance.

Table 24.6 shows the calculation of Pierre's free cash flow for the cash flow discount model. Pierre's $53.6 million of normalized EBITDA has been adjusted for CAPX, taxes, and operating lease expense.

The free cash flow discounted for Pierre is different for two time periods: (1) $43.6 million a year for years 1-10 and (2) $35.6 million a year after year 10 to perpetuity. The free cash flow for years 1-10 assumes Pierre will continue amortizing, for tax purposes, the goodwill/intangible value created in the Madison Deaborn acquisition. This creates a tax shield for years 1-10. After year 10, it is assumed the goodwill/intangible value has been fully amoritized and a tax shield is no longer available.

Part V: Presentation of Alternative Enterprise Value for Pierre

Table 24.6—Free Cash Flow Alternative Plan

(in $ millions)	Alternative Plan Free Cash Flow [a] Annual Years 1 to 10	Alternative Plan Free Cash Flow [a] Annual After Year 10
Normalized EBITDA	53.6	53.6
Add back operating lease expense	$3.6	3.6
Less depreciation on operating leases capitalized [b]	0.7	0.7
Less interest on operating leases capitalized [b]	0.2	0.2
Less depreciation as per Debtor's Plan	11.6	11.6
Less amortization	20.0 [c]	0 [c]
Less interest	13.2 [d]	13.2 [d]
Taxable income	11.5	31.5
Tax rate	40%	40%
Income tax	4.6	12.6
Free Cash Flow to Firm:		
Normalized EBITDA	53.6	53.6
Add back operating lease expense	3.6	3.6
Less taxes	4.6	12.6
+ - Change in working capital	0	0
Less CAPX on balance sheet plus operating lease	9.0	9.0
Free cash flow to firm	43.6	35.6

Source: Estimates developed by author.

(a) The Alternative Plan income statement and cash flow analysis is presented in Chapter 25.
(b) The present value of operating leases at 7% interest rate is $4.6 million based on the analysis of the schedule of current maturities of payments for the 3 years FYE March 2005–2007. The annual interest expense is $0.2 million. The $4.6 million capitalized cost is depreciated over seven years.
(c) As a result of the Madison Dearborn acquistion of Pierre and the Zartic/Covervalue acquistions, the book value of goodwill/intangibles was $357 million at March 1, 2007. For accounting purposes, Pierre charged-off $222 million of the goodwill/intangibles in FYE March 2008 due to impairment. For tax purposes, tha analysis assumes Pierre can continue to amortize the $357 million of goodwill/intangibles over 15 years on the tax return and that 10 years of amortization remains. Pierre's amortization of goodwill/intanbiles was $23.1 million per year. It is assumed that Pierre will continue to have a tax deduction of at least $20 million a year for ten remaining years.
(d) The detailed calculation of interest expense is presnted in Chapter 25.
(e) CAPX is assumed to be $9 million based on historical analysis of an on balance sheet CAPX plus an assumed $1 million a year CAPX for operating leases (operating lease CAPX is not reported as CAPX in the Statement of Cash Flows under genearlly accepted accounting principles, but it represents a cash outflow).

Chapter 24: Alternative Enterprise Value

Pierre's Cost of Capital

Pierre's cost of capital is a blend of Pierre's cost of debt and equity. The debt and equity is weighted by the percentage of debt and equity in the Alternative Reorganizaiton Plan.

The formula for Pierre's weigthed average cost of capital is:

$$[\text{(yield on debt)} \times (1- \text{tax rate}) \times (D)] + [(R) \times (E)]$$

where:
Yield on the debt is the rate on Pierre's debt in the Alternative Plan.
Tax rate is the marginal tax rate for the company. Assumed at 40% for Pierre.

- D = Proportion of the Pierre capital financed with debt.
- E = Proportion of the Pierre's capital financed with equity.
- R = Pierre's cost of equity capital

Build-up Method to Determine the Cost of Equity

Pierre's cost of equity capital under the build-up method is 13.64% as calculated in the Table 24.7 below.

Table 24.7— Build-Up Method for Equity Cost of Capital

	Adder	Description of Premium	Source
+	3.00%	Risk-free rate	Ibbotson 20 year U.S. Treasury income return 1926–2008
+	6.50%	Equity risk	Ibbotson S&P 500 return 1926–2008 less risk-free rate
+	4.11%	Company size	Ibbotson (market cap > $136.5 million and < $218.6 million
+	(2.47%)	Industry risk	Analysis of industry Beta in Chapter 24
+	2.50%	Bankruptcy emergence	Analysis in Chapter 24
=	13.64%	Cost of Equity	

Source: Ibbotson 2009 SSBI Valuation Yearbook and estimates developed by author.

The 13.64% cost of equity compares to 18.0% used by Grant Thronton in its 2001 valuation of Pierre. Grant Thornton did not provide a breakout of the components of 18.5% cost of equity, although Grant Thornton references reliance on the *Ibbotson SSBI 2001 Yearbook*.

The assumptions for the components of Pierre's cost of equity under the Alternative Enterprise Valuation are discussed in the next sections.

Part V: Presentation of Alternative Enterprise Value for Pierre

Risk Free Rate of Return

The *Ibbotson SSBI (Stocks, Bonds, Bills, and Inflation) Yearbook* provides returns for bonds and stocks from 1926 through the end of each year. For the risk-free rate, Ibbotson uses the income return for U.S. Treasury bonds with a 20-year maturity. Ibbotson believes the 30-year U.S. Treasury bond return is the appropriate risk-free rate, but the 30-year bond has limited history; while a 20-year remaining maturity can be traced back to 1926. From 1926 to the end of 2008, the income yield on the 20-year U.S. Treasury bond was 3.00% (Table C-1 in the *Ibbotson SSBI 2009 Valuation Yearbook*).

Equity Risk Premium

The proxy for the equity risk premium is the excess of the return on the S&P 500 over the 20-year U.S. Treasury bond, measured from the beginning of 1926 to the end of 2008. Over this time, the S&P 500 had an average return of 9.50%, resulting in an equity risk premium of 6.5%.

The equity risk premium for Pierre is 2.23% higher than the 4.27% average recommended by the experts (Table 4.3 in Chapter 4). The use of the 6.5% equity risk premium, rather than 4.27%, will result in a 34% lower Enterprise Value.

Size Premium

Ibbotson divides the S&P 500 into deciles based on the market capitalizaition of a firm. Ibbotson then caluculates the equity returns for each decile as compared to the return for the S&P 500. The excess of the return for each decile over the return for the S&P 500 is the size premium. The size premium has ranged between -0.36% for the top decile to 5.81% for the lowest decile. Table C-1 in the *2009 Ibbotson SSBI Yearbook* gives a 2.71% size premium for companies with market capitalizations between $218 million and $453 million. The size premium increases to 4.11% for companies with market capitalizalizatons between $136 million and $218 million. The 4.11% is the assumed size premium for Pierre.

Chapter 24: Alternative Enterprise Value

Industry Premium

Ibbotson has developed an industry premium method that appraisers can reference and cite in their appraisal reports. The Ibbotson industry risk premium relies on an estimation of Beta developed by Ibbotson.

Methodology for Pierre's Industry Premium

In the cost of equity build-up method, a premium can be added or subtracted for industry risk. An industry premium adder is not required under the CAPM model because the Beta in the model is assumed to include the industry risk premium.

The analysis of Pierre's sales volatility and cost structure will be used to determine the appropriate industry risk premium under the build-up method. The industry adder for Pierre will be developed based on an analysis of Betas for Pierre's industry.

Packaged sandwiches are 38% of Pierre's sales and cooked protein products are 56% of sales. Although a breakout by sales channel is not available, it is believed that a significant percentage of Pierre's sales are to grocery stores and convenience stores. Pierre also has sales to quick-service restaurant business; Hardee's accounted for 11% of sales.

Significantly, Pierre's products are quick-convenience items with a smaller ticket price than the average price of a meal at a full-service restaurant. The senstivity of Pierre's sales to economic downturns should be between the food store industry (consumer staples) and the restaurant industry (consumer discretionary), but closer to the the food store industry because of the small ticket size and the fact that 25% of Pierre's sales are to schools which are not expected to fluctuate with the economy.

The *Ibbotson 2009 SSBI Yearbook* shows a grocery/food stores industry adder of -0.10% and a eating places industry adder of -0.57%. Assuming a 50% weight for each for Pierre, the industry premium adder is -0.34% which is not significant relative to the overall discount rate.

The cost structure of a firm is also important in the risk for a firm. For the food and kindred products sector, Ibbotson data shows 116 companies have an average adder of -2.65%. A sub-sector of the food and kindred products sector is the meat packaging industry. Ibbotson shows a positive 2.33% industry adder for the 11 firms in the meat packaging industry. Pierre is not a pure meat processing and packaging firm based on the analysis of Pierre's business.

A proxy Beta will be used for Pierre based on comparable firms in the industry. Three firms in the packaged foods and meats industry have similar cost structures to Pierre.

Part V: Presentation of Alternative Enterprise Value for Pierre

Del Monte, Tootsie Roll, and Cuisine Solutions have an average cost of goods sold of 72.2% and SGA of 17.7%. Pierre had an average cost of goods sold of 72.2% and SG&A of 16.3% from 2005—2007.

The five year average unlevered Beta for Del Monte, Tootsie Roll, and Cuisine Solutions is 0.54—this will serve as the industry proxy for Pierre. The 0.54 unlevered proxy Beta will be levered based on the average leverage for all U.S. non-financial public firms. The average debt (net of cash) to market value of equity for all U.S. publicly traded stocks with revenue of $25 million (excluding financials) is 0.23:1 (see Table 3.2 in Chapter 3). Levering the 0.54 industry proxy Beta with a 0.23:1 debt to equity ratio produces a levered Beta of 0.62 (assuming a marginal tax rate of 40%).

In the capital asset pricing model, the Beta times the equity risk premium for the market equals the equity risk premium for a firm. Therefore, the 6.5% Ibbotson S&P 500 risk premium times the 0.62 levered Beta equals a 4.03% risk premium for the industry proxy, which is 2.47% lower than the 6.5% equity risk premium for the S&P 500. Consequently, the implied industry risk premium for Pierre is -2.47%.

In summary, the analysis showed an insignificant industry premium for the sensitivity of Pierre's sales to the economy. Based on Pierre's cost of goods sold and SGA percentages, Pierre's cost model is similar to Del Monte, Tootsie Roll and Cuisine Solutions. The -2.65% equity risk premium adder that Ibbotson reports for the 116 firms in food and kindred products sector seems more reasonable than the +2.33% adder reported by Ibbotson for the 11 firms in the meat packaging industry.

The final industry risk premium for the build-up equity cost of capital method for Pierre is the -2.47% industry proxy derived from the Beta analysis of comparable companies.

Table 24.8 summarizes the detail of industry risk premiums and five year Betas for the industries and companies previously discussed in the analysis.

Chapter 24: Alternative Enterprise Value

Table 24.8—Industry Premiums for Cost of Equity and Betas

SIC	Industry	Firms Ibbotson Data	Ibbotson Industry Premium	Levered Beta 5 year	Unlevered Beta 5 year
5411	Consumer Staple- food stores sector	15	-0.10	0.77 median [a] 1.03 average	0.58 median 0.78 average
5812	Consumer Discretionary-eating places (restaurants)	61	-0.57	1.61 median [b] 1.41 average	1.41 median 1.24 median
20	Consumer Staples- food & kindred products	106	-2.65		
201	- Sub sector meat products - Packaged foods & meats	11 [c]	+2.33 	1.08 average [d] 0.82 median	0.91 average 0.69 median
	Comparable companies Del Monte, Tootsie Roll, Cuisine Solutions	3		0.80 average [e]	0.54 average

Source: Beta data developed by author based on raw data sourced from Capital IQ. Industry adder data from Ibbotson SBBI 2009 *Valuation Yearbook: Market Results for Stocks, Bonds, Bills, and Inflation 1926-2008.*
Notes:
Unlevered Beta = Beta levered divided [1 + debt/market value equity times (1- tax rate)].

(a) Median Beta from seven grocery stores as of June 1, 2009. Convenience stores are excluded because a majority of their revenue is from gasoline sales. The seven firms have an average 0.53:1 ratio of debt (net of cash) to market value of equity. A marginal tax rate of 40% is assumed.
(b) For 48 restaurants in the U.S. as of June 1, 2009. The 48 firms have an average 0.23:1 ratio of debt (net of cash) to market value of equity. A marginal tax rate of 40% is assumed.
(c) The 11 firms captured in the Ibbotson data for the meat products sector are: Bob Evans Farms; Bridgford Foods Corp; Cagle's Inc.; Hormel Foods Corp.; Pilgrim's Pride Corp.; Sanderson Farms, Inc.; Zhongpin.
(d) 96 firms in the U.S. as of June 1, 2009. The Beta data is on 34 firms with a market capitalization less than $2 billion and revenue greater than $50 million. Pilgrams Pride has been excluded because the company is in bankruptcy. The debt (net of cash) to market value of equity is 0.51:1 for the 34 firms. The assumed marginal tax rate is 35.6% which is the average tax rate for the 20 of the 34 companies that had taxable income.
(e) Average Beta for all there firms as of June 1, 2009. Unlevered Beta is calculated based on the actual debt to market capitalization and tax rate for each firm. The detailed calculation for each firm is in Table 24.91.

Bankruptcy Emergence Risk Premium

Investors typically require a higher return premium for a company that is emeging from bankruptcy. Some courts have allowed valuaton experts to use a bankruptcy emergence premium. A screen has been ran using Capital IQ for non-financial companies trading on all U.S exchanges (including the pink sheets) who filed bankruptcy in the most recent three years and whose stocks contine to trade on U.S. exchanges as of June 1, 2009.

Part V: Presentation of Alternative Enterprise Value for Pierre

The 54 bankrupt non-financial firms have the following Betas:

	Median	Average
5-year	1.97	2.25
2-year	1.57	1.14
1-year	1.63	1.19

The average of the 1, 2, and 5 year Betas is 1.6, implying a bankruptcy emergence risk premium of 3.90% (the Ibbotson equity premium of 6.5% times the Beta of 1.60).

Fundemental business analysis revealed Pierre's bankruptcy was primarily the result of high debt leverage, some difficutly intergrating acqustions, and rapidily rising commodity prices. Pierre's bankruptcy was not due to a broken business model or industry with fundemental flaws. Pierre is insuluated from foreign competition and the company has a well established market niche with substantial market share in conveinience packaged sandwiches. It is difficult to justify a significant bankruptcy emergence premium for Pierre Foods on the basis that some courts and valuation experts have previously assigned an emergence premium. Pierre does not operate in a broken auto industry.

A bankruptcy emergence risk premium adder of 2.50% is assigned to Pierre based on the full analysis of Pierre Foods and its industry. If Pierre were in a broken industry and emerging from bankruptcy, a higher emergence premium might be warranted.

Estimating the Cost of Debt

The cost of debt for the reorganized debtor should be based on the cost of debt for a firm with a comparable credit profile and similar debt instruments. The postpetition debt and financial metrics of the reorganized Pierre in the Alternative Plan will be structured to achieve a credit rating comparable to a Standard & Poor's B rated credit.

The overall cost of Pierre's debt is a weighted average based on: (1) the amount of secured and unsecured debt in the capital structure and (2) the interest rates on the secured and unsecured debt based on a credit rating comparble to an S&P B rated credit.

The Alternative Plan assumes all of the Wachivia Credit Faciltiy debt will be reninsated at par. The Wachovia debt is approximately $250 million.

$98 million (39%) of the $250 million pro-forma debt in the Alternative Plan is treated as debt fully secured by collateral for interest rating pricing puposes (assumes market loan advance rates on receivables, inventory, PP&E.

Chapter 24: Alternative Enterprise Value

See Table 25.3 in Chapter 25). The remaining $152 million (61%) of the Wachovia debt is treated as unsecured for interest rate pricing purposes.

The $250 million debt in the Alternative Plan will be structued to amortize over eight years, for an average loan life of four years. For the 47 years between January 1, 1962 and December 31, 2008, the extrapolated income yield was 6.63% for four-year U.S. Treasury securities (Treasury rates from Federal Reserve Statistical Release H.15). The 6.63% extrapolated four-year Treasury rate will be the base rate. Pierre's interest rate will be the base rate plus a prcing spread (calculated in the next sections).

As of April 3, 2009, the *JPMorgan Daily High Yield Update* (Acciavatti, et al., 2008) reported B rated unsecured bonds were yielding 13.31%, a substantial premium over historical spreads. The unprecedented high spreads were caused by the 2008/2009 financial and economic crisis. The historical average JP Morgan spreads are used for Pierre's valuation rather than current spread, which is consistent with determining the equity cost of capital based on the the longest measurement period possible. The model to value a company should be based on the long-term historical averages that represent normalized long-term expectations. This is consistent with using the longest period possible to measure the equity risk premium rather than using an equity risk premium of -37.6 based on the S&P 500 losing 37.6% of its value in 2008.

For the 21 years from 1987–2008, the *JP Morgan 2008 High-Yield Annual Review Review* (Acciavatti, et al., 2008) reported that an average high-yield S&P B rated credit had a spread of 5.66% over comparable U.S. Treasury securities. Over the same time, leveraged secured loans have traded with an average risk premium of 2.5% over comparable term U.S. securities.

Pierre cost of debt is calculated as follows:
- 39% of the loan is a secured loan. The interest rate is fixed at 9.13%. The rate is calcuated by adding the 2.5% spread to the four-year U.S. Treasuary average yield of 6.63% over the last 47 years;
- 61% of the loan is an unsecured loan. The interest rate is fixed at 12.29%. The rate is calculated by adding the 5.66% spread to the four-year U.S. Treasury average yield of 6.63% over the last 47 years;
- Based on the above pricing, the average weighted cost of debt for the $250 million debt in the Alternative Plan is 11.06%.

Part V: Presentation of Alternative Enterprise Value for Pierre

Discounted Cash Flow Model: Present Value Formula

The last calculation to determine Enterprise Value is the present value formua to discount cash flows. There are a number of models that can be used, including:

- Stable firm model that has a stable rate of earnings or growth in earnings;
- Two stage model that assumes an initial high rate of growth in earnings followed by a stable growth;
- Three stage growth model where the first two stages are higher growth rate time periods and the final stage is a stable growth rate.

For Pierre, the model of stable earnings growth will be used. The stable firm model is:

$$\text{Enterprise Value} = \frac{\text{Normalized Cash Flows Available to all Capital}}{(\text{Required Rate of Return}) - (\text{Growth Rate})}$$

Growth Rate in Model

The Debtor's Plan projects revenue growth of 0% (FYE March 2009), 2.9% (FYE March 2010), 7.4% (FYE March 2011), and 6.9% (FYE March 2012). The average sales growth is 4.3% over the four years in the Debtor's Plan. Based on a Capital IQ custom screen by the author, the five year median sales growth rate is 8.66% for U.S. exchange traded companies with annual sales over $50 million in the packaged foods and meats industry. Historically, Pierre's sales growth has been faster than the industry average. Pierre's acquistions make it difficult to determine its growth rate excluding acquistions. Pierre's sales consist primarily of packaged sandwiches and pre-cooked proteins in a quick-service food industry that have grown faster than the overall U.S. economy.

The Alternative Enterprise Value assumes a 2.96% growth rate for Pierre's sales and free cash flow, a growth rate equal to the historical real compound annual growth rate of the U.S. economy from 1981 to the end of 2008.

Chapter 24: Alternative Enterprise Value

Pierre's Enterprise Value Under Build-up Method

Based on the variables and formula in the Table 24.90, Pierre's Enterprise Value is $572 million based on the build-up method for the cost of capital.

Table 24.90— Calculation of Alternative Enterprise Value for Build-Up Method ($ millions)

Pierre's Enterprise Value based on variables & assumptions below	$572
Free Cash Flow to Firm (average or normalized 2005 – 2007) [a]	$43.6 years 1 – 10 $35.6 year thereafter
Buildup Model for Cost of Equity:	
Ibbotson Risk Free Rate (1926 – 2008)	3.00%
Ibbotson Risk Premium for S&P 500 average stock (1926 – 2008)	6.50%
Ibbotson Risk Premium small cap stock 2009 SSBI Yearbook	4.11%
Industry Risk Premium developed in this book	(-2.47%)
Bankruptcy emergence risk premium developed by author	2.50%
Required Equity Return for Pierre Foods	13.64%
Targeted equity to capital target ratio [b]	0.46
Targeted debt to capital target ratio [b]	0.54
Assumed marginal federal/state tax rate	40%
Pretax debt cost [c]	11.06% [c]
Cost of Debt = cost of debt * (1 – tax rate)	6.63%
Pierre's cost of capital = (cost of equity) * (equity/total capital) + pretax debt cost * [(1 – tax rate) * (debt/total capital)]	9.85%
Less Pierre's assumed sales & cash flow growth rate	2..96%
Discount rate for cash flow to determine Enterprise Value	6.89%

(a) Free cash flow calcuated in Table 24.6.
(b) Target debt to capital ratio is 0.46 for purposes of estimating the cost of capital. Based on the final $514 million Enterprise Value assigned to Pierre at the end of Chapter 24, the actual debt to capital ratio is 0.49:1 ($250 million of debt to $514 million Enterprise Value).
(c) $250 million of pro-forma debt in the Alternative Plan. The loan value of Pierre's assets, assuming prudent lender advance rates, supports a secured loan of $98 million (39% of the $250 million debt). $152 million (61%) of debt is unsecured for interest rate pricing purposes. The $250 million of exit debt under the Altnerative Plan amortizes over eight years, for an average-life of four years. Between January 1962 and December, 2008, U.S. Treauary securities, with a four-year maturity, had an extrapolated income yield of 6.63 (Federal Reseve H15). The JP Morgan High Yield Update (Acciavatti, Linares, Nelson, 2008) reported historical interest rate spreads over comparable term U.S. Treasury securities for unsecured bonds and secured loans for single B rated firms. The JP Morgan historical spreads are based on long periods of time rather than spreads at one point in time. The historical spreads were 5.66% for unsecured bonds and 2.50% for senior secured loans. Therefore, in determining the cost of Pierre's debt, 39% of Pierres debt has a rate of 9.13% (U.S. 4 year Treasury yield plus 2.5%) and 61% of the debt has a rate of 12.29% (U.S. Treasury yield plus 5.66%). The overall blended yield is 11.06%.

Part V: Presentation of Alternative Enterprise Value for Pierre

Enterprise Value Based on Capital Asset Pricing (CAPM) Model

For the CAPM, two cases are presented to estimate a proxy for Pierre's Beta:

- The average five year Beta for Del Monte, Tootsie Roll, and Cuisines Solutions;
- The average and median five year Beta for the packaged foods and meats industry. The proxy Betas have been unlevered and relevered for Pierre's projected leverage.

For the industry proxy, the measurement is on 109 exchange traded U.S. firms in the packaged foods and meats industy. Their Betas have been unlevered based on their average 0.18:1 book value of debt to the market value of equity.

The average Beta is 0.80 for Del Monte, Tootsie Roll, and Cuisines Solution—their unlevered average Beta is 0.54.

For the 109 companies in the packaged foods and meats industry, the Beta is 1.08 (average) and 0.82 (median). The unleverd Beta for the 109 companies is 0.81 (average) and 0.62 (median).

Pierre's Beta is relevered for an projected debt to equity ratio of 0.65:1 (40% marginal tax rate). The following formula has been used to lever Pierre's Beta:

Pierre's Beta = { Beta unlevered * { (1 + [(Debt/Equity) * (1-t)] }

The formula to estimate Pierre' cost of equity under the CAPM model is:

+ Risk free rate
+ Levered Beta x equity premium
+ Small firm capitalization premium
+ Bankruptcy emergence premium
= Cost of equity

The risk-free rate, equity premium, small firm premium, and bankruptcy emergence premium used in the CAPM are identical in amount to the premiums used in build-up method.

Assuming the variables in Table 24.90, Pierre's Enterprise Value estimates are shown in Table 24.91 for three cases:

- $487 million Enterprise Value based on the average Beta proxy for Del Monte, Tootsie Roll, and Cuisines Solutions;
- $425 million Enterprise Value based on the <u>average</u> Beta proxy for the 108 public firms in packaged foods and meats industry;
- $471 million Enterprise Value based on the <u>median</u> Beta proxy for the 108 public firms in the packaged foods and meats industry.

Chapter 24: Alternative Enterprise Value

Table 24.91—Pierre's Enterprise Value under CAPM based on Industry Beta and Comparable Firm Betas

	Five Year Betas Used in CAPM Model		
	Three Peer Firms [a] - Del Monte - Tootsie Roll - Cuisine Solution	Packaged Foods & Meats Industry	
		Average Beta	Median Beta
Pierre's Enterprise Value based on data in this Table	$487 million	$425 million	$471 million
Free Cash Flow to Firm	$43.6 million a year for years 1–10 & $35.6 year thereafter		
Levered Beta			
- Del Monte ($3.7 billion annual sales)	0.60		
- Tootsie Roll ($493 million annual sales)	0.63		
- Cuisine Solutions ($87.5 million annual sales)	1.16		
Avg. for Del Monte, Tootsie Roll, Cuisine Solutions	0.80		
- Packaged Food & Meats Industry	–	1.08 [b]	0.82 [b]
Unlevered Beta			
- Del Monte (1.15:1 debt/equity ratio. 33.8% tax rate)	0.34		
- Tootsie Roll (no significant debt. 30.6% tax rate)	0.63		
- Cuisine Solutions (.34:1 debt to equity ratio. 0% tax rate)	0.68		
Avg. for Del Monte, Tootsie Roll, Cuisine Solutions	0.55		
- Packaged food & meats industry	–	0.81 [b]	0.62 [b]
Risk-free Rate (20-year U.S. Treasury return)	3.0%	3.0%	3.0%
Equity risk premium (Ibbotson 1926 to 2008)	6.5%	6.5%	6.5%
Small cap premium (Ibbotson 1926 to 2008)	4.1%	4.1%	4.1%
Bankruptcy emergence premium developed in this book	2.5%	2.5%	2.5%
Pierre's projected debt to equity ratio	.90 [c]	.90 [c]	.90 [c]
Marginal federal/state tax rate	40% [d]	40% [d]	40% [d]
Levered Beta= Beta unlevered *{(1 + [(Debt/Equity) * (1-t)]}	0.85	1.24	.95
Cost of equity = risk free rate + (levered Beta * equity premium) + small cap premium + emergence premium	15.1%	17.7%	15.8%
Pretax debt cost	11.06	11.06%	11.06%
Cost of debt = pretax cost of debt * (1 – tax rate)	6.63%	6.63%	6.63%
Debt to capital ratio	.47	.47	.47
Equity to capital ratio	.53	.53	.53
Required return = (cost of equity) * (equity/capital) + Pretax debt cost * [(1 – tax rate) * (debt/capital)]	11.19%	12.50%	11.49%
Pierre's assumed growth rate for sales and cash flow	2.96%	2.96%	2.96%
Discount factor for cash flows	8.23%	9.54%	8.53%

Source: Beta data developed by author based on data from Capital IQ

(a) For the 3 years FYE March 2005–2007, Pierre had an average COGS of 72.2% and average SG&A of 16.3%. Within the packaged foods & meats sector, three firms have COGS and SGA percentages comparable to Pierre: Del Monte, Tootsie Roll, and Cuisine Solutions.

(b) As of June 1, 2009. The Beta data is on 34 firms with market capitalization less than $2 billion and revenue greater than $50 million. Pilgrams Pride was excluded because the company is in bankruptcy. Unlevered is based on debt (net of cash) to market capitalization of equity. Equity is as of June 1, 2009 and debt is as of the most recent annual 2008 financial statement. The ratio of debt (net of cash) to market value of equity is 0.51:1 for the 34 firms. Unlevered Beta = Beta levered divided [1 + debt/market value equity times (1- tax rate)]. The average tax rate for 20 of the 34 firms that had taxable income was 35.6% (the marginal tax rate).

(c) Modeled debt to equity ratio of 0.90:1 for Pierre in CAPM. Pierre's final Enterprise Value estimated at $514 million at end of Chapter 24. Debt in the Alternative Plan is $248 million, for a final debt/equity of 0.93:1.

(d) KMPG reports a marginal rate of 40% for firms in the U.S.

Part V: Presentation of Alternative Enterprise Value for Pierre

Final Determination of Pierre's Enterprise Value as of October 1, 2008

Table 24.92 summarizes all of the Enterprise Values for Pierre that have been reviewed in this Chapter based on the following valuations:

- Grant Thornton multiples in 2001;
- Madison Dearborn 2004 acquisition multiples;
- Hormel comparable company multiples;
- Bridgford Food comparable company mutliples;
- Comparable transaction multiples from July 2007 to January 2009;
- Build-up method of cost of capital;
- CAPM model.

Valuation experts are of the opinion that the discounted cash flow is the most preferable method of estimating Enterprise Value.

The build-up method and CAPM models gave Enterprise Values of $574 million and $471 million, respectively. The average of the two methods is $522 million. The $522 million is weighted 50% in the final estimate of the Pierre's Alternative Enterprise Value.

The $482 million Enterprise Value, based on the October 2008 Industry Peer Enterprise Value to EBITDA multiple, is weighted 25% in the final analysis.

The $531 million Enterprise Value, based on the July 2007 to January 2009 comparable transaction Enterprise Value EBITDA, is weighted 25%.

The final Alternative Enterprise Value for Pierre is $514 million and compares to the Perella Weinberg estimate of $232 million for Pierre's Enterprise Value.

The $514 million Alternative estimate of Enterprise Value is equal to 9.6 times Pierre's $53.6 million of normalized EBITDA.

Many distressed equity funds and buyers of corporate assets favor Enterprise Value to EBITDA multiples in the 3.5:1 to 5.0:1 range. Their objective is to buy a company at a bargain price. The purpose of the Alternative estimate of Enterprise Value is not to provide the most conservative estimate for a bargain purchase price; rather the purpose is to determine fair value for the benefit of all the parties to the bankrupt estate.

A plan based on the $514 million Alternative Enterprise Value must be feasible, providing the Debtor with adequate liquidity and a capital structure that will not land the Debtor back in bankruptcy in the near future. The next chapter

Chapter 24: Alternative Enterprise Value

is a presentation of a feasible Alternative Plan based on the $514 million Enterprise Value.

Table 24.92—Summary of Pierre's Enterprise Value Under Different Models ($millions)

(in $ millions)	Enterprise Value Based on EBITDA Multiple	Enterprise Value Based on Sales Multiple	Enterprise Value Based on Discounted Cash Flow
Grant Thornton 2001 multiple	358	348	
Madison Dearborn June 2004 acquisition multiple	399	655	
October 2008 Industry Peer Multiple	482	417	
Hormel October 2008 results	493	507	
Bridgford March 2009 results (annualized)	359	295	
Comparable Transactions July 2007 to Jan 2009	531		
DCF Alternative Enterprise Value Build-up Method			574
DCF Alternative Enterprise Value CAPM			471 [a]
Average of above	437	444	522
Median of above	446	402	522

Source: Prior estimates from in Chapter 24.

(a) Based on industry of 109 firms in the food packaging and meat industry. $471 million is the average estimated Enterprise Value under CAPM.

Part VI
The Presentation of the Alternative Reorganization Plan

Chapter 25

The Alternative Reorganization Plan

"If you want to make enemies, try to change something."
Woodrow Wilson

The Alternative Plan assumes the $514 million Alternative Enterprise Value as estimated in Chapter 24.
The Alternative Plan is as follows:
- It is assumed that Pierre accepts $1 million of prepetition capital leases based on estimates of the rejected leases in the case;
- Wachovia's claim is $248.7 million, after add-back of $2.9 million preference payments recovered from the Wachovia holders;
- The $248.7 million Wachovia claim is exchanged for a $248.7 million loan, secured by a first-lien on all assets. The Wachovia lien is primed by a $6.4 million Exit Revolver, without impairment because Wachovia reduced its letters of credits exposure by $6.4 million during bankruptcy;
- The Wachovia loan is interest-only for six months, followed by an eight-year loan amortization. The Wachovia loan is bifurcated into four tranches of $62.2 million. Each subsequent tranche is subordinate in payment and collateral to the prior tranche. Each tranche fully amortizes as follows: tranche 1 (2.5 years), tranche 2 (4.5 years), tranche 3 (6.5 years), and tranche 4 (8.5 years). Because the loan amortizes, the Wachovia loan will not have an after-acquired lien on equipment and real estate. Wachovia's after-acquired lien extends only to receivables and inventory;
- On December 27, 2008 the book value of receivables and inventories was $85 million—if the book value falls below $85 million at the end of any future quarter, Pierre will pay the amount below $85 million into a

Part VI: Presentation of an Alternative Reorganization Plan

cash escrow account as collateral security for the Wachovia loan. The escrow agent will apply the escrow balance to the loan balance in the event of a loan default. If the value of the collateral increases above $85 million, the escrow agent will transfer the excess funds in escrow to Pierre's unrestricted cash;

- The Wachovia loan has a four-quarter rolling covenant for: (1) EBITDA to interest > 3.50:1, (2) EBITDA to debt service > 1.00:1, and (3) debt to EBITDA < 6.0:1. Measurement begins 3/31/2010. Other covenants: cash balances > $15 million and payables average age < 45 days (measured quarterly, beginning the first quarter after bankruptcy). Annual CAPX < $8 million;

- The Wachovia loan has the same key affirmative/negative covenants as in prepetition Wachovia loan, except a change of control is defined as any party obtaining more than 50% of the stock other than Madison Dearborn or Oaktree Capital. Stock dividends are permitted if the EBITDA to debt service ratio > 1.25:1 (four quarters rolling and most recent quarter) and subject to cash > $25 million (after the dividend payment) and payables < 30 days;

- 100% of Pierre's stock is valued at $264.3 million, the difference between Alternative Enterprise Value of $514 million and funded debt of $249.7 million (Wachovia debt of $248.7 million + capital leases of $1 million). The Alternative Plan distributes Pierre's Preferred stock to claimants as identified in Table 25.0. Preferred Stock carries 9% cumulative dividends, payable quarterly.

Table 25.0—Allocation of Preferred Stock to Classes of Claims

(in $ millions)	Claims	Stock Value	% of Stock
Unsecured Claims:			
Senior Notes	131.3	131.3	49.6%
Interest on Senior Notes during bankruptcy	4.7	4.7	1.8%
Vendor & contract	6.2	6.2	2.4%
Vendor disgorgement recovery claim	9.0	9.0	3.4%
Compensation Woodhams & Naylor	2.4	2.4	0.9%
Contract reject: NASCAR & Interstate Warehouse	5.7	5.7	2.2%
Prepetition Stockholders		105.0 [a]	39.7%
Totals		264.3	100.0%

(a) Prepetition stockholders receive 39.7% of the stock to be held in escrow. The stock is released from escrow on March 1, 2012, if there has not any conversion of the Wachovia debt to equity or if there is a not material event default on the Wachovia loan on March 1, 2012.

Chapter 25: Alternative Reorganization Plan

- The $15.6 million of tranche 1 loan principal payments (due between July 1, 2009 and December 1, 2009) are funded into an escrow account, but funding is not required if Pierre's cash is < $15 million;
- If Pierre's debt service to EBITDA is < 1.0:1 (four quarter rolling or most recent quarter) for the period ending December 31, 2009, Pierre's balance sheet will be restructured as follows:
  - Tranches 2–4 ($186.7 million) exchanged for a newly issued stock that gives Tranches 2–4 ownership of 62.5% of Pierre's stock (calculated in next bullet point). Table 25.1 shows the ownership of the stock in the event of the conversion of tranches 2–4:

Table 25.1—Allocation of Preferred Stock to Classes of Claims if Tranche 2, 3, and 4 Convert to Equity

(in $ millions)	Claims	Stock Value	%
Unsecured Claims:			
Senior Notes	131.3	90.5	30.3%
Interest on Senior Notes during bankruptcy	4.7	3.3	1.1%
Vendor & contract	6.2	4.3	1.4%
Vendor disgorgement recovery claim	9.0	8.3	2.8%
Compensation Woodhams & Naylor	2.4	1.7	0.6%
Contract reject: NASCAR & Interstate Warehouse	5.7	3.9	1.3%
Prepetition Stockholders		0	0%
Converted Wachovia Tranche 2, 3 and 4	186.7	186.7	62.5%
Totals		298.6	100%

Source: estimates and projections by the author.

  - The Distress Enterprise Value is $361.8 million. Pierre's stock is valued at $298.6 million, net of $1 million capital leases and $62.2 million tranche 1 debt. 62.5% of the stock value is $186.7 million, equal to the value of the debt exchanged on tranches 2–4. The DCF valuation model discounts $35.1 million of annual free cash flow ($40.5 million of distress EBITDA per Table 8.0, plus $3.6 million of operating lease expense less $9 million of CAPX). Debt to equity ratio modeled at 0.14:1. Discount rate for cash flow is 9.70% net of growth rate of 2.96%. Cost of capital equals (13.64% cost of equity x 86% equity in capital structure) + (6.63% cost of debt x 14% debt in capital structure).
  - The escrow agent pays the cash in the escrow to tranche 1 after December 31 2009, subject to EBITDA to debt service > 1.0:1 for the most recent quarter and subject to cash balances > $15

Part VI: Presentation of an Alternative Reorganization Plan

million after the payment. If cash in the escrow is short of the required amount, Pierre pays the deficiency when cash balances are in excess of $15 million.

- If tranches 2–4 convert to debt, Pierre has only $62.2 million of remaining debt. The CMLTD on Tranche 1 is $31.2 million (a two-year amortization). Because of the aggressive amortization, a covenant will prohibit principal payments on tranche 1 if cash is less than $15 million.

- Senior management of Pierre will have a five-year incentive compensation package structured to maximize cash flow, liquidity, and return on equity based on the Alternative Plan income statement, cash flow, and balance sheet. If management exceeds the cumulative five-year Alternative Plan cash flow forecast, the maximum bonus is 100% of annual salary. The bonus is payable 50% in cash and 50% in stock.

Tax Implications of Alternative Plan

The Internal Revenue Code disallows the carry-forward of prior year losses as an offset to future income when there is a 50% change in stock ownership. Under the Debtor's Plan, Pierre does not retain prior year loss carry-forwards because Oaktree Capital gains control of 92% of Pierre's stock.

The Debtor's Plan results in an estimated $134 million taxable gain on the cancellation of debt because the Senior Notes and other unsecured claims receive 12½ cents on the dollar in full settlement of their prepetition claims. The Debtor's Plan estimates $25 million of post-emergence tax liability for fiscal years 2010–2012., projected to be paid every two to four months over a three year period (footnotes to Exhibit C to Debtor's October 29, 2009 Plan)

In the Alternative Plan, the stock exchanged for creditor claims has a fair market value equal to the value of the prepetition claims. As a result, Pierre does not have a taxable gain on the settlement of prepetition claims.

Under the Alternative Plan, there is a much better chance the Debtor will be able to carry-forward past tax losses as an offset against future income because the prepetition shareholders are retaining 39.7% of the stock in Pierre and the Senior Note holders are receiving 51.4% of the stock. A final determination of the preservation of the tax losses is subject to further due diligence for the requirement of an 18 month holding period for the prepetition stock and Senior Notes.

Chapter 25: Alternative Reorganization Plan

Amortization of the Wachovia Loan—Alternative Plan

Table 25.2 shows the amortization for each Wachovia loan tranche.

Table 25.2—Amortization of the Four Wachovia Loan Tranches ($ millions)

Date	Tranche 1 Balance	Tranche 2 Balance	Tranche 3 Balance	Tranche 4 Balance	Total Balance
Day 1	62.2	62.2	62.2	62.2	248.7
18 months	31.1	62.2	62.2	62.2	217.7
30 months	0	62.2	62.2	62.2	186.6
42 months	0	31.1	62.2	62.2	155.5
54 months	0	0	62.2	62.2	124.4
66 months	0	0	31.1	62.2	93.3
78 months	0	0	0	62.2	62.2
90 months	0	0	0	31.1	31.1
102 months	0	0	0	0	0

Source: Projection by author based on Alternative Plan.

The bifurcation of the loan into four tranches provides for greater collateral coverage and faster repayment for the two most senior tranches and allows for a tiered loan pricing structure. The bifurcation will also facilitate the syndication of the Wachovia loan.

As of December 27, 2008, Pierre's receivables, inventories, and PP&E had a net book value of $149 million. Assuming a prudent lender would loan 85% of receivables, 50% of inventory, and 50% of the net book value of PP&E, the loan value of the collateral is $98 million (Table 25.3).

Table 25.3—Wachovia Loan: Secured Vs. Unsecured for Purposes of Pricing the Loan

(in $ millions)	Book Value 12/27/08	Prudent Lender Advance Rate	Loan Value
Receivables	35	85%	30
Inventory	60	50%	30
PP&E	76	50%	38
Total	149		98

Wachovia loan secured portion (a)	$98 (39%)
Wachovia loan unsecured portion (a)	$153 (61%)
Total Wachovia loan (a)	$249 (100%)

Source: Pierre's U.S. SEC EDGAR filing for 12/27/08 book value. Author estimate of prudent lender advance rates
(a) For pricing purposes only.

Part VI: Presentation of an Alternative Reorganization Plan

Table 25.4 compares the ratio of the loan value of the assets to the loan balance on each tranche. The purpose of the comparison is to assess the recovery prospects for each tranche in the event of loan default.

Table 25.4—Ratio of Prudent Lender Loan Value to Loan Balance by Tranche

Date	Tranche 1 Balance	Tranche 2 Balance	Tranche 3 Balance	Tranche 4 Balance	Total Balance
Day 1	1.56:1	0.56:1	(0.44:1)	(1.43:1)	0.39:1
18 months	3.11:1	1.06:1	0.06:1	(0.94:1)	0.45:1
30 months	Paid off	1.56:1	0.56:1	(0.44:1)	0.52:1
42 months		3.11:1	1.06:1	0.06:1	0.62:1
54 months		Paid off	1.56:1	0.56:1	0.78:1
66 months			3.11:1	1.06:1	1.04:1
78 months			Paid off	1.56:1	1.56:1
90 months				3.11:1	3.11:1
102 months				Paid off	Paid off

Source: Projection by author based on Alternative Plan

The amortization of the Wachovia loan in 8.5 years is commercially reasonable and in-line with lending practices in the market. Receivables and inventories are non-depreciating assets and the Alternative Plan has a control to maintain minimum assets of $149 million.

It is unfortunate that the Wachovia loan is $248.7 million as compared to the $149 million book value of the collateral, but the Wachovia collateral to loan ratio is no worse off than it was 90 days to bankruptcy or immediately after Wachovia underwrote and funded the acquisitions of Clovervale/Zartic. In fact, the Wachovia Revolver had $19.6 million unfunded exposure when Wachovia prior the Wachovia loan default.

The Alternative Plan has a mandatory 8.5 year amortization. In the event the value of receivables and inventories fall below the level at December 27, 2008, then at the end of each quarter Pierre will be required to place the shortfall into an escrow account as collateral security for the loan.

Chapter 25: Alternative Reorganization Plan

Determining the Interest Rate for each Tranche—Alternative Plan

For the 21 years 1987-2008, the *JP Morgan 2008 High-Yield Annual Review* reported (Acciavatti, et al., 2008) that the average high-yield B rated S&P corporate bond (unsecured) had an average spread of 5.66% over comparable U.S. Treasury securities. Over the same time, leveraged secured loans traded with an average spread of 2.5% over comparable term U.S. Treasury securities.

The first two Wachovia tranches have a risk-adjusted interest rate spread that compares favorably to historical average spread for a senior-secured loan because of: (1) collateral coverage, (2) the short duration of the loan, and (3) the priority of cash flow coverage.

Tranches 3 and 4 are partially secured and the rate for these two tranches is a blend of the spread for senior secured loans and of the spread for unsecured corporate bonds, assuming a B rated credit.

The interest rate for each Tranche is a fixed interest, equal to the comparable term U.S. Treasury rate plus the following margin:

- Tranche 1: 1.50% margin based on:
    - 1.56:1 day one collateral to loan ratio;
    - Priority position on cash flow;
    - 2.5 year loan amortization.
- Tranche 2: 3.00% margin based on:
    - 0.56:1 day one collateral to loan ratio;
    - 1.06:1 collateral to loan ratio in 1.5 years;
    - Priority position on cash flow;
    - 4.5 year loan amortization;
- Tranche 3: 4.66% margin (1.00% below the 5.66% historical spread for unsecured single B rated bonds). The tranche 3 collateral to loan ratio is 1.0:1 in 3.5 years;
- Tranche 4: 5.66% margin (equal to the 5.66% historical spread for unsecured single B rated bonds). The tranche 4 collateral to loan ratio is 1.0:1 in 5.5 years.

Part VI: Presentation of an Alternative Reorganization Plan

Fixed Interest Rate by Tranche

Table 25.5 shows the fixed interest rates for each tranche based on the comparable term U.S. Treasury securities as of December 12, 2008 (the emergence date from bankruptcy).

Table 25.5—Fixed Interest Rate for Wachovia Credit Facility Under Alternative Plan

	Tranche 1	Tranche 2	Tranche 3	Tranche 4
Loan term	2 year	4 year	6 year	8 year
U.S. Treasury rate comparable term	0.97%	1.21%	1.67%	2.50%
Interest rate margin	1.50%	3.00%	4.66%	5.66%
Interest rate fixed for loan term	2.47%	4.21%	6.33%	8.16%

Source: Treasury rates from Federal Reserve Statistical Release H.15. The four-year, six-year, and eight-year rates are extrapolated from the rates provided in the H.15 for three-year, five-year, and seven-year term U.S. Treasury rates as of December 12, 2008.

Liquidity Post Chapter 11 Exit—Alternative Plan

Table 25.6 projects pro-forma unrestricted cash balances of $14.6 million after exit from bankruptcy. The $14.6 million unrestricted cash is net of a $6.6 million cash reserve for letters of credits. Total post emergence liquidity is $21.0 million, consisting of the $14.6 million unrestricted cash balance and $6.4 million availability on the Exit Revolver.

Table 25.6—Projected Cash Liquidity at Exit From Chapter 11 Under Alternative Plan

($ millions)	
5.8	Cash at December 27, 2008 (Pierre's balance sheet filed with Bankruptcy Court)
-8.0	Payout balance of professional fees ($15.9 with $7.9 million paid out through 12/19)
-3.4	Payout of other claim after December 27 (high estimate)
9.0	Disgorgement of prepaid vendor payments 90 days prior to bankruptcy
2.9	Disgorgement of cash paid to Wachovia Credit Facility 90 days prior to bankruptcy
29.8	Claw back of 12% cash payout to Wachovia Credit Facility under Debtor Plan
15.7	Claw back of 12% paid out on $131 million unsecured Senior Notes
(20.0)	Payoff Exit Facility Term Loan balance at 12/27/08 (balance sheet filed in Bankruptcy Court)
(11.7)	Payoff Exit Facility Revolver balance at 12/27/08 (balance sheet filed in Bankruptcy Court)
1.1	Proceeds for sale of equipment closing by 1Q09
21.2	Pro forma cash balance
(6.6)	Less restricted cash required to secured letters of credits
14.6	Unrestricted cash
6.4	Exit Revolver borrowing availability
21.0	Liquidity emergence

Source: Projection by author based on Alternative Plan and estimates from the case information.

Chapter 25: Alternative Reorganization Plan

Working Capital Required For Future Periods in the Alternative Plan

Table 25.7 shows working capital accounts for Pierre's balance sheets dated November 29, 2008, December 27, 2008, and for Pierre's projections for fiscal years March 2009–2011.

The Alternative Plan assumes an increase in inventories from $60 million at December 27, 2008 to $67 million for all future periods, an amount consistent with the Debtor's future projections and the inventories that Pierre maintained at FYE March 1, 2008.

The Debtor's Plan projects sales of $55 million a month for FYE March 2010, 24% more than the average monthly sales of $44.3 million for November/December 2008. Therefore, the Alternative Plan projects receivables will increase 24% for all future periods from the level of receivables at December 27, 2008.

As of December 27, 2008, vendor payables are $7 million (15-day vendor payable turnover). The Debtor plan and the Alternative Plan both assume vendor payables will increase to $17 million by February 28, 2010, providing $10 million of additional working capital within one year as trade terms return.

Table 25.7—Analysis of Working Capital Accounts (Alternative Plan)

(in $ millions)	Actual 11/29/08	Actual 12/27/08	Alternative Plan All Future Periods	Debtor's Plan		
				FYE 2/28/09	FYE 2/28/10	FYE 2/28/11
Receivables	38	35	43	50	52	53
Inventory	61	60	67	67	67	69
Prepaid and other assets	11	11	11	9	10	10
Current assets	110	106	121	126	129	132
Payables - post petition	5	7	17	6	17	19
Accrued marketing	7	6	6	below	below	Below
Accrued wages	4	8	8	below	below	Below
Accrued interest Wachovia	3	0.7	0.7	below	below	Below
Accrued wages	4	8	8	below	below	Below
Other accruals	5	6	6	23	22	22
Current Liabilities	31	36	38	29	39	41

Source: Pierre's U.S. SEC EDGAR filings and the projections in the Debtor's October 29, 2008 Plan.

(a) $8 million of professional fees related to the bankruptcy to be paid post February 28, 2009—the Alternative Plan liquidity assumed the $8 million was paid on December 12 (exit from bankruptcy).

Part VI: Presentation of an Alternative Reorganization Plan

Post Closing Balance Sheet—Alternative Plan

Pierre exited bankruptcy on December 12, 2008. Table 25.8 shows the projected balance sheet in the Alternative Plan post emergence.

Table 25.8—Balance Sheet Alternative Plan Immediately After Exit From Bankruptcy

	(in $ millions)	Footnotes and Comments
Cash unrestricted	14.6	As previously estimated
Receivables	38.2	11/29/08 balance sheet
Inventory	61.4	" "
PP&E & spare parts	76.6	" "
Software	2.3	" "
Other assets	6.7	" "
Restricted cash	6.6	To secure letter of credits
Goodwill	335.9	Total liabilities & equity less all other assets
Total Assets	$542.3	
Trade Payables	6.9 [a]	11/28/08 balance sheet
Accrued marketing	6.3	" "
Accrued wages	8.0	" "
Accrued interest Wachovia	0.7	" "
Accruals	6.4	" "
Professional fees accrued	0 [b]	" "
CMLTD capital lease	0.3	
CMLTD Wachovia debt	31.1	8 year amortization on Wachovia loan
Long-term capital lease	0.7	
Long-term Wachovia debt	217.6	Wachovia loan due after one year
Total debt	249.7	
Total liabilities	278.0	
Shareholders equity	264.3	Enterprise Value of $514 less $249.7 funded debt
Total liabilities & equity	542.3	

Source: Author projections based on Alternative Plan.

(a) Payables are $6.9 at November 29, 2008, for a payable turnover of 6.7 days based on raw material cost of sales. Payables in the Debtor's Plan increase to $17.2 million by March 2010, for a payable turnover of 17 days based on the level of raw material purchases in the Debtor's Plan.

(b) $8.0 million professional fees on the Debtor's balance sheet dated 11/29/08. To be paid in full under the Alternative Plan at the exit from bankruptcy.

Projected Income, Cash Flow, Cash, & Wachovia Loan—Alternative Plan

Table 25.9 shows the FYE 2009–2018 Alternative Plan projected: (1) income statement, (2) cash flows, (3) cash balances, and (4) Wachovia loan balance.

The Alternative Plan projects $53.6 million of annual EBITDA for each of the nine years in the budget, an amount equal to Pierre's historical average Adjusted EBITDA for the three fiscal years FYE March 2005–2007.

Chapter 25: Alternative Reorganization Plan

Table 25.9—Alternative Plan Projected Income Statement, Cash Flow, & Wachovia Loan Balance

($millions)	Yr. 1	Yr. 2	Yr. 3	Yr. 4	Yr. 5	Yr. 6	Yr. 7	Yr. 8	Yr. 9
Sales (a)	643	643	643	643	643	643	643	643	643
Gross Margin (b)	171.7	171.7	171.7	171.7	171.7	171.7	171.7	171.7	171.7
Gross Margin % (b)	26.7%	26.7%	26.7%	26.7%	26.7%	26.7%	26.7%	26.7%	26.7%
SG&A (c)	118.0	118.0	118.0	118.0	118.0	118.0	118.0	118.0	118.0
EBITDA (d)	53.6	53.6	53.6	53.6	53.6	53.6	53.6	53.6	53.6
Depreciation	11.6	11.6	11.6	11.6	11.6	11.6	11.6	11.6	11.6
Operating Income	42.0	42.0	42.0	42.0	42.0	42.0	42.0	42.0	42.0
Interest	13.2	12.6	11.7	10.5	9.1	7.2	5.2	2.7	.4
Pre-tax income	28.8	29.4	30.3	31.5	32.9	34.8	36.8	39.3	41.6
Tax (40% rate)	11.5	11.8	12.1	12.6	13.2	13.9	14.7	15.7	16.6
Net Income	17.3	17.6	18.2	18.9	19.7	20.9	22.1	23.6	25.0
Interest	13.2	12.6	11.7	10.5	9.1	7.2	5.2	2.7	.4
CMLTD	15.6	31.1	31.1	31.1	31.1	31.1	31.1	31.1	15.6
Debt Service	28.8	43.7	42.8	41.6	40.2	38.3	36.3	32.8	16.0
EBITDA/interest	**4.06x**	**4.27x**	**4.57x**	**5.11x**	**5.89x**	**7.44x**	**10.4x**	**20x**	**143x**
EBITDA/debt service	**1.85x**	**1.22x**	**1.24x**	**1.28x**	**1.32x**	**1.39x**	**1.47x**	**1.57x**	**3.33x**
Free Cash Flow:									
+ EBITDA	53.6	53.6	53.6	53.6	53.6	53.6	53.6	53.6	53.6
- Debt service	28.8	43.7	42.8	41.6	40.2	38.3	36.3	32.8	16.0
- CAPX (e)	8.0	8.0	8.0	8.0	8.0	8.0	8.0	8.0	8.0
- Working capital	0	5.0 (f)	0	0	0	0	0	0	0
- Cash Taxes (g)	3.4	3.6	4.0	4.4	5.0	5.7	6.6	7.6	8.5
= Free cash flow	13.4	(6.7)	(1.2)	(0.4)	1.3	1.6	2.7	4.3	21.1
Beginning cash	14.6	28.0	21.3	20.1	19.7	21.0	22.6	25.3	29.6
Ending cash	28.0	21.3	20.1	19.7	21.0	22.6	25.3	29.6	50.7
Wachovia loan begin	248.7	233.1	202.0	170.9	139.8	108.7	77.6	46.5	15.6
Wachovia loan end	233.1	202.0	170.9	139.8	108.71	77.6	46.5	15.4	0

Source: Author estimates based on the Alternative Plan and case information.
Footnotes: Capital lease of $1 million is not included in the analysis. It is not material to overall results.

a) Assumes sales of $643 million in all future periods (equal to sales in FYE March 2008). The Alternative Plan has a monthly sales forecast of $53.6 million. Pierre's sales averaged $54.2 million a month in bankruptcy.

b) Gross margin of 26.7% for all future periods (equal to gross margin for FYE March 2005–2007). Gross margin of 22.7% in FYE March 2008 was distorted by rapidly rising commodity prices. Commodity prices fell significantly in 4Q08 and 1Q09.

c) Alternative Plan forecasts $118 million of SGA for all future periods (equal to the Debtor's forecast for FYE March 2010). The $118 million forecast could be high. SGA could be as low as $109 million based on analysis of SGA in FYE March 2008. The FYE March 2008 SGA had $14.9 million of unusual costs. The Alternative forecast does not assume any decrease in lease expense or contract rejections savings. On March 1, 2009, operating leases are scheduled to deceased $3.6 million a year. Pierre also rejected and renegotiated a number of leases and executory contracts that could save $400,000 to $800,000 a year, if not more.

d) EBITDA for the 5.5 months in bankruptcy was $40.5 million (annualized), or $13.1 million less than the $53.6 million forecast in the Alternative Plan. Pierre will see substantial cost reductions at emergence. See discussion in Chapter 8 for COGS and SGA for detail.

e) Historical CAPX $8.7 million (fiscal 2007) and $7.8 million (fiscal 2008). Pierre may be able to finance 30–50% of CAPX. The Wachovia loan in the Alternative Plan does not have a lien on after-acquired PP&E.

f) $5 million use of cash for working capital, consisting of $8 million increase in receivables, $7 million increase in inventory, and a $10 million increase in trade payables.

g) 40% assumed tax rate. It may be possible to preserve prior year losses for tax purposes. The Alternative Plan does not assume tax losses will not be carried forward. The tax code permits amortization of goodwill/intangibles over 15 years (goodwill/intangibles is not depreciated on the GAAP statements). Pierre charged-off $222 million in 2008 due asset impairment. Pierre can deduct goodwill/intangibles over 15 years on the tax return, estimated at $20 million a year for 10 remainings years.

Part VI: Presentation of an Alternative Reorganization Plan

Adequate Liquidity—Alternative Plan

The Alternative Plan projects $14.6 million of pro-forma unrestricted cash liquidity on a post reorganization basis. Cash liquidity increases to $28 million by the end of year one and reaches a low of $19.7 million at the end of year four. The $19.7 million cash liquidity equals 19 months of interest expense and 5.4 months of debt service.

As a safeguard to protect liquidity, the Alternative Plan has been structured for Pierre to pay into escrow the first six monthly principal payments on tranche 1. Furthermore, if Pierre's EBITDA to debt service is less than 1.0:1 in the fourth quarter of 2009, then the escrow agent cannot pay out the $15.6 million in escrow unless cash is in excess of $15.0 million. If Pierre's debt service to EBITDA is < 1.0:1 (four quarter rolling or most recent quarter) for the period ending December 31, 2009, then Wachovia loan tranches 2–4 will convert to equity.

Immediately after the exit from bankruptcy, Pierre's pro-forma liquidity is $21 million, consisting of $14.6 million unrestricted cash and $6.4 million of Revolver availability. The Debtor's liquidity is satisfactory and is not likely to land the Debtor back in bankruptcy in the near future.

Adequate Cash Flow and Debt Service Coverage—Alternative Plan

EBITDA to interest coverage in the Alternative Plan is satisfactory and is summarized below:

	Year 1	Year 2	Year 3
EBITDA to Interest	4.06:1	4.27:1	4.57:1
EBITDA to Debt Service	1.85:1	1.22:1	1.24:1

All of Pierre's debt pays out within 8.5 years in the Alternative Plan.

Sensitivity Analysis on the Alternative Plan

Pierre's revenue during bankruptcy (on an annualized basis) is comparable to the projected revenue in the Alternative Plan.

The Alternative Plan forecasts a return to $53.6 million of normalized EBITDA. During the 5.5 months in bankruptcy, a time of substantial distress, the Debtor's annualized EBITDA was $40.5 million (Table 8.3 in Chapter 8).

Table 25.91 is a cash flow sensitivity analysis projection that shows Pierre's liquidity will remain satisfactory in the case of $40.5 million of distress EBITDA.

Chapter 25: Alternative Reorganization Plan

Table 25.91—Cash Flow Stress Analysis for Alternative Plan
(in $ millions)

	Year 1 Stress Analysis
Distress EBITDA	40.5
Depreciation	11.6
Amortization goodwill/intangibles	20.0
Interest expense	13.2
Taxable income	(4.3)
Income tax	0.0
Distress EBITDA	40.5
Interest	13.2
CMLTD (6 mo. principal. Interest only first 6 mo.)	15.6
Capital expenditures	8.0
Net cash flow	3.7
Cash at the end of year 1	18.3
EBITDA to Interest Ratio	3.07:1
EBITDA to Debt Service Ratio	1.41:1

Source: Author estimates and projections.

If required, Pierre could curtail CAPX to preserve cash. Pierre would also have access to a $6.4 million Exit Revolver. In addition, Pierre could finance a portion of its $8 million CAPX on an operating lease or a loan.

Safety Net Structure—Alternative Plan

In the event Pierre does not have minimum EBITDA to debt service of 1.0:1 by the fourth quarter of 2009, the $186.7 million of debt on tranches 2–4 will convert to equity. Table 25.92 shows Pierre's cash flow, assuming the conversion of tranches 2-4 to equity and $40.5 million of distress EBITDA.

For this case, Pierre's EBITDA to interest coverage is 27:1. Pierre's net cash flow coverage is $3.2 million a year short of servicing the principal payments on the $62.2 million tranche 1 debt, but the repayment structure on the debt is very aggressive. Pierre will only have $62.2 million of total debt and the principal due in one year is $31.2 million (a two year amortization on all of Pierre's outstanding debt). As a result, a covenant will be in place restricting the payment of principal on the loan if Pierre's cash balance falls below $15 million.

Part VI: Presentation of an Alternative Reorganization Plan

Table 25.92—Cash Flow Stress Analysis for Alternative Plan if Tranches 2-4 are Converted to Equity
(in $ millions)

	Year 1 Stress Analysis
Distress EBITDA	40.5
Depreciation	11.6
Amortization goodwill/intangibles	20.0
Interest expense (interest for 12 mo. on tranche 1	1.5
Taxable income	7.4
Income tax	3.0
Distress EBITDA	40.5
Interest	1.5
CMLTD (12 mo. principal on tranche 1)	31.2
Capital expenditures	8.0
Net cash flow	3.0
Cash at the end of year 1	3.2
EBITDA to Interest Ratio	27.0:1
EBITDA to Debt Service Ratio	1.24:1

Source: Author estimates and projections

Feasibility of the Alternative Plan

The Alternative Plan is feasible because is not likely to be followed by the debtor's liquidation or need for further financial reorganization. The structure provides the opportunity for full recovery to unsecured creditors if the Debtor's operations return to normal. If not, the Alternative Plan provides for the automatic conversion of tranches 2–4 to equity. Assuming distress EBITDA, Pierre cash flow is $3.2 million a year short of covering the $31.1 million annual principal due on $62.2 million debt. This debt amortization is extremely aggressive as it fully amortizes Pierre's total debt in 2 years. The Plan structure has a safeguard preventing the payment of principal on the debt if cash balances are below $15 million.

Credit Ratings Based on S&P Metrics—Alternative Plan

S&P published *CreditStats: Adjusted Key U.S. Industrial Financial Ratios* (January 2007). The report compared S&P median financial ratios to S&P credit ratings for U.S. industrial companies rated BBB to CCC. Table 25.93(a) presents the S&P data and also shows Pierre's projected financial ratios in the Alternative Plan. Table 25.93(b) shows the Alternative Plan projected credit rating for each financial ratio.

Chapter 25: Alternative Reorganization Plan

Table 25.93(a) S &P's Key U.S. Industrial Financial Ratios, Long-Term Debt Three-year (2004 to 2006 averages)								Table 25.93(b) Pierre's Ratios and Credit Rating (a)	
	AAA	AA	A	BBB	BB	B	CCC	Pierre's Ratios	Pierre's Rating
Oper. income/revenue (%)	22.8	25.1	19.9	15.7	17.3	16.4	13.5	6.5	<CCC
Disc. Cash flow/debt (%)	88.9	23.8	16.7	11.7	5.4	(0.1)	(3.7)	n/a	na
EBIT to interest coverage (x)	27.3	18.0	10.4	5.9	3.4	1.5	0.5	3.2	BB+
EBITDA to interest coverage (x)	31.0	21.4	12.8	7.6	4.6	2.3	1.2	4.1	BB
FFO/ debt (%)	174.2	74.3	50.7	35.9	24.9	12.0	4.5	20.0	BB
Free oper. cash flow debt (%)	133.1	43.0	26.0	15.4	7.2	2.2	(4.1)	14.8	BBB
Return on capital (%)	25.2	25.4	19.7	15.1	12.5	8.8	5.2	7.0	B-
Debt/EBITDA (x)	0.5	1.0	1.6	2.2	3.2	5.4	7.7	4.7	B+
Debt/debt plus equity (%)	12.6	6.1	38.4	43.7	51.9	74.9	100.6	49	BB
No. of companies	6	15	118	213	297	345	32		

Source: Table 25.93(a) reprinted with permission from S&P. FFO is defined by S&P as funds from operations.
(a) For Table 25.93(b), the author has calculated Pierre's ratios and assigned a credit rating for each ratios based on the average ratios from Table 25.93(a).

Pierre Credit Ratings—Alternative Plan

The Alternative Plan assigns Pierre a corporate credit rating of B-.

The credit ratings for the four Wachovia loan tranches are notched as follows:

- Tranche 1 is notched up +3 to BB- (100% full recovery);
- Tranche 2 is notched up +1 to B (30%-50% recovery);
- Tranches 3 and 4 are notched down -3 to CCC- (0-10% recovery).

A significant structural enhancement of Pierre's debt structure is the 8.5 year principal amortization on 100% of the debt in the Alternative Plan. As the loan balances amortize in the future, the recovery ratings for the junior tranches are expected to improve.

Recommended Cramdown for Classes of Claims Not Approving the Alternative Plan

The Alternative Plan offers a 100% recovery. The 9% dividend on the Preferred Stock recovers in 16 months the same amount the Debtor's Plan offers for the full settlement of the unsecured claims.

The Alternative Plan projects that EBITDA will return to the average annual EBITDA for FYE March 2005-2007. The Alternative Plan is structured for adequate cash flow coverage and liquidity. The Alternative Plan assigns Pierre a corporate credit rating of B-. The Alternative Plan projects that all of Pierre's debt will be paid off in 8.5 years.

Part VI: Presentation of an Alternative Reorganization Plan

Pierre is not likely to land back in bankruptcy under the Alternative Plan. If Pierre's debt service coverage is not 1.0:1 by the fourth quarter of 2009, $186.7 million of the Wachovia debt is converted to equity.

A cramdown of the Wachovia claim is possible because the net present value of the payments to the Wachovia claim equals the amount of the claim. The Wachovia debt retains its first-lien position on all of Pierre's assets, except to the extent of $6.4 million priming lien for an Exit Revolver. The granting of the priming lien does not impair the Wachovia claim. The Wachovia claim reduced its letters of credit exposure by $6.4 million during bankruptcy when the DIP Lender issued replacement letters of credits.

Chapter 26

Bankruptcy Prediction: Z-Score

The Z-score formula for predicting bankruptcy was originally developed in 1968 by Edward Altman, a professor at the Stern School of Business at New York University.

The Z-score for a private company is a multivariate formula which measures bankruptcy based on the sum of the following factors:

+	3.1070 x Earnings before interest & taxes/assets;
+	0.7170 x (current assets − current liabilities)/assets;
+	0.8470 x retained earnings/total assets;
+	0.9980 x sales/assets.
+	0.4200 x book value of equity/liabilities
=	Z-Score

Z-Score	Zones of Discrimination
Z-Score	Zone of Discrimination
>2.9	Safe Zone
1.23 to 2.9	Grey Zone
< 1.23	Distress Zone

Part VI: Presentation of an Alternative Reorganization Plan

Pierre's Z-Score Prior to Bankruptcy

The Z-Score test results and associated zones of discrimination for Piere's December 2007 and FYE March 2008 finanical statements are shown in the Table 26.0.

Table 26.0—Z-Score Results and Zones of Discrimination

Financial Statement	Z-Score	Zone
December 2007-quarter (annualized)	1.63	grey
December 2007-nine months (annualized)	1.51	grey
FYE March 2008- twelve months	(1.59)	distress

Table 26.1 shows the detailed Z-Score calculation of -1.59 (distress zone) on the FYE March 2008 financial statement. Pierre's auditor classified all of the Pierre's debt in current maturities on the FYE March 2008 financials. Moreover, Pierre charged-off $223.3 million of goodwill/intangibles in FYE March 2008. These factors significantly lowered EBIT and working capital. As a result, the Z-Score moved from the grey zone on the December 2007 quarterly financials to the distress zone on FYE March 2008 financials.

Table 26.1—Pierre's Z-Score FYE March 2008 & Quarter December 3, 2007
($ millions)

	3/31/08 12 months			12/3/07 Quarter End		
Current Assets	146.8			150.9		
Current Liabilities	421.4			41.8		
Working Capital	(274.5)			109.1		
Total Liabilities	441.3			446.7		
Book Value equity	(91.8)			129.8		
Total Assets	349.5			596.4		
Sales	643.3			708.5		
Retained Earnings	(243.0)			129.8		
EBIT	(245.9)			0.6		
	T Value	Factor	Value	T Value	Factor	Value
T1	-0.7855	.7170	-0.5633	0.1829	.7171	0.1312
T2	-0.6954	.847	-0.5890	0.2176	.847	0.1843
T3	-0.7039	3.107	-2.1871	0.0010	3.107	0.0032
T4	-0.2080	.42	-0.0874	0.2906	.42	0.1204
T5	1.8407	.998	1.8371	1.1879	.998	1.1855
Total Z-Score			-1.59			1.63 (a)
			Distress			Grey
Conclusion			Zone			Zone

Chapter 26: Bankruptcy Prediction Z-Scores

Z-Score—Alternative Plan

Table 26.2 shows the calculation of Pierre's Z-score based on the Alternative Plan EBIT and the Alternative Plan distress EBIT.

Pierre's Z-score is 1.90 based on the Alternative Plan's $42 million of EBIT and 1.82 based on $28.9 million of distress EBIT. The Z-score for the Alternative Plan is above the 1.56 average for the Z-Score grey zone.

Table 26.2—Pierre's Z-Score: Based on the Alternative Plan Normalized and Distress EBTIDA

($ millions)	Alternative Plan Distress EBITDA			Alternative Plan Normalized EBITDA		
Current Assets	114.2			114.2		
Current Liabilities	59.7			54.5		
Working Capital	54.5			56.7		
Total Liabilities	278.0			277.9		
Book Value equity	264.3			255.4		
Total Assets	542.3			533.3		
Sales	643.3			643.3		
Retained Earnings	0			0		
EBIT	28.9			42.0		
	T Value	Factor	Value	T Value	Factor	Value
T1	0.1050	.7170	0.0720	0.10498	.7171	0.0720
T2	0	.847	0	0	.847	0
T3	0.05329	3.107	0.1656	0.07744	3.107	0.2406
T4	0.95072	.42	0.3993	0.95072	.42	0.3993
T5	1.18624	.998	1.1838	1.18624	.998	1.18387
Total Z-Score			1.82			1.90
Conclusion			Grey Zone			Grey Zone

Z-score Assuming Tranche 2, 3, & 4 Loans Convert to Equity

Table 26.3 shows the Z-Score calculation assuming distress EBIT and the conversion of loan tranches 2–4 to equity. The Z-Score improves to 3.50 (safe zone.

Part VI: Presentation of an Alternative Reorganization Plan

Table 26.3—Pierre's Z-Score: Based on Alternative Plan Distress EBITDA With Conversion of Tranche 2, 3, & 4 to Equity
($ millions)

Current Assets	114.2		
Current Liabilities	59.7		
Working Capital	54.5		
Total Liabilities	91.0 (a)		
Book Value equity	450.0		
Total Assets	542.3		
Sales	643.3		
Retained Earnings	0		
EBIT	28.9		
	T Value	Factor	Value
T1	0.1005	.7170	0.0721
T2	0	.847	0
T3	0.05329	3.107	0.1656
T4	4.94450	.42	2.0776
T5	1.18624	.998	1.1838
Total Z-Score			**3.50**
Conclusion			**Safe Zone**

(a) Convert Wachovia loan Tranche 2, 3, 4 ($187.2 million) to Equity

Chapter 27

Condensed Version of Pierre's Bankruptcy, the Alternative Plan & Concluding Comments

"Simplicity is the most difficult thing to achieve in this world. It is the last limit of experience and the last effort of genius." George Sands

Pierre Foods' Business

Pierre manufactures and sells processed food solutions. Pierre's sales grew from $358 million in 2004 to $643 million in 2008.

Microwavable sandwiches and pre-cooked proteins are 38% and 56% of Pierre's sales, respectively. Pierre's pre-cooked proteins include burgers, meatloaf, chicken strips, and barbeque pork ribs.

Pierre's sales to schools are 25% of sales. Pierre's sales to the Hardee's and Carl's Jr. fast-food restaurants are 10% of Pierre's sales. The remaining 65% of Pierre's sales are primarily to vending operators, convenience stores, and grocery stores.

On-site prepared food at convenience stores is a $16 billion market, with $2 billion of packaged sandwich sales. Pierre has a leading market share in packaged microwavable sandwiches, but no single firm dominates the industry. The packaged sandwich and pre-cooked food convenience industry have potential for consolidation.

The 2008 U.S. economic recession and Pierre's bankruptcy did not cause any significant decrease in Pierre's sales.

Madison Dearborn's Acquisition of Pierre in June 2004

Private-equity firm Madison Dearborn managed $8 billion in investments when it acquired Pierre Foods in a June 2004 leveraged buyout for $422 million. Madison Dearborn contributed $142 million in cash and leveraged Pierre with $275 million of debt to acquire the company. The debt consisted of $125 million of unsecured Senior Subordinated 9.875% Notes and a $150 million Wachovia secured Credit Facility.

Madison Dearborn's 2004 acquisition price was:
- 16.8 times 2004 EBITDA
- 9.3 times 2005 EBITDA
- 7.5 times pro-forma EBITDA

Industry peers were trading at 7.3 times EBIDTA in 2004.

Acquisition of Clovervale and Zartic

In 2006, Pierre acquired Clovervale and Zartic for $117 million. The holders of the Wachovia Credit Facility approved a $124 million increase in the Wachovia Term Loan to finance the acquisitions. Pierre's debt increased from $234 million to $370 million.

Pierre's High Debt Burden

The acquisitions increased Pierre's debt to EBITDA ratio to 5.98:1 for fiscal year-ending March 2007. The Wachovia Credit Facility had an aggresseive target for future decreases in the debt to EBTIDA ratio. The covenant gradually tightened each year, reaching 3.25:1 by November 2009.

Pierre's secured debt to EBITDA ratio of 2.70:1 was reasonable compared to EBITDA acquisition multiples in the industry.

Wachovia Secured Credit Facility — Collateral

The $250 million Wachovia Credit Facility was presented as a senior-secured loan. Based on prudent lender loan values, the Wachovia loan was undersecured by $140 million, implying a 44% recovery in the event of default.

$125 Million Senior Notes (Unsecured)

The $125 million unsecured Senior Notes had minimal prospects for recovery in a liquidation of the business. The unsecured Senior Note lenders were attracted by the 9.875% interest rate and the B credit rating assigned by

Chapter 27 Condensed Version of Pierre's Bankruptcy & Alternative Plan

Standard and Poor's (S&P). In the event of distress and default, the unsecured Senior Notes were in an undesirable place in Pierre's capital structure.

Pierre's Credit Rating

Valuation: Measuring and Managing the Value of Companies (Koller, Gooedhart, Wessels, 2005) has found that the interest coverage ratio is the key variable explaining credit ratings by S&P, with more than 45% of the rating differences explained by interest coverage.

On July 18, 2007, Pierre released its June 2007 quarterly financial results. Pierre reported an EBITDA to interest ratio of 1.42:1 for the June 2007 quarter. The 1.42:1 EBITDA to interest ratio implied a corporate credit rating of CCC based on the EBITDA to interest ratio for the typical U.S. industrial company rated CCC by S&P. Nevertheless, it was not until September 25, 2007 that S&P downgraded Pierre's corporate credit rating from B+/Negative to B/Watch Negative. S&P downgraded Pierre to B/Negative on October 11, 2007.

S&P considers many factors in the assignment of credit ratings. Although Madison Dearborn did not guarantee any of Pierre's obligations, Madison Dearborn had a $142 million cash equity investment in Pierre to protect from loss. S&P may have considered, among other factors, Madison Dearborn's investment, financial strength, and reputation as an intangible factors in maintaining Pierre's credit rating at B/Negative.

Pierre's EBITDA to interest ratio continued to deteriorate. Pierre's EBITDA to interest ratio decreased to 0.65:1 for the September 2007 quarter and 1.08:1 for the December 2008 quarter.

S&P downgraded Pierre's corporate credit rating from B/Negative to CCC+/watch/developing on June 3, 2008 — one day after Pierre gave notice it would be late in filing its fiscal year-end March 2008 financial statements.

Pierre's Credit Agency Ratings and Implications

A credit rated below BBB- is a speculative credit and S&P rated Pierre as a speculative credit. Although regulators and financial institutions have increasingly relied on the ratings of credit rating agencies for risk assessment, a credit agency rating is an opinion and not a guarantee of the current or future credit rating. Creditors have not been successful in suing credit rating agencies for harm caused by the reliance on credit rating opinions unless there is gross negligence or fraud on the part of the rating agency.

An investor has a fiduciary responsibility to perform its own independent credit analysis and evaluation of risk.

Events Leading to Bankruptcy Filing

Robert Naylor had served as Pierre's Senior Vice-President of Sales and Marketing for nine years. In October 2007, Pierre issued a press release announcing his retirement at the age of 55. A subsequent U.S. Securities & Exchange filing by Pierre showed that Naylor and Pierre had entered into a termination and severance agreement.

In February 2008, Cynthia Hughes joined the company to become Pierre's new Chief Financial Officer. Ms. Hughes had previously worked for Pierre in 2003. In June 2008, Pierre terminated the employment of Joe Meyers. Meyers had served as Pierre's Chief Financial Officer until the appointment of Hughes. Meyers had worked for Pierre for more than 10 years in high level accounting positions.

Early in fiscal year 2008, skyrocketing energy and industrial commodity costs, combined with sharp increases in raw material pricing, translated into significant pricing pressure for Pierre. In fiscal 2008, the price Pierre paid for beef, chicken, pork, and cheese increased 1.5%, 24.6%, 7.4%, and 37.1%, respectively. As the spike in oil and natural gas prices continued to escalate, Pierre continued to experience increased pricing for packaging materials and distribution costs.

In May 2008, Pierre began working with Madison Dearborn to come up with a plan. Pierre's management knew the company would be in default on its financial covenants when Pierre reported its fiscal year-end March 2008 financial results to Wachovia.

Madison Dearborn made the decision not to invest more cash in Pierre. The skyrocketing commodity costs and the interest expense on the 9.875% unsecured Senior Notes were too much of a burden on cash flow. The discussions then turned to bankruptcy.

On June 2, 2008, Wachovia sent a notice of loan default to Pierre for failure to deliver the March 2008 fiscal year-end financial statements. Wachovia increased the loan interest rate to the default interest rate. The higher interest rate was applied retroactively back to February 2008, resulting in an additional $1.2 million of interest expense.

The default caused Pierre to lose access to $19 million of borrowing availability on the $40 million Wachovia revolving line of credit. The default also caused a cross-default on Pierre's debt Swap Agreement. A $3.6 million swap termination payment was due on July 31, 2008.

With access to the revolving line of credit cut-off, Pierre did not have cash available for the $1.2 million Wachovia interest payment, the $3.6 million swap termination fee, and funds to secure an additional $2.3 million of bonding

Chapter 27 Condensed Version of Pierre's Bankruptcy & Alternative Plan

required by the U.S.D.A. for school sale programs. Pierre also had a $6.2 million interest payment on the $125 million Senior Notes due on July 15, 2008.

Oaktree Capital Begins Buying Debt and Works on a Bankruptcy Plan

Prior to bankruptcy, Oaktree Capital began buying the Wachovia secured debt. By June 2008, Oaktree Capital had purchased $60 million (24%) of the Wachovia debt.

In June 2008, without additional money coming from Madison Dearborn, Oaktree Capital began working on a restructuring plan with Pierre and the 44 holders of the $250 million Wachovia debt. The proposal included a debtor-in-possession (DIP) loan from Oaktree Capital and a restructuring plan for bankruptcy. Oaktree planned to exchange its $60 million of Wachovia debt for stock in Pierre and inject new cash in return for stock. The remaining Wachovia debt holders would have their debt reinstated at par value.

Pierre, Oaktree Capital, and Wachovia worked on a restructuring plan for bankruptcy through June 2008. Certain Wachovia holders were against linking an Oaktree Capital DIP loan to the restructuring plan. A few of the parties were also concerned with the possibility of a fight over Pierre's Enterprise Value with the Senior Note holders. The negotiations fell apart and Pierre filed bankruptcy on July 15, 2008, the same day the $6.2 million interest payment was due on the Senior Notes.

On July 16, 2008, Pierre's attorney, John Henes, with Kirkland & Ellis, argued in Court (Bankr. D. Del., Court transcript) for Pierre's use of cash collateral: "If we shut this Company down because we do not have access to cash collateral, we would have spoiled smelly beef."

On July 16, 2008, Oaktree Capital provided Pierre with a $35 million DIP line of credit. The DIP line had superpriority claim status and a lien on all of Pierre's assets, priming the lien held by the Wachovia Credit Facility. The Wachovia Credit Facility was granted adequate protection in the form of: (1) payment of interest, (2) a continuing security interest in all of Pierre's assets, and (3) superprioity status for any loss of collateral value because of the priming lien. The superprioity status was subordinate to the DIP loan and certain professional fee carveouts.

Oaktree Capital continued buying the Wachovia debt and acquired 92% of the Wachovia debt.

Oaktree Capital's Investment Strategy

Oaktree Capital, a Los Angeles based private equity firm, is one of the leading U.S. firms investing in distressed investments. The firm manages $51 billion of investment funds in high-yield debt, convertible debt, distressed debt, private equity, real estate, and listed equities. Oaktree Capital typically seeks to have a seat on the board of directors or observation rights in its portfolio of companies.

Oaktree Capital's investment strategy is explained on the Oaktree Capital website:

> Investment opportunities in distressed debt typically arise as a result of lowered credit standards and the unwise extension of credit, followed by the onset of economic weakness or some other igniter. When both elements are in place, distressed debt can be the market in which negativism is most crystallized and concentrated, giving us unusual opportunities for bargain purchases. Directed by the same management since the strategy's inception 19 years ago, Oaktree Capital's industry leading distressed debt team has invested successfully through several full cycles in the distressed debt market. The team is comprised of professionals with diverse backgrounds in portfolio management, law, accounting, valuation and banking. They combine extensive experience in distressed bank debt, defaulted securities and bankruptcy situations with proven expertise in valuing companies and assets, negotiation and restructuring. The team benefits from a large and expert staff, from Oaktree's proprietary analytical capability, and from a unique and superior access to deal flow. We favor large, fundamentally sound companies that are overleveraged. Oaktree Capital often assumes a leadership role in the financial restructuring process, investing at every level of the capital structure, in foreign or domestic securities, in companies or hard assets, in stressed securities and in unusual instruments and special situations. Oaktree Capital seeks to avoid losses through an emphasis on secured or senior debt, a mix of public and private debt, an insistence on protection from underlying asset values or franchise value, and limited concentrations of positions."

The Creditors Committee, Oaktree, and Pierre Agree to a Speedy Plan

After Pierre filed bankruptcy on July 15, 2008, the Creditors Committee was formed on July 28, 2008 and hired Imperial Capital as its financial advisor two days later. In the December 10, 2008 Court confirmation hearing for the

Chapter 27 Condensed Version of Pierre's Bankruptcy & Alternative Plan

Debtor's Plan, Eric Carson, managing Director of Imperial Capital, testified (Bankr. D. Del., Court transcript) that Oaktree Capital provided a term sheet proposal to the Creditors Committee in late August 2008. The proposal offered a small recovery to the unsecured creditors in the form of Pierre's stock. Oaktree Capital gave the Creditors Committee one week to respond to the offer.

Abid Qureshi, an attorney with Akin Gump who represented the Creditors Committee, characterized the Oaktree Capital offer in Court on behalf of Carson, as "a take-it-or-leave-it offer, the alternative to which was a cramdown."

Oaktree Capital and the Creditors Committee reached an agreement for a plan that paid 12 cents on the dollar in cash to all of the unsecured creditors. The plan would require any Wachovia debt holder, who accepted a settlement under the plan, to release their right to require the recovery amount received by Senior Note holders to be paid over to the Wachovia class. The Senior Notes were subordinate to the Wachovia debt and this plan provision permitted the Senior Note holders to receive a recovery.

The Creditors Committee reached agreement on Pierre's Plan one month after Oaktree Capital had presented its August term sheet proposal to the Creditors Committee. Pierre filed its first Plan on September 29, 2008 and Oaktree Capital was listed as the sponsor of the Plan.

Pierre's final Plan was filed on October 29, 2008. The final Plan kept the same 12% payout to the unsecured creditors but increased the payout to the Wachovia secured claim.

Debtor's Final Plan of Reorganization

Pierre incurred $15.9 million of professional fees during its five-month stay in bankruptcy. The professional fees were 8.3% of tangible assets.

Pierre's final Plan paid 12 cents on the dollar in cash for unsecured claims. Pierre's Plan reported a recovery of 73% to 92% for the Wachovia loan. The cash payout for the Wachovia loan was not clear in the Debtor's Plan. It appeared that the cash payout could range from 0–12%. The Plan did not include a sources and uses of funds statement for the emergence from bankruptcy.

The Wachovia loan recovery has been estimated at 81%, as follows:
12% Cash payout
34% $85 million, 14% Note due in 2014
35% 100% of Pierre's stock, in the form of Preferred Stock (8% dividend)
81%

The Debtor's Plan estimated the Wachovia loan would recover 35% in a liquidation of the business, taking up to one year and consuming up to 17% of Pierre's tangible assets. The independent analysis (Chapter 14) estimated a Wachovia loan recovery between 39% (three month liquidation) and 48% (nine month liquidation).

Form of Wachovia Recovery

A financial insitution, underwriting the extension of first-lien, interest-paying debt typically prefers to be paid in cash and/or debt securiites with a structure similar to its prepetition debt.

The Debtor's Plan estimated recovery did not take into account the form of the securities received by the Wachovia claim. The Wachovia claim received 100% of Pierre's stock and an $85 million Note that was subordinated to a $95 million Exit Credit Facility. The interest on the $85 million Note could be paid in cash or added to the Note balance, at the option of Pierre. The Wachovia holders receiving Pierre's stock also had an 18-month constraint on selling Pierre's stock and could be forced to sell their stock at the same price Oaktree Capital chose to sell its stock.

Plan Vote and Approval

Oaktree Capital controlled 92% of the Wachovia class of claims and could vote for any plan it desired, subject to the individual holders of the Wachovia claims receiving a recovery under a plan at least equal to what they would receive in a liquidation of the business. Rabobank, who held 2.5% of the Wachovia claim, was the only no vote in the Wachovia class. Approximately 99% of the dollar amount of unsecured class of claims voted in favor of the Plan.

Pierre emerged from banktuptcy five months after its bankruptcy filing.

Why the Rush for a Bankruptcy Plan by the Debtor?

Structure of Financial Advisor Fees

The financial advisor compensation was structured for faster case resolution. As financial advisor to the Creditors Committee, Imperial Capital received compensation of $1 million. The fee arrangement was $100,000 a month and a $500,000 success fee. Pierre's Investment Banker, Perella Weinberg Partners, received a $300,000 initial fee, a $150,000 monthly fee, and $2,000,000 transaction fee payable at the end of the case. The Imperial Capital and Perella Weinberg compensation represented 20% of the payout to unsecured creditors.

Chapter 27 Condensed Version of Pierre's Bankruptcy & Alternative Plan

Creditors Committee and Vendor Claims

The unsecured Creditors Committee was represented by three vendors and four Senior Note holders. The Senior Notes held 86% of unsecured claims.

The vendors significantly improved their position prior to bankruptcy and during bankruptcy. Vendor payables were $22.9 million on March 1, 2008 and $15 million when Pierre filed bankruptcy. Prepaid amounts to vendors were zero on March 1, 2008 and $7.5 million when Pierre filed bankruptcy. In first-day Bankruptcy Court Order, $9 million was approved for payment to critical vendor prepetition claims and for other vendor claims.

In the Pierre bankruptcy, no parties of interest filed a motion to recover preference payments. The Alternative Plan assumes an $11.9 million cash recovery of preference payments from vendors and Wachovia debt holders. $2.9 million is recovered from the Wachovia debt holders. The $9 million vendor recovery assumes a recovery equal to 60% of the $15.2 million vendor preference payments.

The vendors benefited from an improvement in their position prior to bankruptcy, during bankruptcy, and would benefit from future sales to a financially sound Pierre. A trade vendor's paradigm is 31% gross profit margins and sales turnover of six times a year. It would be rational for the vendors to support Pierre's Plan.

No Fight Over Enterprise Value From Senior Note Holders

A higher estimate of Enterprise Value for Pierre would allow the Senior Note Holders to argue for a greater recovery, subject to the Wachovia claim receiving a full recovery and a feasible plan structure.

Josh Scherer, Investment Banker for Perella Weinberg, testified on December 10, 2008 in the Plan confirmation hearing, that he was involved in the estimate of Pierre's Enterprise Value. Scherer testified that Pierre never pushed Perella Weinberg to come up with a lower or higher Enterprise Value. He also acknowledged that Oaktree Capital was involved in the valuation process. Nevertheless, in his opinion, Oaktree Capital did not control the valuation process.

According to Mr. Scherer, Pierre's management had assured its customers and vendors the bankruptcy would be quick. Pierre's management was worried that a protracted public fight over Enterprise Value could result in the loss of customer and vendor support.

Mr. Scherer also testified that the Senior Note holders believed that Pierre's Enterprise Value should be significantly higher than Perella Weinberg's estimate.

A key issue for the Creditors Committee agreeing to a plan was a plan provision that allowed the unsecured Senior Note holders to retain a 12% cash recovery under a plan without being required to pay the amount over to the Wachovia claim as required by the Senior Note subordination. The Senior Note holders agreed to accept a 12% cash settlement rather than fight over Pierre's business valuation.

Loss of Customer and Vendor Support

Pierre's liquidity was not an issue for Pierre by November 2008. By the end of November 2008, Pierre had $14 million of cash and a zero balance on the DIP Revolver.

Pierre's cash flow was not an issue in bankruptcy. In the five months of bankruptcy, Pierre had $18.2 million of EBITDA. Pierre's only cash interest expense during the five-month bankruptcy was $9 million for the Wachovia loan. Pierre's operations were building cash in bankruptcy, during the worst economic recession since the Great Depression.

Pierre's customer warranty and products claims were not an issue in bankruptcy. A consumer was not likely to delay buying a sandwich for immediate consumption because of Pierre's financial condition.

Oaktree Capital's DIP Loan Trigger for a Debtor Plan Submittal

Oaktree Capital had a default trigger in the DIP loan if a reorganization plan was not filed by the end of September 2008. The DIP loan also included an event of default if Pierre refinanced the DIP loan. The refinance default was removed prior to final approval of the DIP loan because of an objection by the Creditors Committee.

On a monthly basis, Pierre continued to increase its cash and reduce its exposure under the DIP Credit Facility exposure, as follows:

	(in millions of dollars)		
	Cash	DIP Loan	Reserve Letters Credits
September 27, 2008	$ 4.4	$10.4	$8.7
November 1, 2008	$ 8.3	$ 6.5	$9.1
November 29, 2008	$14.2	$ 0.0	$9.1

If Oaktree Capital called the DIP loan at the end of September for the failure of Pierre to submit a Plan, then according to the liquidation analysis in the Debtor's Plan, Oaktree Capital would have recovered 35% of its 92% investment in the Wachovia loan. Based on the trading prices of Pierre's debt prior to bankruptcy, it is estimated that Oaktree Capital paid 67% to 83% of the

Chapter 27 Condensed Version of Pierre's Bankruptcy & Alternative Plan

par for the Wachovia debt. Given Pierre's liquidity and financial performance in bankruptcy, it was unlikely that Oaktree Capital would call the DIP loan and take a loss.

Pierre had until November 15, 2008 to submit a Plan under the Bankruptcy Code. Moreover, Bankruptcy Courts will typically grant a debtor reasonable extensions of time for plan submittal. Pierre was building cash balances in bankruptcy.

By November 29, 2008, Pierre had $14.2 million in cash and a $9.1 million obligation under the DIP loan for letters of credits. Pierre's $193 million of tangible assets would have adequately covered a $9.1 million DIP loan with super-priority status and a priming lien.

Did Oaktree Capital's Proposed Cash Investment Rush a Plan?

Oaktree Capital was not proposing any cash injection into Pierre's capital structure in the Debtor's Plan. Moreover, Pierre paid for all of Oaktree Capital's expense in connection with the Debtor's Plan.

Hypothesis for Debtor's Speedy Plan

The case analysis reveals that Pierre's management held a minimal amount of Pierre's prepetition stock.

Although Pierre's management had a fiduciary responsibility to its shareholders, management did not own a significant amount of prepetition stock in Pierre to protect from loss. The following hypothesis is offered: in addition to the DIP default deadline for rushing a Plan, Pierre's management was operating on the belief, assumption, or hope that Oaktree Capital would be the new ownership group because of Oaktree Capital's significant debt ownership and reputation as a large, successful distressed investor who had access to capital and the public markets. Under the circumstances, Pierre's management most likely believed the prepetition shareholders would receive a zero recovery; Oaktree Capital would be the new boss. The best plan for management and employees would be a remerged Pierre with as little debt in the capital structure as possible.

Management Role in Debtor's Plan

In the December 10, 2008 confirmation hearing for the Debtor's Plan, Cynthia Hughes, Pierre's Chief Financial Officer, testified that she relied on the financial experts and advisors hired by Pierre. Hughes was asked if Pierre's financial advisors had communicated to her that Oaktree Capital's goal was to make an equity play for Pierre to take over ownership. The attorney representing Pierre objected to question to the extent the question asked her to disclose any legal advice she may have received from her advisors in response to the question.

In a Chapter 11 bankruptcy, the Bankruptcy Code gives Pierre's management the exclusive right to submit and recommend a plan of reorganization in the first 120 days. The bankruptcy courts typically grant reasonable extensions beyond 120 days. Pierre's financial advisors did not have the exclusive right to submit and recommend a plan.

In the Plan confirmation hearing on December 10, 2008, John Henes, the attorney representing Pierre, commented that Pierre's management felt very fortunate to have a company such as Oaktree Capital buy Pierre's debt, make a DIP financing commitment, and negotiate with the Creditors Committee for a plan to de-lever the balance sheet, allowing Pierre to emerge from Chapter 11 in a stronger position and able to thrive in the future.

Registration Rights Agreement

A Registration Rights Agreement and Management Services Agreement between Oaktree Capital and Pierre offered the hope of bigger plans for the future of Pierre.

The Registration Rights Agreement gave Oaktree Capital the right to require Pierre's management to file for an initial public offering of stock. Moreover, Pierre agreed to pay Oaktree Capital a $1.5 million annual management fee in connection with a Management Services Agreement. Under the Management Services Agreement, Pierre was also required to pay a $4.5 million fee to Oaktree Capital should Pierre consummate an initial public stock offering or sell one or more of the Pierre companies (through merger or otherwise), or sell all or substantially all of Pierre's assets.

The payment of the management fees to Oaktree Capital under the Management Services Agreement was disclosed in the October 29, 2008 Plan Disclosure Statement as follows: "the Shareholders Agreement between the Debtor and Oaktree Capital provides for the payment to Oaktree Capital of customary management fees for sponsored deals."

In the December 10, 2008 confirmation hearing on the Debtor's Plan, Hughes testified that she was not aware of the Management Services Agreement. The Chief Financial Officer of Pierre was not aware of an agreement that would pay Oaktree Capital an annual management services fee of $1.5 million and an initial public offering success fee of $4.5 million. The Management Services Agreement was filed with the Bankruptcy Court

Chapter 27 Condensed Version of Pierre's Bankruptcy & Alternative Plan

on December 8, 2008 in a Second Amended Plan for Technical Modifications—three days after the final date for voting on the Debtor's Plan.

The hope that Oaktree Capital might support a future public offering for Pierre may have been an incentive for Pierre's management to be anxious to move fast on a plan sponsored by Oaktree Capital. Oaktree Capital was bringing human capital to the table — its reputation and experience as a possible future equity sponsor for a public offering.

Management and Director Incentive and Severance Program

There may have been more incentive for Pierre's management to agree to a speedy plan. The Debtor's Plan disclosed a Management and Director Incentive and Severance Program. A copy of the compensation program was not included in the Debtor's Plan or Plan Supplements. Rabobank, who objected to the Debtor's Plan, received a copy of the compensation plan several days prior to the December 10, 2008 confirmation hearing for the Plan (Bankr. D. Del, Ct. transcript), but the compensation plan was not filed as a document with the Bankruptcy Court. If the management compensation program included a provision to compensate management with stock, then a future public offering of Pierre's stock could provide management with a possible opportunity to monetize a future stock award.

An Alternative Plan of Reorganization

Pierre's bankruptcy was not the result of falling sales or a broken business model. The bankruptcy resulted from high debt leverage, difficulty integrating acquisitions, and the unusual period of rapidly rising commodity prices in 2007 and 2008. The Alternative Plan projects that Pierre's EBITDA will return to the normal level experienced from 2005 to 2007.

Comparison of Pierre's EBITDA to the Industry & U.S. Firms

The Alternative Plan assumes $53.6 million of normalized annual EBITDA based on Pierre's historical results for the three years FYE March 2005–2007. The $53.6 million of EBITDA is 8.3% of Pierre's sales. Pierre's EBITDA as a percentage of sales is reasonable compared to peers and other U.S. industrial firms.

The median EBITDA to sales ratio is 12.1% for U.S. exchange traded and U.S. based non-financial firms with annual sales over $25 million.

Pierre operates in the packaged foods and meats industry. The EBITDA to sales ratio is 11% for 21 publicly traded companies in the packaged foods and meats industry with market capitalizations under $2 billion.

Estimate of an Alternative Enterprise Value

A comprehensive analysis of Enterprise Value was performed in Chapter 24 to determine Pierre's Alternative Enterprise Value under three methods: (1) comparable company basis, (2) comparable transaction basis, and (3) discounted cash flow analysis.

Many courts have cited the U.S. Supreme Court's opinion in the 1941 case of Consolidated Rock when determining the value of a debtor at the date of the plan of reorganization. Consolidated Rock established the key criteria in valuing a company is its earning capacity rather than its market value during the bankruptcy because market value will be harmed by the bankruptcy. According to the Supreme Court, this estimate of earning capacity should be based on an informed judgment that embraces all facts relevant to future earning capacity, including, the nature and condition of the properties, the past earning records, and all circumstances which indicate whether or not these records are a reliable criterion of future performance.

The $514 million final Alternative Enterprise Value for the Alternative Plan was 9.4 times Pierre's $53.6 million average annual EBITDA for the three years FYE March 2005–2007. The Debtor Plan was submitted in October 2008. As of October 1, 2008, publicly traded industry peers were trading at an EBITDA multiple of 9.0 times.

Perella Weinberg Partners, Pierre's hired valuation expert, estimated Pierre's Enterprise Value at $232 million in the Debtor's Plan. The Debtor's Plan did not disclose the assumptions and details of the Perella Weinberg valuation that are critical in order to evaluate Enterprise Value.

Chapter 24 provides a comprehensive analysis of the $514 million Alternative Enterprise Value, with full disclosure of details and assumptions.

Alternative Plan Structure

The Alternative Plan reinstates the $248.7 million secured Wachovia claim as debt on an 8.5-year loan amortization.

The Alternative Plan provides the unsecured claims and prepetition stockholders 100% of the Preferred Stock that carries a 9% cumulative dividend.

Chapter 27 Condensed Version of Pierre's Bankruptcy & Alternative Plan

The recovery to the classes of claims is set forth in the Table 27.1.

Table 27.0—Allocation of Preferred Stock to Classes of Claims

(in $ millions)	Claims	Value of Stock	% of Stock
Unsecured Claims:			
Senior Notes	131.3	131.3	49.6%
Interest on Senior Notes during bankruptcy	4.7	4.7	1.8%
Vendor & contract	6.2	6.2	2.4%
Vendor disgorgement recovery claim	9.0	9.0	3.4%
Compensation Woodhams & Naylor	2.4	2.4	0.9%
Contract reject: NASCAR & Interstate Warehouse	5.7	5.7	2.2%
Prepetition Stockholders		105.0 (a)	39.7%
Totals		264.3	100.0%

Source: author estimate based on Alternative Plan and case information on claims

(a) Prepetition stockholders receive 39.7% of the stock to be held in escrow. The stock is released from escrow on March 1, 2012, if there has not any conversion of the Wachovia debt to equity or if there is a not material event default in the Wachovia loan on March 1, 2012.

Pierre's Enterprise Value in the Alternative Plan is $514 million. The value of the stock is $264 million net of the $249.7 million of reinstated debt. The reinstated debt is the $248.7 million of Wachovia debt and $1 million of capital leases.

Recovery Debtor Plan vs. Alternative Plan

In contrast to the Debtor Plan, the Alternative Plan does not pay 12% cash to the secured and unsecured claims but the Alternative Plan provides a 100% recovery to unsecured claims. The unsecured claims receive Preferred Stock and the right to 9% cumulative dividends, subject to the liquidity and cash flow covenants in the Alternative Plan. It only takes 16 months of dividend payments to equal the 12% recovery offered in the Debtor's Plan.

The Debtor's Plan pays out $47.2 million of cash for the 12% settlement of claims; the Alternative Plan eliminates the payout and Pierre retains the $47.2 million of cash for working capital to be used in the business.

Alternative Plan Structure: Wachovia Loan Four Tranches

The Alternative Plan presented in Chapter 25 reinstates the $248.7 million prepetition Wachovia loan in four tranches of $62.2 million, with each succeeding tranche subordinate in collateral and to cash flows. Each tranche is interest only for the first six months. The loan amortization for each tranche is tranche one (2.5 years), tranche two (4.5 years), tranche three (6.5 years), and tranche four (8.5 years).

$6.4 Million Exit Revolver without Impairment to Wachovia Loan

The Alternative Plan provides the Wachovia loan with a first-lien on all of Pierre's assets, with the exception that the collateral securing the Wachovia loan is subordinate to a $6.4 million Exit Revolver. The carve-out is without impairment to the prepetition Wachovia Credit Facility because Wachovia was able to reduce its letters of credit exposure by $6.4 million when the DIP Lender (Oaktree Capital) issued replacement letters of credit immediately after the bankruptcy filing.

Feasibility Test: Liquidity in the Alternative Plan

The Alternative Plan forecasts a zero balance on the $6.4 million exit line of credit. Pierre's liquidity is $21 million on a post emergence basis, consisting of $14.6 million in cash and $6.4 million of borrowing availability.

The Alternative Plan projects a low cash balance of $19.7 million in the fourth year. Cash balances increase to $50.7 million in the ninth year. The debt is paid off in 8.5 years.

Feasibility Test: Cash Flow Coverage in the Alternative Plan

Based on the $53.6 million of normalized EBITDA projected in the Alternative Plan, Pierre's cash flow and leverage metrics are satisfactory, as follows:

Cash Flow/Leverage Metric	Ratio Year 1	Ratio Year 2
EBITDA to interest	4.06:1	4.27:1
EBITDA to debt service	1.85:1	1.22:1
Debt to EBITDA:	4.60:1	4.60:1

Pierre's Corporate Credit Rating B- for Alternative Plan

The Alternative Plan assigns Pierre a corporate credit rating of B-. The credit ratings on the four Wachovia loan tranches are notched based on priority of collateral and cash flow. The credit rating for tranche one is notched up +3 to BB- (100% full recovery); tranche two rating is notched up +1 to B (30% to 50% recovery); tranche three and four are notched down -3 to CCC- (0% to 10% recovery).

Chapter 27 Condensed Version of Pierre's Bankruptcy & Alternative Plan

Structural Enhancement in Alternative Plan

A significant structural enhancement in the Alternative Plan is the 8.5-year amortization on 100% of Pierre's debt. The recovery ratings for the junior tranches are expected to improve in the future as the loan balance amortizes.

The tranche structure will enhance the ability of the Wachovia holders to sell off the senior tranches and reduce credit exposure.

Bankruptcy Prediction Model for Alternative Plan

A bankruptcy prediction model was performed on the Alternative Plan. The Altman Z-Score model was used for the analysis. Pierre's Z-Score of 1.90 for Alternative Plan is in the grey zone but the score is above the 1.56 average score for the grey zone.

Alternative Plan Structured for Distress Event

During the distress period in bankruptcy, Pierre's EBITDA was $40.5 million on an annualized basis. The Alternative Plan projects Pierre's EBITDA returns to the normal levels experienced in FYE March 2005–2007 because:

- Many costs in FYE March 2008 were unusual one-time expenses.

- Commodity prices decreased by the end of 2008 and into 2009. The Debtor's Plan projections were prior to the decrease in prices;

- $2.7 million of one-time expense in FYE March 2008 related to the Wachovia loan;

- $1.4 million of expense in FYE 2008 because of a plant fire;

- $1.5 million of expense in FYE 2008 for the Cedartown plant closure;

- Savings from the rejection and renegotiation of burdensome supply contracts. Pierre rejected more than 400 individual marketing and rebate agreements. The Debtor's plan did itemize the specific cash flow savings.

- The Alternative Plan estimates cash flow savings from the rejection of capital leases of $400,000 to $800,000 a year;

- $200,000 of annual savings on a NASCAR advertising contract;

- Certain operating leases are scheduled to expire in the next two years. Operating lease expenses could decrease $3.6 million a year beginning March 1, 2009 and by an additional $1.6 million the following year;

If Pierre's EBITDA does not recover, the Alternative Plan has a provision requiring a mandatory change in Pierre's capital structure. If EBITDA to debt service coverage does not exceed 1.0:1 by the December 2009 quarter, the Alternative Plan requires:

- $186.7 million of the Wachovia debt (tranches 2–4) is exchanged for 62.5% ownership of Pierre's stock;
- Cancellation of the stock held in escrow for the benefit of prepetition shareholders;
- Remaining prepetition claims will retain their stock for 37.5% ownership of Pierre.

The Alternative Plan provides the opportunity for management to return EBTIDA to normalized levels, and if this does not happen, the Alternative Plan converts an additional $186 million of secured debt to equity, reducing interest expense by an additional $11.7 million a year. The Z-Score improves to 3.50 and is in the bankruptcy safe zone.

Tax Impact of Alternative Plan

The Alternative Plan also increases the likelihood that Pierre will retain its tax loss carry-forwards. In the Debtor's Plan, Pierre cannot use its prior-year tax losses to offset future income because Oaktree Capital became the owner of 92% of Pierre's Preferred Stock.

The Debtor's Plan results in an estimated $134 million taxable gain on the cancellation of debt because the Senior Notes and other unsecured claims receive 12½ cents on the dollar in full settlement of their prepetition claims.

The Alternative Plan does not create any gain on the cancellation of debt or the exchange of debt for stock.

Concluding Comments on Alternative Plan

The purpose of the estimate of Pierre's Enterprise Value in the Alternative Plan was not to determine a bargain purchase price for a distressed equity investment fund; rather the purpose of the valuation was to determine the fair market value of Pierre's business on a normalized basis in accordance with the 1941 Consolidated Rock Supreme Court decision on valuation of a business in bankruptcy.

The Alternative Plan projects that EBITDA will return to the historical levels for 2005-2007. The Alternative Plan Enterprise Value of $514 million is in-line with the valuations of industry peers.

Chapter 27 Condensed Version of Pierre's Bankruptcy & Alternative Plan

The Debtor's Plan offers a 12% recovery to the unsecured claims; the Alternative Plan offers a 100% recovery.

The Alternative Plan: (1) is a feasible plan based on extensive credit and financial analysis, (2) is structured for adequate cash flow coverage and liquidity, (3) assigns Pierre a corporate credit rating of B-, and (4) projects that all of Pierre's debt will be paid off in 8.5 years.

Pierre is not likely to land back in bankruptcy under the Alternative Plan because of the automatic conversion of debt tranches 2-4 to equity if Pierre's debt service coverage is not 1.0:1 by the fourth quarter of 2009. The conversion of the debt to equity results in bankruptcy Z-Score that is in the safe zone.

A cramdown of the Wachovia claim is possible in the Alternative Plan because: (1) the net present value of the payments to the Wachovia claim equals the amount of the claim and (2) the Wachovia claims retains its first-lien position on all of Pierre's assets, except to the extent of $6.4 million priming lien for an Exit Revolver. The granting of the priming lien does not impair the Wachovia claim because the claim benefited during bankruptcy when the DIP Lender replaced the letters of credits issued under the Wachovia Credit Facility.

Analysis of Oaktree Capital's Investment in Pierre

Oaktree Capital controlled 92% of the Wachovia secured debt. There were unsubstantiated allegations in the case that Oaktree Capital also held 30% to 40% of Pierre's Senior Notes which would have allowed Oaktree Capital to block voting approval of an alternative plan. From the voting record, there was no evidence of Oaktree Capital's ownership of Senior Notes.

Karen Boyer, Executive Director of Special Assets for Rabobank, testified in the December 10, 2008 Plan confirmation hearing that on November 18, 2008 Oaktree Capital offered 30 cents on the dollar for Rabobank's $6.7 million position in the Wachovia Credit Facility.

The cash price that Oaktree Capital paid for its 92% of the Wachovia loan is unknown. The Wachovia loan was trading between 67% and 83% of par between March 31, 2008 and June 30, 2008. Oaktree Capital owned at least 24% of the Wachovia loan prior to the July 2008 bankruptcy filing. Assuming Oaktree Capital aquired 92% of the Wachovia debt at 75 cents on the dollar, Oaktree Capital would have paid $188 million for its 92% ownership in the $250 million Wachovia loan. Oaktree Capital received an estimated cash payout of $27 million (92% of the estimated 12% cash payout for the $245 million Wachovia claim). Therefore, assuming Oaktree Capital purchased its 92% interest in the Wachovia loan for 75 cents on the dollar, Oaktree Capital's net investment was $161 million net of the cash payout.

Oaktree Capital also received a $78 million PIK Note (92% of the $85 million Note), reducing its investment from $161 million to $83 million for 92% ownership and control of Pierre.

The Debtor's Plan estimated Pierre's Enterprise Value at $232 million, equal to 4.3 times Pierre's average annual EBITDA for the three years FYE March 2005–2007. The $232 million Enterprise Value implied a value of $91 million for 100% of the Pierre's stock ($232 million Enterprise Value less the Debtor Plan pro-forma debt of $141 million). Oaktree Capital's 92% stock ownership therefore had a value of $85 million as compared Oaktree Captial's $83 million estimated net investment.

The value of 92% of Pierre's stock in the Alternative Plan is $245 million vs. Oaktree Capital's $83 million investment. The Debtor's Plan also entitles Oaktree Capital to 8% annual dividends on the Preferred Stock, a $1.5 million annual management fee, and a $4.5 million public offering success fee.

Lessons for Institutional Lenders

The institutions that underwrote the $250 million Wachovia loan and the $125 million Senior Notes were operating in the syndicated lending market. These institutional lenders can be quick to sell at the first signs of trouble. This allowed Oaktree Capital to accumulate 92% of the Wachovia secured debt. Traditional relationship banks are more likely to be willing to restructure problem loans.

The non-relationship lenders are more likely to buy and sell loans based on credit agency ratings and loan pricing spreads. Non-bank institutional lenders also look for exit strategies based on a refinance of debt, a sale of a company or division, and issuance of equity.

In Pierre's case, a swap of equity for the unsecured debt was the primary required repair to Pierre's capital structure. For a pre-bankruptcy exchange of debt for equity to be successful, consent of 100% of the participants is almost always required in the loan agreement. The 100% consent is difficult to achieve when there are many debt holders. Many loan agreements allow for the replacement of non-consenting debt holders. The Wachovia Credit Facility had 44 lenders at loan origination. Some debt holders may have different objectives.

A distressed equity investor who controls the secured debt in the capital structure, and who can successfully argue for impairment of its secured debt claim, may desire more than the reinstatement of the secured debt at par. The distressed investor may bargain for stock ownership of the debtor.

In underwriting the first-lien Wachovia Credit Facility, it was critical for each lender to plan for the future possibility of a distressed workout, especially in

Chapter 27 Condensed Version of Pierre's Bankruptcy & Alternative Plan

light of Pierre's high ratio of total debt to EBTIDA. It was important to analyze the type of institutions intially holding the secured Wachovia debt as well as the hold sizes for each lender.

The Wachovia loan could have been underwriten with a provision to restrict the sale and assignment of the loan to eligible assignee. Eligible assignees could have been limited to commercial banks, savings and loan associations, insurance companies, mutual funds, and commercial finance companies. A sale to a vulture fund or a distress debt purchaser could have been prohibted or required the approval of a majority of the holders in the facility.

These types of restrictive or prohibitive restrictions should be weighed carefully as they could limit the marketability and pricing of the debt. On the other hand, the restrictive assignment provisons could be more appealing to traditional relationship lenders who have concerns about the possiblity of their secured loan turning into a Pierre Foods/Oakhill Capital-type of recovery. Even with these protections, because most loan agreements require 100% lender consent for a change in the loan structure, it remains difficult to restructure a company's capital structure outside of bankruptcy. Holders of the secured debt may be unwilling to compromise because they may have purchased a swap that pays if the borrower files bankruptcy. The loan agreement should contain a provision allowing the replacement of a non-consenting debt holder.

Epilogue

As of August 2009, Pierre operates as a privately held company and continues to be owned primarily by Oaktree Capital Management. Pierre's most recent financial statements were filed with the Bankruptcy Court for the month ending December 29, 2008.

In June 2009, The Wall Street Journal reported (Kelly, 2009) that Oaktree Capital had invested 60% of the $10.9 billion it raised in May 2008 for its OCM Opportunities Fund VIIb and that Oaktree Capital was planning to raise an additional $4 billion for fund VIII.

In May 2009, Mergers & Acquisitions Magazine awarded the 2008 acquisition deal of the year to Oaktree Capital's acquisition of Pierre Foods (MacFadyen, 2009).

References

References

Acciavatti, Peter D. and Linares, Tony and Jantzen, Nelson R. (2008). *J.P.Morgan 2008 High-Yield Annual Review. North American High Yield Research and Leveraged Loan Research*. In JPMorgan.com.

Altman, Edward, I. The Use of Credit Scoring Models and the Importance of a Credit Culture. Stern School of Business, New York University. Retrieved from: http://pages.stern.nyu.edu/~ealtman/Presentations.htm

Altman, Edward I. and Hotchkiss, Edith S. (2006). *Corporate Financial Distress and Bankruptcy*. 3rd Edition. Hoboken: John Wiley & Sons, Inc.

Ayotte, Kenneth and Morrison Edward, R. (2008). Creditor Control and Conflict in Chapter 11. *Columbia Law and Economics Research Paper No. 321. Northwestern Law & Econ Research Paper No. 08-16*.

Consolidated Rock Products Co. v. DuBois (1941) 312 U.S. 510, 61 S. Ct.

Damodaran, Aswath. (2006). Damodaran on Valuation. *Security Analysis for Investment and Corporate Finance*. Hoboken: John Wiley & Sons, Inc.

Bankruptcy Court, District of Delaware. Case 08-11480 (KG). Retrieved from Kurtzman Carson web tracking site. http://www.kccllc.net/Pierre.

- Debtors First-Day (July 15, 2008) Court motions.
- Court transcripts dated July 16, 2008, August 13, 2008, and December 10, 2008.
- Interim Order (July 16, 2008) and Final Order (August 13, 2008) authorizing the Debtors to obtain postpetition financing on a senior secured basis, superpriority basis, authorizing the use of cash collateral, and granting adequate protection to prepetition secured parties.
- Interim Order (July 16, 2008) and Final Order (August 13, 2008) authorizing the Debtors to pay certain prepetition claims of vendors PSA/PACA claimants and lien claims and lien claimants and approving procedures related thereto.
- Interim Order (July 16, 2008) and Final Order (August 13, 2008) authorizing Debtors to pay certain: (1) prepetition wages, salaries, (2) other compensation, and (3) other reimbursable employee expenses, and employee medical and similar benefits.

References

- Interim Order (July 16, 2008) and Final Order (August 13, 2008) authorizing Debtors to pay certain prepetition claims of vendors, PSA/PACA claimants and lien claimants and approving procedures related thereto.
- Debtors Schedules of Assets and Liabilities filed September 3, 2008;
- Debtors Statements of Financial Affairs filed September 3, 2008;
- Debtor's Plan of Reorganization filed September 29, 2008;
- First Amended Plan of Reorganization filed October 28, 2008;
- Second Amended Plan of Reorganization filed on October 29, 2008;
- Second Amended Plan Supplement filed December 12, 2008 for the Second Amended Plan;
- Second Amended Plan with technical modifications filed on December 8, 2008;
- Debtors Plan Supplement filed November 20, 2008;
- Objection of Cooperative Centrale Raiffeisen-Boerenleenbank B.A. "Rabobank International" to Confirmation of Debtors Second Amended Plan dated October 29, 2008;

Dimson, Elroy and Marsh, Paul, and Staunton. (2002). *Triumph of the Optimists: 101 Years of Global Investment Returns.* Princeton University Press.

Dimson, Elroy and Marsh, Paul, and Staunton. (2009). *The Credit Suisse Global Investment Returns Yearbook 2009.* Switzerland: Credit Suisse Research Institute

In re Exide Technologies (Bankr Ct. Del. 2003), 303 B.R.

Gilson, Stuart, C. and Hotchkiss, Edith, S. and Ruback, Richard, S. (Spring 2000). Valuation of Bankrupt Firms. *Review of Financial Studies,* Volume 13, Number 1, Pages 43-74.

Ibbotson SBBI 2009 *Valuation Yearbook: Market Results for Stocks, Bonds, Bills, and Inflation 1926-2008.* Chicago: Morningstar, Inc.

Kelly, Keenan, (June 10, 2009). When $10.9 Billion Just Isn't Enough, *The Wall Street Journal.*

Koller, Tim, and Gooedhart, Marc, and Wessels, David. (2005). *Valuation: Measuring and Managing the Value of Companies.* Hoboken: John Wiley & Sons, Inc.

References

Kurtzman Carson Consultants. Pierre Foods, Inc., et al., on-line case tracking website maintained by Kurtzman Carson for case information, including documents filed with the Delaware Bankruptcy Court and official claims register. In http://www.kccllc.net/. Retrieved http://kccllc.net/Pierre

Lattman, Peter and McCracken, Jefferey. (December 31, 2008). *Buyout Firms Swoop in for Feast on the Cheap*, Wall Street Journal, Retrieved http://online.wsj.com/article/SB123068444351344245.html

MacFadyen, Ken, (May 1, 2009). Deal of the Year. *Mergers & Acquisitions.* Retrieved online from:
http://www.mergersunleashed.com http://www.sourcemedia.com/

Nellson Nutraceutical, Inc. (2007). Bankr D. Del. 303 B.R.

QSR. Report Says Sandwich Market Worth $121 billion. December 18, 2006. http://www.qsrweb.com/article.php?id=6430

Standard and Poor's. (Chinn, Wesley, E., and Lugg, David). *Standard & Poor's CredStats: Adjusted Key U.S. Industrial Financial Ratios for 2003 to 2005.* Published January 27, 2007.
In www.corporatecriteria.standardandpoors.com

Standard and Poor's. (Chinn, Wesley, E., and Lugg, David). *Standard & Poor's CredStats: Adjusted Key U.S. Industrial Financial Ratios for 2004 to 2006.* Published September 9, 2007.
In www.corporatecriteria.standardandpoors.com

Su, Gordon, L. (September 2007). Bankruptcy Implications of Second Lien Loans. *The Journal of Corporate Renewal.*

Taleb, Hassim, N. (2004). *Fooled by Randomness.* New York: Random House.

U.S. Bankruptcy Code. http://uscode.house.gov/download/title_11.shtml.

Bibliography

Branch Ben and Ray Hugh. (2007). *Bankruptcy Investing: How to Profit From Distressed Companies.* Washington: Beard Books.

Brealey, Richard, A. and Myers, Stewart, C. (2002). *Capital Investment and Valuation.* London: McGraw-Hill.

Broude, Richard, F. (1986). *Reorganizations Under Chapter 11 of the Bankruptcy Code.* Law Journal Press.

Capital IQ, Division of Standard & Poor's, Screening & Analytics. Capitaliq.com

Cornell, Bradford. (1999). *The Equity Risk Premium.* New York: Wiley.

Das, Satyajit. (2006), *Traders Guns & Money.* England: Prentice Hall.

DePamphilis, Donald, M (2008). *Mergers, Acquisitions, and Other Restructuring Activities.* Oxford: Elsevier.

Epstein, Kenneth and Raftery, Michelle. (April 2004). True Lease or Secured Financing: Recovering Meaningful Residual Value. *Law Journal Newsletters Equipment Leasing Newsletter.* Volume 23, Number 3.

Federal Reserve. Federal Reserve Statistical Releases Selected Interest Rates H15. Retrieved from: http://www.federalreserve.gov/releases/h15/data.htm

Friedland, Johnathan, P. and Bernstein, Michael, L. (May 2008). Chapter 11– 101: The Nuts and Bolts of Chapter 11 Practice: A Primer. *NACM Oregon Informational Brief.* Issue 8.3.

Garbade, Kenneth, D. (2001). *Pricing Corporate Securities as Contingent Claims.* Cambridge: Massachusetts Institute of Technology.

Ginsberg, Robert, E., Martin and Martin, Robert, D., and Kelley Susan, V. (2008) *Ginsberg and Martin on Bankruptcy.* Gaithersburg: Aspen Publishers.

Jakubowski, Steve. May 5, 2009. Chrysler Bankruptcy Analysis Part III: Will the Absolute Priority Rule Kill The Sale. In *BankruptcylitigationBlog.com.* Retrieved May, 5, 2009, from
http://www.bankruptcylitigationblog.com/archives/bankruptcy-in-the-news-chrysler-files-bankruptcy-part-i-assessing-the-financial-carnage.html

Bibliography

Jakubowski, Steve. April, 30, 2009. Chrysler Bankruptcy Analysis–Part II: Testing The Limits Of Section 363 Sales. In *BankruptcylitigationBlog.com*. Retrieved May, 5, 2009, from http://www.bankruptcylitigationblog.com/archives/bankruptcy-in-the-news-chrysler-files-bankruptcy-part-ii-testing-the-limits-of-section-363-sales.html

Jakubowski, Steve. April 30, 2009. Chrysler Files Bankruptcy–Part I: Assessing The Financial Carnage. In *BankruptcylitigationBlog.com*. Retrieved May, 5, 2009, from http://www.bankruptcylitigationblog.com/archives/bankruptcy-in-the-news-chrysler-bankruptcy-analysis-part-iii-will-the-absolute-priority-rule-kill-the-sale.html

Klee, Kenneth, N. (2009). *Bankruptcy and the Supreme Court*. Newark: LexisNexis.

Kohn, Richard, M. and Solow, Alan, P. and Taber, Douglas, P. (December 1995). Pure Debtor-In-Possession Financing. *The Secured Lender*.

Lipman, Frederick, D. (2005). *Valuing Your Business*. Hoboken: John Wiley & Sons, Inc.

Moyer, Stephen G. (2005). *Distressed Debt Analysis: Strategies for Speculative Investors*. Boca Raton: J. Ross Publishing, Inc.

Mulvaney, Michael, J. and Fahy, William V. and Gates, Daniel. (March 2009). *Rating Methodology Debtor-In-Possession Lending*. Moody's Global Corporate Finance. Moody's Investor Services.

Oaktree Capital Management, L.P. website. Oaktreecapital.com

Pierre Foods website. Pierrefoods.com

Powlen, David, (October 2008). Triple Trouble: Valuing Companies in Chapter 11. *The Journal of Corporate Renewal*.

Pratt, Shannon, P. and Grabowski, Roger, J. (2008). *Cost of Capital*. Hoboken: John Wiley & Sons, Inc.

Reilly, Robert, F. and Schweihs, Robert P. (1999). *Handbook of Advanced Business Valuation*. New York: McGraw-Hill.

Ryan, Bob. (2007). *Corporate Finance and Valuation*. Bedford Row: Thomson Learning.

Bibliography

Sable, Robert, G. and Roeschenthaler, Michael, J., and Blanks, Daniel F. When the 363 Sales Is the Best Route. In *McGuireWood.coms*. Retrieved May 1, 2009, from
http://www.mcguirewoods.com/newsresources/publications/financial_services/jblp.15.02.pdf.

Schlerf, Jeffrey, M. and Glassman, Neil, B. and Ward, Christopher, A. Equity Committees: A Consequence of the Zone of Insolvency. *ABI Journal*, Volume XXIV, No. 10, December/January 2006.

Shea, James, P. and Carlyon, Candace, C. and Hansen, Randon, D. (September 2004). Section 363 and the Path to World Domination; Can All Be Achieved in the Sale Motion? *ABI Southwest Bankruptcy Conference*.

Skeel, David, A, Jr., (2003). Creditors' Ball: The 'New' New Corporate Governance in Chapter 11. University of Pennsylvania Law School. Scholarship at Penn Law. Paper 29.

Standard & Poor's. *Criteria & Methodologies*.
In www.corporatecriteria.standardandpoors.com

Standard and Poor's. *Recovery: Results of Revisions To Recovery Rating Scale and Issue Level Rating Framework*. (June 12, 2007).
In www.corporatecriteria.standardandpoors.com

Standard & Poor's. *Standard & Poor's Encyclopedia of Analytical Adjustments for Corporate Entities*. (May 31, 2007).
In www.corporatecriteria.standardandpoors.com

Standard & Poor's . CreditStats: Packaged Foods & Meats—U.S. Published August 28, 2008. In www.ratingsdirect.com.

Tabas, Joel, L. (December/January 2004). The §1111(b) Election: A Decision-making Framework. *American Bankruptcy Institute Journal*. Volume XXII, Number 10.

WeinBerg, Kenneth, P. (July/August 2003). Lease Vs. Loan Analysis Under the Uniform Commercial Code. *Monitor*.

Whitman, Martin, J. and Diz, Fernando (2009). *Distress Investing*. Hoboken: John Wiley & Sons, Inc.

Bibliography

Woolner, Ann. (May 6, 2009). Chrysler's Greedy Hedge Funds Holdouts Get It Right. In *Bloomberg.com*. Retrieved May 6, 2009.
http://www.bloomberg.com/apps/news?pid=20601039&sid=azVYi8YEXsAc&refer=home

U.S. House of Representatives
Downloadable U.S. Code. *11 U.S.C Title 11 - Bankruptcy*.

U.S. Securities and Exchange Commission. Edgar Company Search. Pierre Foods, Inc. Pierre's filings with the SEC, including all 8-K, 10-K, 10-Q, S-4/A, S-4, and 424B3 filings.

About the Author

Joe Gensor has 30 years of experience in the asset based lending industry in commercial loan underwriting and analysis. His lending career has included employment with commercial banks, asset-based receivable and inventory lenders, and asset based equipment lenders.

Prior his undertaking the Pierre's Food case analysis, Mr. Gensor was not familiar with Pierre Foods. Although Mr. Gensor was generally familiar with Oaktree Capital through news articles, he did not have any business relationship with Oaktree Capital or any of its employees.

www.ingramcontent.com/pod-product-compliance
Ingram Content Group UK Ltd.
Pitfield, Milton Keynes, MK11 3LW, UK
UKHW051256180426
11947UKWH00020B/1741